KNOWING
SUBJECTS

 volume 57

KNOWING SUBJECTS

Cognitive Cultural Studies

and Early Modern

Spanish Literature

Barbara Simerka

Purdue University Press
West Lafayette, Indiana

∞ The paper used in this book meets the minimum requirements of American National Standard for Information Sciences—Permanence of Paper for Printed Library Materials, ANSI Z39.48-1992.

Printed in the United States of America
Design by Anita Noble

Front cover image Copyright Lightspring, 2013. Used under license from Shutterstock.com.

Library of Congress Cataloging-in-Publication Data

Simerka, Barbara, 1957–
    Knowing subjects : cognitive cultural studies and early modern Spanish literature / by Barbara Simerka.
        p.   cm. — (Purdue studies in Romance literatures ; v. 57)
    Includes bibliographical references and index.
    ISBN 978-1-55753-644-0 (pbk. : alk. paper) — ISBN 978-1-61249-267-4 (epdf) — ISBN 978-1-61249-268-1 (epub) 1. Spanish literature—Classical period, 1500-1700—History and criticism. 2. Cognitive learning theory. 3. Picaresque literature, Spanish—History and criticism. I. Title.
    PQ6066.S525 2013
    860.9—dc23   2012039055

Contents

Preface

The seeds for this book were planted at the University of Michigan in the late 1970s. I have a phobia about Bunsen burners and microscopes, so a very understanding advisor allowed me to fulfill my natural science requirement by taking four nonlaboratory classes instead of two lab courses. I chose courses in biological approaches to anthropology and psychology; that was the beginning of a lifelong fascination with the fields of learning theory and primate behavior. When I discovered that current approaches to cognitive studies incorporate both, I was immediately ready to sign on!

As I worked to catch up with twenty years of advances in these fields, Howard Mancing was a constant source of information and encouragement. He shared an early version of his *magnum opus* on cognitive theory, "Voices in Everything," which helped me greatly in developing my focus. I cannot thank him enough. Professor Reid Strieby introduced me to the work of Erving Goffman and has provided many hours of stimulating discussion on psychology and literature. Several people read drafts of individual chapters and provided invaluable feedback; I am grateful to Ellen Spolsky, Bruce Burningham, Cory Reed, and Nieves Romero-Diaz. Christopher Weimer helped me to better frame my explications of cognitive theory for a literary audience. Angela Curran, Amy Williamsen, Catherine Connor, and Lisa Vollendorf have also been valued supporters and sounding boards. Julio Ramirez, a neuropsychologist, provided important bibliographical suggestions and corrections to my theoretical introduction. I have benefitted from the discussions following numerous conference panels; Sidney Donnell and Emile Bergmann offered especially useful observations at the GEMELA conference at Mt. Holyoke. Mariana Erickson was a dedicated and meticulous research assistant.

In Chapter 6, a portion of the material, which has now been substantially revised, appeared earlier as "Metatheater and Skepticism in Early Modern Representations of the Saint Genesius Legend," *Comparative Literature Studies* 4.1 (2005): 50–73. Copyright © 2008 by the Pennsylvania State UP. Rpt. by permission of the Pennsylvania State University Press.

PSC-CUNY, the union that represents Queens College, recently negotiated a contract that supports full-year sabbaticals. I could not have undertaken such a complex project without the extended release time; additional summer research grants from PSC were also very beneficial. I am grateful to Dean Tamara Evans and my department for approving the sabbatical and for respecting a true reprieve from college responsibilities. Susan Y. Clawson at Purdue Studies in Romance Literatures provided substantial support during the editing process, for which I am truly appreciative.

I thank my parents, Charles and Dorothy Simerka, and my late father-in-law, Ken Smith, for their love and support. My husband, Steve, has provided treasured technical advice, over twenty years of encouragement, and the occasional gourmet meal to keep me going. During the five years that I have been working on this project, my daughter Rachel has been passing through her teenage years with spirit and grace, allowing me to devote sustained attention to scholarship.

List of Abbreviations and Cognitive Terms

AI: Artificial Intelligence

A model of the human mind that arose in the late 1950s that views the mind as mechanistic and likens it to a computer devoted to information processing.

Contextualism

The contextualist model describes cognition as simultaneous, parallel, networked, and interactive nonconscious processes. It is an updated version of the modularity model, based on the most recent advances in brain imaging technologies.

Ecological Cognition

The ecological model proposes an interactive model of evolved brain, individual psyche, and sociocultural environment. This model is embodied but antideterministic, and describes the hardwired and experiential aspects of cognitive functioning as interdependent and mutually sustaining.

Immersion

Cognitive models of reading propose immersion as a common but stigmatized form of excess engagement with fictional characters and story worlds, usually in response to leisure or genre fiction. Immersive reading practice is escapist; the reader does not maintain normative cognitive boundaries between reality and fiction.

MI: Machiavellian Intelligence

A specific form of mind reading, when advanced minds seek to understand mental processes, emotions, or beliefs in order to better deceive or manipulate others for material and/or social advantage.

MR: Mind Reading

The study of how humans living in complex social systems conceptualize the thoughts and rationales behind other people's actions and use those insights to negotiate social relationships. MR enables us to interpret and predict actions, feelings, and motivations. Also known as Theory of Mind (ToM). MR has been proposed as the cognitive activity unique to advanced primates that justifies our much larger brains.

Modularity, modular mind

A model proposed by Jerry Fodor in 1983, based on early scanning technologies, of cognition as modular rather than linear. Separate compartments (modules) of the brain work simultaneously but independently—at a nonconscious level—to process different types of information.

p-response: Participatory Response

Richard Gerrig's model for a continuum of normative to anomalous responses to fiction. Responses range from expressing hopes and fear about the outcome, to gap-filling mental activities, to discussions about characters as if they were living humans, to trying to live like the characters in a story world.

Radiant Ignition

Elaine Scarry studies the cognitive processes by which readers bring to life the words on the printed page. Radiant ignition is the technique through which writers illuminate a scene or a figure part by part, like a spotlight moving across a space or object, to control readers' visualization.

SI: Social Intelligence

An umbrella term for mentalist activities (ToM, MR, MI) when used for altruistic or cooperative rather than selfish or competitive purposes.

ST: Simulation Theory

One proposed model of MR. ST views mind reading as a form of imaginative identification, whereby we "place ourselves in others' shoes" in order to project what people might think or how they might react. This model posits that humans anticipate the reactions of others based on our own reactions.

ToM: Theory of Mind

See Mind Reading (MR) above. The two terms are used interchangeably.

TT: Theory Theory

One proposed model of MR. TT posits mind reading as a capacity that requires development of a set of theories concerning predictable patterns of human thought and reaction. This model requires the ability to represent and conceptualize someone else's mental representations

Chapter One

Introduction
Cognitive Cultural Studies

Since the advent of cognitive sciences after World War II, several different new models have been proposed to describe the way the human mind and brain function, some complementary and others diametrically opposed. The emerging model of "contextualized" or "ecological" cognition stands in polar opposition to both the behaviorist model of the human mind popular until the 1960s, as well as to the Artificial Intelligence (AI) model that arose in the 1950s (Mancing, "Voices"). Both of the latter paradigms are strictly empirical in nature; they incorporate mind/body dualism, posit a mechanistic brain, and focus on reason and analysis as the primary cognitive functions. By contrast, the contextualist approach embraces embodiment rather than Cartesian binarism, emphasizes context, connectivity, and the construction of meaning, and depicts thought as metaphorical and narrative in nature (Mancing, "Embodied" 26–27). Even with this cursory description of the crucial differences between the two models of cognitive functioning, it is apparent that contextualism offers rich possibilities for literary study.

The behaviorist model created research situations in which cognition was measured based on strictly controlled environmental manipulations (such as pigeons pecking at food levers) and the nature of reasoning processes was explained based on extrapolations from such data. However, actual thoughts were considered private, nonquantifiable and hence unknowable. In the behaviorist model, the mind was seen as primarily mechanistic and analytic in nature. The behaviorist model of human psychology corresponds in many ways to the New Critical tenet of "intentional fallacy," which posited authorial intention as beyond empirical knowing and therefore as a forbidden territory for analysis. It is likely that this model arose in part to correct the excesses of the previous paradigm, which had employed Freudian or Jungian psychoanalytic tactics upon author biographies in order to discern textual meaning. In addition, behaviorist assumptions seem to underlie the related tenet of "affective fallacy," which viewed the analysis of reader response as subjective rather than empirical and thus equally objectionable. Both behaviorist cognitive models and New Critical literary analysis models appear in retrospect to be over-reactions to the spectacular successes of the natural and physical sciences in the first decades of the twentieth century. In an attempt to reclaim a more central role for their respective disciplines, many humanistic scholars emphasized the objective aspects that psychology and literary study could share with the more prestigious "hard" sciences.

The Artificial Intelligence (AI) model shares many of these empirical and mechanistic assumptions. The popular metaphor of the mind as a computer sets the framework for a paradigm in which the most significant cognitive activity is information processing. The development and standardization of the computational language of the binary unit (in which all information is reduced to concepts that can be represented as either the digit 0 or 1) reinforces the notion of thought as mechanistic, linear, computational, and symbolic rather than embodied (Mancing, "Embodied" 26–27; Varela et al. 7). The AI model gave rise to half a century of scientific research aimed at producing computers or robots that could reproduce human thought processes (computers that could write literary texts would surely have been the next step). This effort, and the grandiose projections and promises by early researchers, engaged the imagination of science fiction authors like Philip K. Dick and Arthur C. Clarke, who wrote dystopic novels about future societies in which nefarious thinking machines or androids wreaked havoc. The AI endeavor also inspired the more optimistic musings of Gene Roddenberry's *Star Trek: The Next Generation* and Julian May's *Galactic Milieu* trilogy, who created hybrid beings such as Data the Android and Jack the Bodiless in order to explore the connections between mind, body, and humanity. Both types of fictional speculation, like the projections of the researchers themselves, proved to be premature. Because the AI model focuses on computation, the type of thought that can be achieved is highly limited; for this reason the greatest success to date has been the defeat of a world chess champion by the IBM computer "Big Blue." The game of chess is a highly scripted activity in which success is achieved by the ability to rapidly compare the success of a large number of possible moves; for this reason the lightening-fast processing speed of a large computer provides the necessary advantage. In order to move beyond mere computation, IBM announced that it has created the next generation "Watson," designed as a "question answering machine" (C. Thompson). Designed to perform reasoning processes rather than mere calculations, its first challenge was to take on *Jeopardy* quiz show champions. The competition was televised in February 2011; although Watson did defeat the human champions, it is my opinion that this victory was based on speed of access and a large data library rather than true analytic skills. The humans bested Watson on questions that required inferential thinking. Similarly, in most contexts for which scientists have tried to create scriptlike programs to elicit human responses, the results to date have not been promising (Varela et al. 147; Mancing, "Embodied" 29). After dedicating many years to the study of AI, Roger Schank has become a leading voice for more holistic approaches. His titles provide clear indications of his research conclusions: his book is entitled *Tell Me a Story: Narrative and Intelligence* and the first chapter is "Knowledge Is Stories." Mancing cites Schank's explanations for the current and probable future failure to create true human intelligence in a machine, an endeavor to which Schank dedicated over two decades before conceding defeat: "knowledge [...] is experience and stories, and intelligence is the apt use of experience and the creation and telling of a story" (Shank 16, cited in Mancing, "Voices" ch. 15). This model of intelligence as narrative corresponds in many ways to the contextualist model of cognition and is of obvious relevance for literary study.

In the move away from AI models of intelligence as computation, one alternative that has emerged is the embodied mind. Varela et al. point out that while a processor model may be sufficient for "propositional knowledge" or "knowledge *that*," this is an incomplete picture that in fact focuses upon the least important aspects of intellect. Far more significant is "knowledge *how*" based on material experience as well as rational processes (146). They assert that "context-dependent know-how" [should not be conceived of] as a residual artifact that can be progressively eliminated [from cognitive models] by the discovery of more sophisticated rules but as, in fact, the very essence of *creative* cognition" (148; emphasis in original). This contextual proposition, grounded in hermeneutical philosophy (especially Merleau-Ponty and Gadamer) views knowledge as being "inseparable from our bodies, our language, and our social history—in short, from our *embodiment*" (149; emphasis in original). The embodied cognitive process is neither biologically nor culturally determined, but rather a "codetermination of animal and environment" (203). Or, as Howard Mancing astutely reiterates on several occasions, the most successful cognitive models propose knowledge as always "100 percent nature and 100 percent nurture" ("Embodied" 39). The model of embodied cognition has inspired numerous literary scholars. Mark Turner's seminal text, *Reading Minds,* explores the relationships between aspects of embodiment and literary structure, such as bilateral symmetry in human limbs and literary structures such as binarism, narrative symmetry, and metaphor. In addition, Turner points to recurrent plot patterns, such as the journey or quest, and prominent metaphors, such as the container, as related to the embodied experiences of locomotion and the human body as a container for the human essence. Other important studies of literature and cognitive theory include: Blakey Vermeule's *Why Do We Care about Literary Characters?,* which explores novels that elicit "high mind reading"; Patrick Colm Hogan's and David Herman's studies of narrative; Reuven Tsur's and Norman Holland's work on poetry; Elaine Scarry and Ellen Esrock's analyses of cognition and the reading process; and Janet Murray and Mary Thomas Crane's books on Shakespeare and cognition. Recent anthologies offer nuanced surveys of the vast terrain of literary cognitive study, including: *The Work of Fiction* by Alan Richardson and Ellen Spolsky, *Theory of Mind and Literature* from Paula Leverage et al., Lisa Zunshine's *Introduction to Cognitive Cultural Studies,* and *Cognitive Cervantes.*

This book proposes cognitive study as a supplement to, and not as a replacement for, current historically based and ideological approaches. My approach is similar to Lisa Zunshine's paradigm of "cognitive cultural studies," which takes into account the interconnectedness of the evolved human brain, social communication, and aesthetics (*Cultural Studies* 14). Zunshine asserts that Raymond Williams's model of cultural materialism, as developed in *Marxism in Literature* and other works, is highly compatible with cognitive approaches (*Cultural Studies* 5–15). She points to the homologies between Theory of Mind and materialist studies, both sharing "a denial of teleology... emphasis on indeterminacy and on ongoing, *mutually goading* transformations of individuals and their environments" (*Cultural Studies* 13; emphasis added). The highlighted text emphasizes that this new model of textual analysis is neither deterministic nor bioreductive; it seeks to incorporate new knowledge about the brain and about human cognitive practices into the already interdisciplinary practice of cultural studies. The anthology includes several essays in which contributors link representations of cognition with specific historical moments. Mary Thomas Crane links the emergence of new forms of metaphor and analogy in Donne's poetry to the "new science" of the seventeenth century, which demonstrated significant gaps between the epistemologies of common sense or embodied experience and the "counter intuitive" Newtonian model of physical reality ("Analogy" 188). Ellen Spolsky grounds her materialist cognitivism in a rejection of Sir Philip Sidney's assertion that art is separate from "nature" ("Making" 84). The model of cognitive cultural studies that I offer incorporates many of these lines of inquiry; I propose a tripartite system of "mutually goading" transformation, entailing: an embodied, networked, and highly flexible cognitive structure strongly predisposed to cultural interaction; a newly urbanized and imperial social structure; and literary texts that foreground anxieties about cognitive activity.

Theory of Mind and Social Intelligence

Cognitive theories of Social Intelligence incorporate anthropological, psychological, and pedagogical studies of human cognitive development as well as evolutionary biological studies of primate mental development. In *Mindreading: An Investigation into How We Learn to Love and Lie*, Sanjida O'Connell describes a recently discovered but nearly universal cognitive faculty, "thinking about what is going on in [another's] head" (6). A Theory of Mind enables humans (and advanced primates) to predict what others are likely to do, feel, think, and believe; this capacity is a necessary precursor to a wide variety of human interactions—both positive and not—including projecting and empathizing as well as lying and cheating. Theory of Mind (ToM) or Mind Reading (MR), is not at all related to the popular concept of telepathy, but rather entails the study of how primates, including humans, conceptualize the thoughts and rationales behind other people's actions and use those insights to negotiate social relationships (Whiten 150). The Autism Spectrum disorders, including Asperger's syndrome, derive from an impairment in the cognitive faculties, blocking its victims' awareness that other people have separate mental activities. It was not until research on autism revealed that persons suffering from this malady *lack* a Theory of Mind (ToM), that we became aware of this cognitive function as an essential aspect of social interaction (Zunshine, *Why* 8–17). The model of MR enriches our understanding of human consciousness by making visible certain behaviors that previously had gone unremarked (Zunshine, "Richardson" 142). A science journalist, O'Connnell seeks to adapt cognitive research conducted with primates and impaired children by anthropologists and psychologists for a popular audience; nonetheless, one of her first examples of flawed "mind reading" (MR) is King Leontes' misreading of his brother's and wife's behavior in *A Winter's Tale* (1–2).

Researchers from many disciplines have long sought to specify the cognitive activity that requires human brains to be so much larger than those of our nearest primate cousins; the benefit has to be substantial because of the vastly increased need for calories to support this leap in cerebral size; ToM has emerged as a leading explanatory contender (Byrne, "Technical" 291; Gigerenzer 265). This type of "Social Intelligence" has been posited as the unique attribute that separates humans from other highly intelligent species; however, rudimentary MR has been observed among some animals. Psychological study has focused upon the norms and variations of ToM in 3 groups: (1) primates, in order to get a clearer understanding of the increasing sophistication of mental abilities among lesser and greater apes and humans; (2) injured or mentally disabled human adults, especially autistics; (3) the development of a ToM in young children. This model of intelligence arising from social interactions was proposed to replace earlier paradigms that emphasized hunting and food gathering, tool use and creation, or warfare (Byrne and Whiten 1997, 18).

Cognitive scholars have proposed two separate processes for human ToM or MR. One model, known as Theory Theory, is abstract, positing mind reading as a capacity that requires development of a set of theories concerning predictable patterns of human thought and reaction. The Theory Theory model requires "representational thought"; the ability to represent and conceptualize someone else's mental representations (Davies and Stone, "Introduction" 30). In Janet Astington's definition, Theory Theory entails formation of "concepts of mental states [that] are abstract and unobservable theoretical postulates used to explain and predict observable human behavior" (185). According to Alison Gopnik, the cognitive process for understanding MR is similar to Chomsky's model for language acquisition,

> The basic idea is that children develop their everyday knowledge of the world by using the same cognitive devices that adults use in science. In particular, children develop abstract, coherent, systems of entities and rules, particularly causal entities and rules. That is, they develop theories. These theories enable children to make predictions about new evidence, to interpret evidence, and to explain evidence. Children actively experiment with and explore the world, testing the predictions of the theory and gathering relevant evidence. Some counter-evidence to the theory is simply reinterpreted in terms of the theory. Eventually, however, when many predictions of the theory are falsified, the child begins to seek alternative theories. If the alternative does a better job of predicting and explaining the evidence it replaces the existing theory. (240)

Other proponents of Theory Theory assert that humans are born with an innate capacity or cognitive module for mentalizing, similar to that posited by linguists for speech (Carruthers 24; Saxe and Baron-Cohen iv).

Scholars in all fields of cognitive study who question or reject the Theory Theory model share a common doubt, based on the assertion that young children can demonstrate awareness of the mental activity of others at an age when it is believed that they do not yet have the cognitive capacity to develop formal principles—concerning MR, linguistics, basic science, etc. (Gopnik 241). The most prominent alternative, Simulation Theory, views the mind reading process as a form of imaginative identification, whereby we "place ourselves in others' shoes" in order to project what people might think or how they might react. Advocates of Simulation Theory assert that humans "represent" the mental states of others in an "offline" simulation, and anticipate the reactions of others based on our own reactions. This model was first advocated by philosophers Robert Gordon and Jane Heal in 1986, and further developed by Alvin Goldman, and Stephen Stich and Shaun Nichols in the following decade. According to the Simulation Theory model, the ability to simulate another's mental process emerges in young children as a byproduct of play acting and role playing—acts of mentalism performed even in the early toddler years (Goldman 95). As people mature, their competence in Simulation Theory depends upon developing the ability to take into account differences between themselves and those they observe, in order to be able to simulate accurately. Neurological studies support the Simulation Theory model by confirming the existence of "mirror neurons" in the premotor cortex of apes; these neurons activate equally when an animal performs a task or when it observes another engaged in that same task (Gallese and Goldman 493–98).

To further undermine the likelihood that Theory Theory is the primary form of mentalizing, Goldman even asserts that formation of ToM principles among preschoolers would not be possible because adults do not instruct children explicitly concerning mentalist activity (78–81). This contention is easy to refute; a key element of early childhood socialization involves helping children to discover the connections between the behaviors of others and the thoughts and feelings that cause those reactions—initially, for the purpose of preventing actions that provoke tears or anger in others. Children's television programs and storybooks also provide instruction in this area; for example, one of the most popular *Sesame Street* characters, Elmo, is a fuzzy red monster whose primary plot function is to help children label emotions. Astington cites Vygotsky's findings that children's early and frequent exposure to "mentalistic" conversation from both family members and other members of their social group is essential to the formation of a culturally specific (rather than universal) Theory Theory model of mentalism (194). In addition many cognitive scholars, including Stich and Nichols, assert that the formation of MR "rules" (like the deduction of basic grammar rules and physics laws) is largely tacit, rather than conscious ("Folk" 124).

In recent years, cognitivists have begun to assert that a fully functional ToM involves the use of *both* types of projections (Carruthers and Smith 4–5). Jason Mitchell rejects the argument that Theory Theory and Simulation Theory are mutually exclusive, and that cognitive functions tend toward the simple and unified (known as the "Parsimony Argument"), explaining:

like all biological systems, the brain has been cobbled together through natural selection, a process notorious for tinkering with existing mechanisms without much regard for Occam's razor. And indeed, much of the progress made by cognitive neuroscience over the past three decades has been of a decidedly non-parsimonious nature, in particular the repeated observation that complex cognitive processes—such as memory, cognitive control, and semantic knowledge—do not reflect the operation of unitary mechanisms but rather of multiple processes with distinct neuroanatomical correlates. (363)

Stich and Nichols agree that Simulation Theory is "only one component in a very complicated story" and assert that "mindreading depends on a motley array of mechanisms" (Nichols and Stich, *Mindreading* 212–13). There is a consensus that the repertoire of mind-reading activities is situation-dependent; that is to say, the utility of Simulation Theory or Theory Theory is not absolute but depends on the circumstances in which one mind seeks to understand and influence another. For example, Paul Harris believes that Simulation Theory can be used to improve the sophistication of Theory Theory, and Carruthers sees Simulation Theory as a supplement to Theory Theory in situations that call for "fine grained predictions" (Harris 207; Carruthers 25). The next step in this field of research should entail studies to determine whether or not there exist statistically significant rules or trends concerning when and how each approach is used. Jane Heal asserts that a valid model will answer the question, "What is the appropriate realm of each and how do they interact?" and will offer "systematically organized insight into the difference between our responses in usual and unusual cases" (75–83). In applying the ToM paradigms of Theory Theory and Simulation Theory to the mentalistic activities of early modern Spanish literary characters, I will indeed attempt to delineate "organized insights" concerning the patterns of cognitive activity, exploring situational uses and also seeking to delineate trends among the representations of characters from particular social subgroups: picaresque rogues and their victims and associates, *damas* and *galanes*, and aspiring courtiers.

Advocates of both forms of ToM agree that most mentalist activity is performed at a semiautomatic or tacit level of cognition (Goldman 88; Stich and Nichols, "Folk" 124). In literature as in life, only in the most novel social situations do characters and humans employ MR in a highly conscious manner and make deliberate choices of Theory Theory or Simulation Theory. It is my contention that studying early modern literature from the vantage point of cognitive theory is productive precisely because there is an unusually intensive representation of deliberate acts of mentalizing in texts that highlight new forms of social interaction in Golden Age Spanish urban and court society. My study follows in the footsteps of scholars who have applied this paradigm to texts written in other spaces and eras: Zunshine's *Why We Read Fiction* (2006) provided the earliest detailed analysis of ToM and literature, followed by Vermeule's *Why Do We Care about Literary Characters* (2009) and Alan Palmer's *Social Minds in the Novel* (2010). The Leverage et al. anthology *Theory of Mind and Literature* includes two articles on early modern Spain. In addition, Zunshine's recent anthology *Introduction to Cognitive Cultural Studies* (2010) includes several articles that use the ToM paradigm for analysis of English-language texts.

Both with real beings and with literary characters, studies of MR have focused upon this activity as highly individualistic: one person or character projects the thoughts and reactions of a specific and unique other individual. Sanjida O'Connell uses the term "folk psychology" to describe a set of cultural norms for ascribing specific mental states to "pre-existing categories of behavior" (33). Folk psychology entails explaining individual mentality and behavior by reference to generalized social models, but does not appear to make projections based on positing particularities for specific subgroups. Within the field of literary studies, interest in the possible existence of period- or culture-specific models of how different identity groups think has focused on the by now well-known binaries that portray dominant groups as mentally superior and denigrates outgroups as having a lower intellect and less reasoning capacity (Jaggar 149–51). Scholars of cognitive psychology have just begun to explore the ways that a person or character forms projections based on cultural stereotypes concerning how a specific social subgroup thinks. Alan Palmer uses the term "intermental thinking" to describe shared thoughts or beliefs among social subgroups, and points to incompatibilities between intermental groups as a source of literary and social conflict (229). This model can be taken one step further by noting that these discrepancies can form the basis for formation of derogatory or marginalizing ToMs among incompatible groups. I will demonstrate that in early modern Spanish literary texts, there are myriad examples of characters who employ an MR that depends on projections of a group mentality (according to gender, religion or social ranking) rather than an individual mind.

Machiavellian Intelligence

One primary component of ToM is known as Machiavellian Intelligence (MI) or Social Intelligence (SI). MI serves as a "banner" term for a cluster of ToM studies within the social sciences, which share the belief that "*possession of the cognitive capability we call intelligence is linked with social living and the problems of complexity it can pose*" (Byrne and Whiten, "Machiavellian" 1; emphasis in original). MR transforms into MI or Social Intelligence (SI) as advanced minds living in complex social systems seek to be the most successful at understanding rivals' mental processes in order to better deceive one another for material and/or social advantage (Byrne and Whiten, "Tactical" 208 and "Manipulation" 211). The drastic social dislocations and increase in social complexity that Spain experienced during the early modern era are well known and have been documented extensively. Although the *topos* of deception or *engaño* has been explored in many early modern literary studies, most recently by Donald Gilbert-Santamaría, who discusses a "poetics of engaño" in the picaresque, such analyses have tended to present this topic from a perspective that is dehistorized and abstract (108).

A crucial step in the development of a sophisticated ToM is the moment of understanding that other minds can hold beliefs that are different from one's own. Many studies (of children and primates) have explored the phenomenon of false belief: the ability to understand that others have ideas that differ from the (perceived) state of the world (Wimmer and Perner 103–20). One common test employed to measure this ability involves object permanence: a test subject watches while an examiner places an item in a specific location, and also sees that another subject is watching this. While the other subject is out of the room, the examiner moves the item to a new location, then asks the first text subject: where will the other subject look for the item? A subject displays understanding of false belief at the point when she is capable of understanding that even though she knows that the item has been moved, the other subject will hold a false belief about its location because he did not see when it was moved. Comprehension of false belief, on the part of apes or children, is believed to be the first step in the development of the ability to deceive.

Once the false belief phenomenon is fully understood, advanced primates can begin to influence the minds of others—to deliberately create false beliefs—for a variety of purposes including foraging (economic) success, hierarchical advancement, and sexual satisfaction or reproduction. The form of ToM used for purposes of deception is known as Machiavellian Intelligence (MI). In its most general sense, this term implies the negative, colloquial understanding of Machiavellianism associated with the Italian philosopher, "a strategy of social conduct that involves manipulating others for personal gain, often against the others' self interest" (Byrne and Whiten, "Machiavellian" 12). The more nuanced conceptual framework currently in use is often referred to as Social Intelligence (SI) and includes "not only relatively short term personal gain, such as deception, but also acts such as helping and co-operation that are conventionally seen as alternative strategies … geared to maximizing 'personal' gain in the ultimate currency of reproductive success" (Byrne and Whiten, "Machiavellian" 12–13). In this study, I will use the term MI to describe the "narrow" forms of deception that are short term, selfish, and harmful to those upon whom they are practiced; while SI will be employed to describe the "broad" array of complex and indirect manipulative or cooperative tactics (Strum 74).

Laboratory and field observations of the great apes have uncovered many cognitive activities that entail deceiving others concerning one's actions or motivations (LaFrenière 239). In primate societies where MI was first studied, great apes in the wild were observed looking away from a food source and then returning later in order to eat it privately rather than sharing (because social cooperation mandates the sharing of food discoveries), low ranking males carefully chose seating places in order to perform courtship displays or even fornicate without being detected and sanctioned by dominant males (they chose sites where some body parts could be seen, so that they did not appear to be hiding, but used large rocks or trees to screen genitalia so that sexual activity would not be noticed), and apes were observed forming strategic alliances with nonrelative group members in order to preserve or enhance social status (LaFrenière 240). In captivity, ToM-based deceptive tactics included feigning a need to use the restroom so a trainer would take an ape past a room where a favorite simian companion was performing tasks or playing (Byrne and Whiten, "Manipulation" 211). These studies have demonstrated a considerable level of Social Intelligence among great apes, but not among lesser monkeys such as vervets. It is noteworthy that in the vast majority of cases, it is primarily lower-ranking group members who use MI to negotiate survival and advancement, while dominant males had far less need for subterfuge or cooperation (Miller 328).

Zunshine describes ToM within literary studies as "the ability to explain behavior in terms of the underlying states of mind—or *mind reading* ability" (*Why* 4). While the research concerning MI in ape societies and as part of the mental development of children is well established, the application of the MI paradigm to literary study is in a nascent phase, especially within Hispanism. Mancing has provided a keen analysis of the way Sancho Panza uses SI in the second volume in order to convince Don Quixote that a smelly peasant girl is an enchanted Dulcinea ("Sancho" 125–26). The squire bases his particular deception on his knowledge of his master's specific mental quirks and on the correct projection that because of his particular form of madness, he will accept the discrepancies between the girl's appearance and his fantasy of Dulcinea's beauty by blaming an enchanter. Within early modern Spanish texts, SI is rampant in texts which represent courtship or the pursuit of social advancement, two arenas of primate and human activity in which deception is most prevalent—and productive.

Cognitivists who study MR and SI in primates offer several theories concerning why this function arises in great apes but not lesser monkeys (Gigerenzer 265–67). The theory that I find most convincing—and not coincidentally most relevant to the study of early modern literature—links the need for advanced mental capabilities such as MR to large social groups with complex and hierarchical dominance systems (Boehm 358). Human society will always have its share of Machiavellian figures, but certain historical moments of major societal transition, such as the early modern, project an unusually intense emphasis upon ToM and SI. Studies by J.H. Elliott, Fernand Braudel, Henry Kamen, and John Lynch have shown that the early modern period was marked by the gradual decay of feudal social organizations. With the emergence of larger urban, commercial, and courtier population centers, the opportunities for contact with a wide variety of individuals increased, even as direct knowledge of individuals and families necessarily decreased. This marks a drastic shift from a society in which the members of local aristocracies were well known to one another and endogamous marriages were the norm. A related factor is the substantial increase in the number of titled nobility, as a result of efforts to ease financial pressures during the reigns of Philip II and III, which brought unfamiliar new families to court (including some whose fortunes were obtained in the Americas). The already complex act of MR becomes more difficult when there is a lack of intimate knowledge of most of the people one encounters. At the same time, skilled MR becomes more necessary in a social environment that provides far more opportunity for lying or breaking the rules without detection. An increased awareness of and concern about MR and SI, a product and symptom of the drastic demographic changes of the sixteenth century, is an unrecognized but fundamental aspect of the early modern obsession with *engaño* in writings of all types.

I am offering the model of ToM and SI as a supplement to, and not as a replacement for, current historically based approaches. At its most basic level, the MI paradigm posits certain types of social manipulation as a *universal* aspect of primate and human cognitive activity and behavior, arising from evolutionary pressures that selected for individuals that were most successful in particular forms of social interactions. In highly evolved human societies, the universal aspects of human cognitive processes will not manifest themselves equally at all times and in all situations; rather, specific material conditions call forth the most appropriate of a large variety of survival responses and related cognitive processes. Thus, in applying ToM to early modern texts, I am interested in exploring the ways that authors focused upon particular types of deceptive behavior and the deceitful mindsets of particular social groups, which were described as *newly* intense or problematic at that specific historical moment. Chapters 2, 3, and 4 will focus upon three genres, the *comedia*, the picaresque novel, and the conduct manual, in which representations of deception and SI play a key role in the scrutiny of the dramatic social transformations that Spain undergoes during the early modern age. In all three genres, SI is depicted in a paradoxical manner, both as a skill that virtuous protagonists use to their benefit, but also as a Machiavellian form of dishonesty or lack of authenticity. Each genre explores, albeit from a different perspective, the anxieties that arise at this specific historical moment in response to a new type of court structure and new modes of urban life—and to the resultant modifications in the norms associated with gender and class identity. Cognitive theory emphasizes the importance of MI and SI for survival during periods of environmental change; although anthropologists refer to the geographic factors of droughts and ice ages, I will demonstrate that this model can also be used to explore the early modern urban court as a site of equally drastic social dislocations that elicited an increase in the use of and concerns about SI.

Overview

Chapter 2 unites previously unconnected areas, ToM, MI, and *comedia* study. The few studies to date that have addressed cognitive theory and theater have not used ToM as a paradigm (Connor 155). Zunshine mentions theater only in passing, in order to highlight the differences between novel and play, observing that in place of a narrator the stage offers embodied characters whose gestures, facial expressions, and tones of voice are the foundations of MR activity (*Why* 23). For this reason, this chapter will offer a new direction in literary applications of ToM and MR, scrutinizing how cognitive behavior is represented in the dramatic characters of Spain's "Golden Age." Because courtship drama so heavily emphasizes the relationship between gender, deception, and MR, this chapter will provide a comparison of representative dramas by male and female authors. In patriarchal cultures, cognitive mechanisms are presented through gender-biased filters, so that texts often highlight and condemn "female" forms of deception while minimizing the deception that male characters perpetrate. Male-authored plays that represent a deceptive *galán*, such as *La verdad sospechosa* and *El burlador de Sevilla*, depict Don García and Don Juan as satirical figures to be punished or exiled; this construct implies that the Machiavellian male is the exception that proves the patriarchal rule of masculine superiority. Or, as in the case of *El desdén con el desdén*, masculine deception is presented as socially beneficial. By contrast, the plays of Ana Caro *(El conde Partinuplés)*, María de Zayas *(La traición en la amistad)*, and Angela de Azevedo *(El muerto disimulado; La margarita del Tajo que dio nombre a Santarén)* depict a wide range of appropriate and harmful deceptions on the part of characters of both genders.

Chapter 3 provides an exploration of the function of ToM and SI within the urban contexts presented in *Lazarillo de Tormes*, *Guzmán de Alfarache*, and *La vida del Buscón*. In picaresque literature, mental maturation coincides with a moment when the protagonist, newly immersed in a corrupt urban setting, becomes aware that humans often seek to deceive and that for this reason he needs to develop a ToM. Thus, a key moment in the trajectory of nearly all picaresque narrative is the initial moment of illumination when an innocent youth realizes that the social world is a game of wits in which MI, the ability to anticipate and avert the machinations of others, is the minimum requirement for survival. The pícaro realizes that to survive and prosper he must always assume that those he meets are using their ToM against him, and devise ways not only to avoid their traps but also to create his own scams. All three of the major picaresque protagonists, Lazarillo, Guzmán, and Pablos, experience this perverse form of epiphany within the initial chapters of their respective narratives. The chapter incorporates recent research on poverty, hunger, and charity to trace the connections between new social discourses concerning indigence and the cognitive skills that a pícaro must develop to survive in highly stratified urban societies.

Chapter 4 highlights moments when characters use MI and SI to move beyond economic survival and pursue higher levels of social status within shifting hierarchies of power and dominance. In the early modern era, manuals for courtier advancement provide a blatant representation of advanced minds competing to be the most successful at understanding rivals' mental processes in order to better influence and even deceive one another for material and/or social advantage. In applying the concept of SI to early modern courtier manuals, I trace the homologies between this new cognitive paradigm and the particular types of cognitive behavior that Gracián represents as necessary for survival and advancement at court in his collection of maxims, *Oráculo manual y arte de prudencia*. The chapter also makes use of recent studies by Francisco Sánchez and Felipe Ruan to analyze the parallels between courtier manuals and the social advancement tactics that pícaro protagonists employ. In addition, it explores picaresque and courtier deception in relation to Stephen Greenblatt's model of self-fashioning and Erving Goffman's paradigm of performance and impression management as tools for social advancement.

In dramas, novels, and manuals alike, ToM and deceptive cognitive functions are characterized as giving rise to new modes of thought and manner. Thus, in applying MI to early modern texts, I am interested in exploring the ways that authors focused upon particular types of deceptive behavior and the deceitful mindsets of particular social groups, which were described as *newly* intense or problematic at that specific historical moment of intensive urbanization.

Chapter 5 provides a detailed exploration of the interrelations between two modes of cognition: early modern skepticism and contemporary contextualism. The contextualist model of cognitive functionality is dependent upon new models of the brain itself. In recent decades, new paths of research on brain-injured patients and new insights gained from ever-improving technologies such as positron emission (PET) scans of the brain and magnetic resonance imaging (MRI) have drastically reshaped scientific knowledge of brain structures and functions, highlighting the engagement of numerous areas of the brain in mental activity (Damasio 14; Sacks 62–63). One early model, by Jerry Fodor, proposed that thinking is "modular" rather than linear in nature; that is to say, that at any given time, separate compartments of the brain work simultaneously but independently—at a nonconscious level—to process different types of information (37–46). The nonconscious level is automatic, like the brain level that controls breathing, and is not in any way related to the Freudian unconscious mind. Subsequent research in several different fields has shown Fodor's model to be incomplete; however, all of the theories that have enriched and developed Fodor's modularity reinforce the tenet that consciousness derives from simultaneous or parallel and multifaceted nonconscious processes that provide the conscious mind with varied and even conflicting knowledges.

Ellen Spolsky uses the paradigm of modularity to explain the basis of skepticism as a philosophical system; she notes that this school is based upon the premise that sensory information is unreliable and often contradictory. Spolsky attributes the conflicting information streams that skepticism highlights to the varying data provided to the conscious mind by different modules. She writes that for many Shakespearean characters, quandaries about judgment and knowledge arise from "the multiplicity of knowledge itself" (*Satisfying* 80). Spolsky emphasizes concerns about absolute knowledge of the female mind and its potential for true virtue as a key epistemological fault line where early modern literary characters apply skeptical modes of inquiry. She cites various written and visual reinscriptions of the Roman myth of the rape and subsequent suicide of Lucretia in the sixteenth century, as well as the plot line of a spouse who errs in believing his wife has been unfaithful as presented in *Othello* and Shakespeare's late romances, to illustrate this thesis ("Women's Work" 51; *Satisfying* 68*).*

Spolsky's approach to Shakespeare also helps to shed new light on early modern Spanish texts that present conflicting modalities of cognition as the basis for their critiques of the early modern obsession with honor. The *motif* of unjustified suspicions against a faithful wife is at the forefront of early modern Spanish honor literature; I will focus upon the canonical honor texts *El médico de su honra* and "El curioso impertinente" episode of *Don Quixote* and the feminist reinscription of these works found in María de Zayas's wife murder novellas. In "La más infame venganza," and "El verdugo de su esposa" she identifies epistemological flaws in the honor code as a key factor in women's oppression, which lead to uxoricide.

Spolsky asserts that many honor dramas point to "the impossibility of knowing the things one most needs to know by seeing alone—by judging outward appearances" and suggests that in the late romances, Shakespeare chose tragicomedy as the genre that allows for an embodied knowledge that is "sufficiently satisfying so as to avoid the death of innocent women" ("Women's Work" 78). In early modern Spain, "tragicomic" resolutions to the skeptic's dilemma can be found in many honor plays, as well as in a few of the novellas in Zayas's *Desengaños amorosos*. I will explore Lope de Vega's *El animal de Hungría*, and Zayas's "La inocencia castigada" and "La perseguida triunfante" as representative examples of the tragicomic solution. The tragic and tragicomic texts foreground the problem of how to evaluate complex and conflicting data about gender and honor, highlighting epistemological quandaries that bear a strong relation to the contextualist paradigm.

Chapter 6 examines Lope de Vega's highly self-referential drama, *Lo fingido verdadero*, through the lens of contextualist skepticism. Metatheater is a key element of early modern Spanish dramas that address the problems of cognition and knowledge. One of the defining features of Spanish "baroque" literature of all genres is its emphasis on the text as a set of arbitrary conventions, rather than as a direct or "natural" imitation of reality. In this way, metatheater highlights the problematic nature of the boundary between the real and its many opposites: the illusory, the feigned, the misperceived, the deceptive. Although the metatheatrical aspects of early modern Spanish drama have been studied extensively in recent decades, there has been much less interest among Hispanists in the exploration of philosophical skepticism in the *comedia* or of the symbiotic relationship between artistic self-referentiality and epistemology. In Lope's play, the protagonists inhabit the shadowy borderlands where "real life," acting, and epistemological confusion meet and mingle. Because this play dramatizes a miracle that leads a Roman actor to convert to Christianity, the boundaries between the real and its shadow companions are even more difficult to delineate. This analysis will enable a fuller appreciation of the homologies between self-reflexive literature, early modern skepticism, and the current model of knowledge as derived from embodied, contextualist, and networked cognitive processes. In addition, I will argue that the play depicts the conversion from pagan to Christian as a trope or metaphor for the conversion of Spain's *morisco* population. Lope wrote this play at the end of the tumultuous decade when Catholics debated the sincerity of the *morisco* conversions and ultimately chose to expel the entire group. This chapter links anxieties about the performance of religious identity to the self-fashioning of class and gender roles as explored in previous chapters.

Chapter 7 brings together several strands of cognitive approaches to reading in order to explore the way that Cervantes represents an emergent form of engagement with narrative entertainment. In recent decades, cognitive theorists have moved beyond theoretical speculation to conduct research about what readers actually do (László 150). Victor Nell's *Lost in a Book* analyzes leisure reading, from a theoretical and experimental perspective, in order to reconceptualize this activity and to destigmatize some forms of leisure reading. Nell links concerns about entertainment fiction to moments of religious reform: during both the Reformation era in Germany and the Puritan movement in England, the scrutiny of popular fiction was linked to social discourses that praised industry and disparaged leisure activity as a form of idleness that could foster sinful activity (26–27). Nell's study does not include consideration of post-Tridentine Spain; however, Counter Reformation Spain was equally suspicious of worldly pleasures. And, of course, the topic of "idleness" is ubiquitous in the Cervantine novel, where it is depicted as provoking a socioeconomic crisis as well as a spiritual decline. The importance of unproductive leisure arises at key moments, beginning with the very first sentence of the prologue, which simultaneously apostrophizes and reprimands its "desocupado lector." Don Quixote himself, as well as the pseudo-shepherds who follow Marcela into the woods, and the Duke and Duchess, are denigrated with the adjective "ocioso." The forms of unhealthy reading with which these characters indulge themselves is intimately linked to the idleness of their social groups.

Zunshine applies the ToM paradigm to reading practices, as readers employ MR on characters and narrators. She delineates source monitoring and source tagging as key components of the act of reading; these are the processes by which both characters and readers use their ToM to gauge the reliability of narrators and characters as they are presented over the course of a novel (*Why* 50–60). Source tagging is a central activity for character development, which often hinges upon the moments when a character forms and then later "reweighs" beliefs or feelings (*Why* 61). Source monitoring is also an essential tool for *readers* of texts whose aesthetic interest derives from monitoring the narrator(s) and characters as reliable or not (*Why* 76). Zunshine identifies *Don Quixote* as the initiator of this technique and thus terms all such subsequent texts, from *Clarissa* to *Pale Fire*, as Cervantes's "progeny" (*Why* 75).

Elaine Scarry studies another form of cognitive engagement, the processes by which readers bring to life the words on the printed page. Her particular interest is the types of language that provide readers with concrete and detailed instructions for creating visual images. One of her examples is "radiant ignition," the technique by which words are used to illuminate a scene or a figure part by part, like a spotlight moving across a space or object (80–81). This illuminative practice resembles the medieval blazon and

Petrarchan "dismemberment" tactics by which authors provided numerous vivid metaphors to aid readers' creation of a mental image of each of a woman's important physical attributes. Cervantes utilizes radiant ignition to parody the dismemberment tactic, using both exaggeration and mockery in his depictions of female figures, most of them noteworthy either for supernatural beauty or grotesque ugliness. While many studies have analyzed various aspects of female beauty or its opposite, application of Scarry's concept adds a new dimension to our appreciation of Cervantine inscriptions of gender and class norms (Richardson 43–47).

Concerns about the validity of cognitive approaches to literature are common among literary scholars who associate neuroscience with deterministic models of human behavior, which can be used in particularly deleterious discourses against persons occupying marginalized gender and class positions. The contextualist paradigm of interactive cognition and the newly emerging discipline of "Social Neuroscience" (a journal by that name was launched in 2006) are two important indicators that facile determinism is on the wane. Both of these approaches are consistent with "ecological" cognitivism, which proposes an interactive model of brain, individual psyche, and environment. This approach is embodied but resolutely antideterministic. The ecological model goes beyond both the Cartesian model of the brain as the dominant cognitive force, and simple models of environmental determinism as the determining factor. The readings I offer of the social functions of cognition in early modern texts posit interactive and hence ecological forms of cognitive theory. The ecological approach to cognitive cultural studies is a deliberate rejection of Foucauldian and New Historicist models that posit humans as powerless or hapless in the face of structures of domination. The essays in *Introduction to Cognitive Cultural Studies* envision this praxis as a continuation and development of British cultural and feminist materialism, offering explorations of cognition as an additional factor to consider in exploring literary representations of social resistance and individual agency. I have used this model of interactivity as one of the bases for analysis of the ideological dimensions of early modern literature. Each chapter delineates the ways in which authors support or challenge early modern Spain's normative projections concerning the cognitive functions of humans who are born into specific subject positions related to class or caste and gender. Each chapter demonstrates that challenges to the status quo in early modern Spanish literature include scrutiny, critique, and even outright condemnation of the validity and veracity of patriarchal and hierarchical models of subjectivity and cognitive function.

This book brings together several strands of cognitive theory and delineates the synergies among neurological, anthropological, and psychological discoveries, which provide new insights into human cognition. This interdisciplinary focus of "cognitive cultural study" enables us to better understand the relationship between cognitive function and social responses to and representations of the major social transformations of early modern Spain. In each chapter, the insights of contemporary cognitive theory enable new levels of analysis concerning how early modern writers conceptualized the mental activities of a variety of social groups. In particular, each chapter focuses upon the way that a specific literary form delineates the relationship between an urbanizing culture, unstable subject positions and hierarchies, and social anxieties about the relationship between cognition and cultural transformation.

Chapter Two

Theory of Mind, Social Intelligence, and Urban Courtship Drama

Cognitive research emphasizes that social interaction within complex and hierarchical habitats frequently features extensive recourse to Theory of Mind (ToM) and Machiavellian (MI) or Social Intelligence (SI), both to protect oneself from others and to deploy deception for selfish as well as altruistic purposes (see Chapter 1 for a detailed presentation). This chapter seeks to open new avenues of study concerning the connections between gender norms and the use of SI in early modern dramatic literature. Lisa Zunshine links literary study of ToM specifically to narrative texts, beginning with the courtship novels of Jane Austen, because the novel is the form that most consistently devotes attention to "numerous interacting minds" (*Why* 10). While the assertion that ToM is more prevalent in narrative than in drama may be true for literature written since 1800 (although I suspect George Bernard Shaw and Oscar Wilde would disagree), in the early modern period it is equally common to encounter complex courtship plots on the stage. Like the social novel, *comedias* also foreground interacting minds; indeed, Zunshine herself subsequently published an essay on ToM in Dryden's early modern drama ("Essentialism"). As I demonstrate in Chapter 1, literary texts are most likely to foreground deception and SI at historical moments where significant social mobility leads to instability and uncertainty concerning the markers of group status and to discrepancies concerning cultural norms for courtship. Periods of urbanization also create a drastic increase in social encounters among strangers; William R. Blue's *Spanish Comedy and Historical Contexts in the 1620s* provides the most comprehensive exploration to date of the role of urbanization and gender relations in the *comedia*. These two factors shape the material worlds and the representation of courtship both in Austen's novels and in the *comedia*; the plays analyzed in this chapter highlight anxieties concerning cognitive practices and "gender disorder" on the part of *damas* and *galanes* alike (Perry, *Gender*). I will explore the representation of the uses of SI among male and female protagonists created by both male and female playwrights. The chapter will begin with three plays that foreground feminine cognitive competence: Ana Caro's *El conde Partinuplés*, and Angela de Azevedo's *El muerto disimulado* and *La margarita del Tajo que dio nombre a Santarén*. It will continue with a scrutiny of *La traición en la amistad*; this play by María de Zayas y Sotomayor has proven problematic for feminist scholars because of the female protagonist's duplicity. A cognitive reading of this play offers new insights, if not definitive answers, to this quandary. The chapter concludes with studies of deception and manipulation in two canonical male-authored comedies, *La verdad sospechosa* and *El desdén con el desdén*. I will demonstrate that there is significant evidence of bias on the part of authors of each gender concerning the uses of deception by characters of the opposite gender. However, the treatment of the *enagño* motif and SI ranges across a continuum, and the aesthetic norms of various dramatic subgenres also play a decisive role in the presentation of cognitive activity and gender ideology.

As indicated in Chapter 1, ToM entails two related activities: (1) Simulation Theory, the mental act of projecting the thoughts and reactions of a specific person in a *unique* situation by "placing oneself in another's shoes" and (2) Theory Theory, which entails the deployment of culturally established paradigms of normative group behaviors in order to project how a person (or character) will react in a *typical* situation. The use of both forms of ToM is pervasive in urban courtship drama. Characters frequently use Theory Theory to explain an act of ToM by referring to the cognitive norms of males or females as a group. For example, in *Valor, agravio, y mujer*, Leonor employs Theory Theory in order to induce Juan to fulfill his prior vow to marry her even though he had lost interest in her after the initial conquest. She projects, correctly, that Juan will regain interest in her if he discovers that another man wants her. Nowhere does Leonor state that Juan as an individual is particularly jealous or prone to dog-in-the-manger behavior; instead, it appears that she applies knowledge of cultural stereotypes of aristocratic masculine attitudes. The attribution of gender-based group Theory Theory can be seen in all the dramas to be addressed in this chapter. Simulation Theory is most often used where Theory Theory cannot suffice; when characters' actions are anomalous for persons in their social situation and so projection (and manipulation) of their thoughts requires a more specific analysis. Simulation Theory is often used with "deviant" comic protagonists, such as Fenisa in *Traición en la amistad* or Don García in *La verdad sospechosa*, in order to re-establish social control. One important aspect of the representation of gendered cognitive competence in these plays is the ability (or lack thereof) on the part of male and female characters to know when to apply each Theory. The least insightful characters studied in this chapter are the fathers and suitors who make poor choices concerning when and how to use different forms of ToM, while a key component of the feminist ideology in the plays by *dramaturgas* is the creation of heroines who excel in all aspects of SI.

Machiavellian or Social Intelligence (MI, SI), which entails the use of both forms of ToM to deceive others, is highly relevant to mating rituals, in real life and in literature. Alain Schmitt and Karl Grammer have pointed out that this form of mentalism is prevalent during mate selection in primates and humans; because evolution has structured the female brain to prefer males who possess wealth or prestige in order to assure the survival of her children, males most often use MI to deceive women about their status (104–05). Cognitive research helps to shed light on the *mudanza* theme that is central to early modern literature, demonstrating that in spite of all stereotypes about fickle women, it is in fact male humans and higher apes who show a strong tendency toward neophilia—attraction to what is novel. Geoffrey Miller notes that this is a neurochemical response, linked to a dopamine receptor gene (331). The tendency within courtship ritual to prefer and pursue disinterested or disdainful partners seems to be linked to the neophilia response. For this reason, the conventional female trait of feigning a lack of interest may be in part an evolutionary mechanism to appear novel and thus elicit interest. In survival-oriented societies, this response is curbed because danger often accompanies novelty, while in early modern society and courtship drama, codes of honor pose an obstacle to unrestrained pursuit of amorous variety (Miller 331). In addition, Miller's research into "protean strategies" indicates that primates of both genders engage in deliberately unpredictable behaviors in order to block MR and Machiavellian manipulation, especially in courtship situations (327). Cognitive research indicates that both genders employ deceptive practices in order to facilitate their reproductive success, although in different ways. I want to emphasize that I am in no way suggesting that these cognitive tendencies constitute a gender-based neurological determinism; clearly, in advanced human society many other factors shape norms and discourses of gendered behavior. After providing an exhaustive overview of the vast terrain of cognitive study, Howard Mancing proclaims the superiority of "contextualist" models of human behavior, which emphasize that the individual personality is a product of a complex and interdependent web of evolved physical structures and processes, individual experience and sociocultural formation ("Embodied" 39). For this reason, I will reiterate the quotation from Mancing cited in Chapter 1, behavior is "one hundred percent nature and one hundred percent nurture" ("Embodied" 39). My modest claim is merely that awareness of these cognitive mechanisms enables us to better understand the origins of the normative discourses concerning social manipulation—and thus, to offer a possible explanation for the continuing prevalence of gender stereotypes concerning the types of deception that play a prominent role in early modern courtship literature (and, sadly, that persist in contemporary narrative media such as television sit-coms and Hollywood film). In patriarchal cultures, these cognitive mechanisms are presented through gender-biased filters, so that texts often highlight and condemn "female" forms of deception, and even project neophilia onto women, while minimizing the scale and significance of deception on the part of male characters.

One important contribution to literary applications of ToM is Daniel Dennett's model of levels of intentionality. Dennett explains that human beings process two or three levels of intentionality without even noticing, including such thoughts as

> "I hope he doesn't know that I know about his lie." Beyond three levels the task becomes more complex, as this example indicates, "You wonder [1] whether I realise [2] how hard it is for you to be sure [3] that you understand [4] whether I mean to be saying [5] that you can recognise [6] that I can believe [7] you want me to explain [8] that most of us can keep track of only about five or six orders [of intentionality] under the best of circumstances." (Dennett 243, cited by Mancing, "James" 129)

The highly convoluted plots of many early modern comedies depend upon the presentation of multiple levels of intentionality and deception. Where Dennett's example describes an apparently truthful situation, it is more common in early modern drama to encounter situations involving lies or other types of deception and manipulation, in which one character wonders [1] if the other is aware [2] that s/he is deceiving the other [3] concerning whether or not s/he is aware [4] of a prior deception perpetrated by the other [5]. This example demonstrates that even at the fifth level of intentionality, spectator or reader comprehension is strained. The endless variants on this model of multilevel intentionality, which can be found in fleshed-out form in many early modern dramas, most often entail young men and women deceiving their fathers, or courting couples manipulating each other or their rivals. The ubiquity of complex intentionality within early modern plays indicates a keen awareness of this particular form of deception as an important component of early modern aristocratic culture, even though they lacked contemporary research modalities and cognitive vocabularies. Of course, comic dramas often exaggerate the problem by presenting improbably complex and interwoven strands of intentionality, for the purposes of aesthetic experimentation and pushing the artistic envelope (see also Richardson; Vermeule).

Wise Women in *El conde Partinuplés*

In Ana Caro's *El conde Partinuplés*, Princess Rosaura must be able to form an accurate ToM of the men who court her; her cognitive capacity is crucial both to a successful marriage and to the security of her nation. When Rosaura learns that she must marry in order to maintain her claim to the throne, she proclaims to her cousin Aldora that she wishes she could examine her suitors and "verle[s] el alma hacia dentro" in order to select the fittest mate and sovereign (I.271). Rosaura is even more concerned than the usual *dama* or princess, because a prophetic dream has revealed the potential tragic outcome of a bad choice. Aldora is a *maga* but with limited power; she has a magical mirror that enables Rosaura to view her potential spouses, but she can show the princess only what each man is doing at that specific moment. Rosaura must use this opportunity to form a comprehensive ToM for each man—not merely to intuit the immediate mental activity of a man based on how he is behaving at that moment, but to perform a broader reading in which that one activity is the key to the contender's entire character. In this instance, the more detailed insights of

Simulation Theory are most applicable, and this is the path that Rosaura chooses. Feminist interpretations of this "dating game" scenario highlight the numerous elements of plot reinscription as central to Caro's scrutiny of gender norms (Simerka, "Early Feminist" 498). Juan Pablo Gil-Oslé astutely analyzes this moment as a feminist version of the Judgment of Paris. Teresa Soufas highlights the political aspect of this drama rather than the courtship process, asserting that Caro critiques patriarchal norms that declare females unfit for governing (*Dramas* 41). An exploration of Rosaura's advanced cognitive skills complements these feminist readings.

One key aspect of successful mind reading is to establish a valid relationship between an observed behavior and the underlying mental activity to be interpreted. The Simulation Theory that the princess employs to reject three of the suitors as too vain, too bookish or too bellicose to be a good husband also produces valid reasons for considering them unsuitable as monarchs. An even more important example of mind reading is that which Aldora has performed on Rosaura, although the *maga*'s MR activity is never directly mentioned. Aldora shows Rosaura four men, but tells her that the last, Partinuplés, is actually not available because he is already engaged to another woman. Her cousin responds on two separate occasions that for this precise reason he is the perfect mate, for her character compels her to pursue "un imposible" and "yo lo difícil intento / lo fácil es para todos" (I.383, 420–21). While Rosaura explicitly uses mind reading to evaluate candidates, we can also infer that Aldora uses Simulation Theory, applying her knowledge of Rosaura's love of a challenge (neophilia), to present the man she believes to be the best candidate in a light that will assure that he is also Rosaura's choice. This play, which derives from a French chivalric novel in which the magical elements were more prominent, presents the sorceress as a figure who will use her enhanced knowledge and ability to produce benefit rather than harm (De Armas, *Invisible*). However, her MR ability concerning Rosaura is presented as a human rather than supernatural trait.

Aldora's preference for Partinuplés and her skillful use of ToM, while understated and implicit, become more and more important as the play progresses, as she sets the stage for the unconventional courtship and prevents Rosaura from having Partinuplés killed unjustly. In the end, the mind reading abilities of Rosaura and

Aldora, who used Simulation Theory to judge the proclivities of Partinuplés, are validated when he rejects the throne of France out of love for Rosaura and thus reveals himself to be the ideal mate and ruler. It is a critical commonplace that Caro's *Valor, agravio y mujer* offers a feminist reinscription of *La vida es sueño*; Christopher Weimer and Mercedes Maroto Camino propose that *El conde Partinuplés* is a less obvious reinscription (Weimer 124; Maroto Camino, "Negotiating" 199). In assessing gender and cognition, it is productive to compare Rosaura's MR ability to King Basilio's as he attempted to form a ToM for Segismundo. This is a directly feminist revision of Basilio's flawed MR in *La vida es sueño*; at the play's end the King finds himself prostrated at the feet of the son he so grossly *mis*read. Basilio used an unreliable interpretive lens, astrology, to form his initial judgment of his infant son. Later, he made no attempt to know his son as a maturing individual, and once Segismundo was brought to the palace, Basilio judged him as ungovernable and hence unfit to rule based on a single act. Caro's reinscription, a fusion of Calderonian tragicomedy and the chivalric novel, produces a unique generic hybrid in which the mortal ability of ToM is shown to be more powerful than magic or social codes of honor. This revision of male-authored texts makes clear that women excel in the important intellectual capacity of mind reading, a statement that is further highlighted by granting this ability to not one but two women. In this play, successful ToM is presented as the force that enables a woman to overcome significant obstacles and to achieve a truly comic outcome at both the personal and political levels. Caro makes the strongest claims of any play to be addressed in this chapter concerning both the power of ToM for establishing social harmony and the accuracy and even superiority of female cognition. Facilitating the highly buoyant tone of this play is the lack of references to the specific challenges of mate selection in an urban locale. Neither of Caro's source texts focuses on the court environment as a specific locus of deception, and she follows the Calderonian source in presenting deception and betrayal as a metaphysical rather than social issue, even as she drastically rewrites the tragicomic conclusion. *El conde Partinuplés* celebrates ToM as the force that assists female characters in avoiding *engaño* and that enables *dramaturgas* to achieve unambiguous comic closure (Carrión, "Portrait" 216).

Cognitive *enredos* in Azevedo's
El muerto disimulado

Angela de Azevedo's *El muerto disimulado* features a plethora of variants of cognitive activity, including both Simulation Theory and Theory Theory forms of mentalism. The connection between MI and urban settings is highlighted through this play, beginning with the heroine's description of how she met her true love at the neighboring church, which she was allowed to attend with only her maid for protection (or surveillance), and continuing with many references to the labyrinthine nature of urban geography and society. In the first scene, a father uses various Machiavellian strategies to try to persuade a reluctant daughter to contemplate marriage. Don Rodrigo states in an aside that he will use tenderness rather than threats, "que a veces muestra el remedio, / más que el rigor la blandura" (I.31–32). He seeks to assure his parental devotion, proclaiming Jacinta as "del corazón / única prenda querida / de mi edad envejecida / alivio y consolación" (I.33–34). The gentle touch might have been more effective if the play had not opened with the enraged father chasing after his offspring, as the stage directions specify "con una daga en la mano." Rodrigo continues with a reminder of filial obligation, "son / los padres de Dios figura" (I.61–62). He also employs guilt, "que aquel hijo que disgusta / a su padre y no se ajusta / a su querer no es buen hijo" (I.70–72). Finally, he presents himself as a model of parental restraint: rather than forcing her to marry a specific man of his choice, as custom allows, he leaves her "la elección" (I.108). All of these tactics feature a Theory Theory approach focused on the normative cognitive proclivities of sons and daughters. Rodrigo makes no attempt to use Simulation Theory to find out why his daughter trespasses social norms in her lack of interest in marriage. When his tactics fail, Rodrigo returns to brute tactics, telling Jacinta's maid that if she does not find a way to persuade her mistress, then Jacinta will die. This scene reveals paternal affection to be a Machiavellian *engaño*, a strategic ploy for dominance rather than a true emotional bond. Many studies have pointed to Azevedo's challenges of patriarchal codes of family structure and marriage (Múzquiz-Guerreiro 147; Maroto Camino, "Transvestism" 315). Soufas observes that within the world of the *comedia,* it is generally fathers or other "male overseers" who coerce their daughters into undesirable marriages (*Dramas* 126). John Gabriele notes that

Azevedo's text critiques paternal "tyranny" and the use of daughters as mere objects (129). In Gabriele's view, Azevedo challenges gender norms of character by endowing Jacinta with a very strong will, in contradiction to stereotypes of feminine passivity (129–30). As a supplement to her determination, Jacinta's skill at SI helps her to achieve success in the goals she pursues; her cognitive competence stands in direct contrast to her father's incompetence.

While many early modern comedies place the blame for courtship complications on fickle young lovers employing MI against each other, this play also offers an additional dimension of comic emplotment, in which MI is used by members of different generations against each other as they wrestle for control over the marriages that will determine familial succession. In this scenario, the fidelity of the primary young couple is not in question; Jacinta avoids marriage because she wishes to remain faithful to the memory of Clarindo, who had been shipped off to battle and then killed before they had been able to publicize their love and marry. Of course, *comedia* plots rarely settle for a single blocking element, and so a rival for Jacinta's love emerges as the second figure to employ MI in an effort to break her bond to Clarindo. Don Álvaro does try a unique Simulation Theory angle, appealing to a shared love for the deceased man as an important bond, "en cuya pérdida nos ha hecho / a los dos iguales en la desdicha" (I.474). This attempt at empathetic MR is a spectacular failure, for Jacinta responds with an increased level of hostility, "si hasta aquí con desagrado / he mirado su persona, / este papel me ocasiona / más fastidio y más enfado" (I.477–80). Jacinta's own Simulation Theory approach to mind reading enables her to deduce that this rival must also be the murderer, for the death has not yet been made public. She combines that approach with Theory Theory, to project the reason that Clarindo would have confided in Álvaro about their secret love, and to excuse him for this error, because "el que es amigo perfecto / nada esconde de su amigo" (I.511–12). Jacinta assumes that in all situations where cultural norms support virtuous activities, her lover would be in conformity and hence Theory Theory would suffice to understand his motivations. Further use of this theory concerning the cognitive norms of spurned suitors enables her to interpret Álvaro's motivation for the homicide as a desire to avenge himself upon the woman who had rejected him. This succession of valid inferences enables Jacinta to construct a deliciously apt punishment that entails multiple levels of SI: she writes that she will not marry Álvaro until he finds Clarindo's murderer for her. At this point, Jacinta ascends to the fourth level of intentionality (she knows that he doesn't know that she knows that he sought to deceive her).

Álvaro's Simulation Theory fails, because it is based on his incorrect projection of how Jacinta might respond in her unique situation; on the other hand, even though Jacinta's MR is based mostly on Theory Theory projections concerning how men as a group will behave in certain stereotypical situations, it is entirely accurate. This scene reveals that one type of extrapolation is not inherently superior to the other, but rather that a skilled mind reader knows when to focus on the individual mind and when it is safe to rely on group stereotypes. This scene sets the stage for the entire play, for Jacinta and the other female characters are consistently shown to be skilled at using multiple levels of MR and MI to achieve their desired outcome.

In order to evaluate the feminist dimension of such a portrayal, it is useful to compare Jacinta to Lisarda, the sister of the slain man, who also seeks to identify the murderer and who dresses as a man to pursue her investigation. Both Soufas and Gabriele identify the cross-dressing *motif* as an important element of Azevedo's gender politics; cognitive theory enables us to scrutinize this practice from a new angle. When Lisarda, or any female *comedia* character, dresses as a male in order to pursue a goal that requires unrestricted mobility in the social world, two aspects of MR are intertwined. All such episodes of concealed identity depend upon Theory Theory to project that because social interaction is superficial, no one will look closely enough to penetrate such disguises; Soufas has pointed out that cross-dressing "can be only successful only as long as it [goes] unrecognized" (*Dramas* 140). Clarindo makes this same assumption later in the drama when he dresses as a woman for reasons to be explored below; although Jacinta is shocked by a woman's resemblance to her presumed dead lover, referring to her as a "copia viva," she nonetheless appears not to suspect the truth (II.1696). Early modern authors employ a related from of Theory Theory on their audience or readers; they are confident that aesthetic norms have conditioned respondents to accept such disguises' success at face value and not to question the verisimilitude of this plot device. (But—see Chapter 7 for an analysis of Cervantes's deconstruction of this motif). In addition, authors use Theory Theory to project that courtly love precepts about the power of love at first sight will induce the audience or reader to accept that a female character can continue to love a man even after she learns he has brutally murdered her brother. This assumption is reinforced when Álvaro's sister Beatriz discusses a duel between her brother and her lover; she feels that her maid should easily be able to use Theory Theory to predict where her support lies, for "siempre obligan más / que la sangre amantes veras" (I.1200–01). Multiple levels of ToM, MI, and intentionality are put into play as Álvaro seeks Lisarda/o's aid in resolving his dilemma. Even though the two have just met, Álvaro uses his Theory Theory concerning valiant aristocratic men to assume that this person will conform to the norms of courtier friendship; any man who defends another with his sword will be a loyal friend for life. Lisarda/o of course remains silent about the incorrect projection concerning her gender, but does voice a legitimate problem about Álvaro's assessment that uses Simulation Theory to designate this situation as atypical: how can he expect Lisarda/o's cooperation in this matter, given that "a un amigo vuestro / distes muerte tan osada" (I.1070–71). Again, Álvaro depends on the norms for noble male mentality to justify his ToM; certainly his new friend will pardon the murder because Clarindo was a rival and "no hay amigo, siendo amante" (I.1072). Álvaro once more appeals to friendship codes to convince Lisarda/o to take the blame for the murder now, because in the future "cuando de aquí os suceda / alguna fortuna mala, / me obligo yo a deshacerla" (I.1104–06).

Lisarda/o must engage her own SI in order to pursue the conflicting goals of obtaining justice for her brother's murder and preventing her new love from marrying another woman. To this end, we see Lisarda/o employ complex levels of intentionality: Álvaro does not know that she plans to invent a lie to Jacinta about his infidelity in order to prevent the marriage—and she knows that he believes in her support because he does not know that she is a woman who is in love with him. The irony of these levels is foregrounded as Álvaro tells his "friend," "a vuestra nobleza hidalga / mi amor y mi vida debo" and Lisarda/o responds in an aside that this conventional protestation is literally true in a way he cannot imagine, "sin duda no te engañas / cuando Lisarda te quiere, / y por eso no te mata" (I.1133–37). The baroque *topos* of deceiving with the truth is intimately connected to MI. Here, Álvaro is revealed as an amateur in the mind war games, for his reliance on Theory Theory as the basis for MR is hopelessly naïve compared to Lisarda/o's sophisticated approach. It is important to highlight that the two female characters who use multiple levels of MR and MI are portrayed as employing these deceptions for virtuous ends, in direct contradiction to the patriarchal marriage manuals of the era that characterized female intellect as malevolent in intent. The introduction of the subplot of Álvaro's sister Beatriz and her lover Alberto provides additional evidence of capable female MR. When Beatriz decides to flee for her life after Álvaro discovers her in a totally innocent encounter with Alberto, it is based on knowing that she must use Simulation Theory analysis of Álvaro's specific character, "sin por qué ni para qué / siempre ha sido escrupulosa" (I.1174–75).

Even servants are shown to have the ability to use ToM for positive ends; when the valet Papagayo finds out that Clarindo survived the murder attempt, the *gracioso* tells him that his sister has gone to a convent rather than that she has dressed as a male and gone out in public to investigate his murder, "pues si la verdad le cuento, / aunque por su causa hizo / Lisarda tan grande exceso, / sera la pena doblarle" (II.1291–94). He must then invent a new master to justify his own presence at court. Here, a servant uses SI for altruistic reasons, to protect his mistress rather than his own skin. Azevedo provides Papagayo with an aside, "no hay poeta, vive Dios / que mienta como yo miento" that foregrounds not only his cunning but also her own skill at creating a play with so many levels of complex human interaction (II.1320–21).

The audience might expect that with Clarindo's "resurrection," he and Jacinta could begin to put in place a series of maneuvers that would lead to Álvaro's punishment and support from her father for their wedding. However, Clarindo decides that the best form of MI to use upon Álvaro is to pretend to be an avenging ghost, so he does not seek Jacinta's support. Instead, he decides to further complicate her life by remaining dead so that he can test her loyalty. His Machiavellian tactics are presented very blatantly, as he ponders his exact procedure "para hacer más exacta / esta experiencia que emprendo / de su firmeza y constancia, / ¿qué traza hallar? ¿Qué medio?" (II.1424–27). Here, Clarindo seems to hold an implicit Theory Theory that all women are prone to fickleness;

he doesn't utter a word that would imply use of Simulation Theory to recognize his fiancée's exemplary, Penelope-like loyalty.

By creating scenarios in which even the "good" male characters use Theory Theory to the detriment of women, Azevedo emphasizes that patriarchal stereotypes concerning masculine and feminine modes of and motivations for deception are seriously flawed. Male characters actively seek out opportunities to deceive and manipulate women, and often choose incorrectly between Theory Theory and Simulation Theory modes of ToM, while *dama*s and sisters alike employ MI skillfully but defensively, to defend themselves or the men in their lives. When Beatriz takes refuge from her brother's wrath at the home of Jacinta's family, Don Rodrigo decides to try a new form of MI to turn her plight to his advantage. Here, Theory Theory concerning the bonds of female friendship lead him to project that sympathy for her friend might finally induce Jacinta to wed Álvaro, if this acquiescence on her part is used to bribe Álvaro into allowing his sister to wed happily. Jacinta immediately rejects this notion, but only in an aside, so Rodrigo does not realize immediately that he has once again failed to read his daughter correctly.

In plays that concern themselves with public honor, the issue of ToM can be expanded to a contemplation of the mind of one's entire social group via Theory Theory. When Rodrigo and Álvaro dispute whether it is better to incarcerate Beatriz in a convent or allow her to marry beneath her, both substantiate their cases based on which approach will be least likely to risk damage to her public reputation. When Álvaro asserts that enclosure is best, Rodrigo argues, "Eso es dar ocasión / para que de Beatriz, contra el decoro, / alguna presunción / se atreva a concebir ..." (II.1979–82). When Álvaro responds that allowing the marriage to take place will incite rumors because of the disparity in fortunes, Rodrigo replies that this would not cause gossip because their social status is equal even if their incomes are not. Further, he asserts that if the wedding is described as a love match, there will be no public suspicions at all, "no se agravian primores / de honor, que muchos casan por amores" (II.2001–02). This scene makes visible the link between ToM and the early modern obsession with *fama*. Because maintenance of the appearance of conformity to social norms within the aristocratic social world is crucial to successful courtship and marriage, characters monitor and even obsess over the thoughts and reactions of their peers. In many situations, the appropriate course of action is determined by the head of the family according to projections concerning the courtier micro-society as a whole, often to the detriment of individual agency. Thus, while the deployment of Social Intelligence on the part of enterprising *damas* and *galanes* against individual parents or potential mates is often depicted as the force that makes possible comedic closure, ToM concerning possible damage to familial honor can also be used by blocking characters to justify oppressive regulation of courting couples.

In this instance, it appears that Rodrigo does not consider his arguments concerning group ToM as sufficient; in addition, he appeals to Álvaro's emotions by offering his daughter as further enticement. At this point, control over MI moves from the older to the younger man, as Álvaro reveals Jacinta's relationship with Clarindo in order to frame himself as the hero who will restore Jacinta's tarnished honor rather than a swain receiving a prized woman as a favor. He states triumphantly, "yo me ofrezco" in order to emphasize that he has gained the upper hand (II.2051). In this case, Simulation Theory is not used merely to reach a goal, for Rodrigo had already offered his daughter, but to gain personal power. My own Theory Theory reading of this moment indicates that every *galán,* not only a Machiavellian operator like Álvaro, would take advantage of an opportunity to enter into a new familial relationship from a position of strength, as a benefactor rather than a supplicant.

Clarindo decides to remain dead and to continue with his disguise as an offended victim, in order to continue to test Jacinta's loyalty. This complication can be accounted for primarily as an opportunity for Azevedo to flaunt her plotting abilities. In the final act, the Machiavellian strategies of the cross-dressed siblings Lisardo/a and Clarindo will compete with each other and with Jacinta's own efforts to manipulate her father, all in order to block Álvaro's marriage to Jacinta. For example, the second act closes as Jacinta assuages her father's anger by promising that she will marry Álvaro, if it can be proven that he did not murder Clarindo and that he has made a vow of marriage to no other woman. Jacinta presents caveats that conform to social norms, relying on Theory Theory of her father as a conventional father whose strict adherence to the honor code will prevent him from pressing her further until both questions are resolved.

The final act provides far fewer examples of ToM and MI, as the strategies generated in the first two acts are brought to fruition or *fracaso*. Don Rodrigo and Álvaro still hope that their series of machinations will succeed, based on an erroneous use of Theory Theory concerning Jacinta's emotional loyalty. The audience will know by this point that their approach is flawed, in part because they know of the competing Machiavellian strategies that have been set in motion. In addition, the numerous examples of Rodrigo's flawed ToM highlight that this form of intergenerational mis-Mind-Reading is in fact a *comedia* convention, as are the false hopes of the villains, who present themselves as rivals. Jacinta, as befits the *dama* role, remains faithful to her first love, "solamente se inclina / una vez un pecho noble" (III.3216–17). Comic heroines rarely abandon the love object of the first act, and as a crucial component of comic resolution, fathers and unscrupulous rivals generally move from a negative Theory Theory concerning all women to a respectful Simulation Theory of one particular female character capable of unswerving devotion.

In some situations, analyzing the ToM of others is simply a parlor game for those characters who must sit and wait as the more important conflicts are resolved. For example, when Alberto is told that other matters must be addressed before his own concerns, he uses Simulation Theory to speculate about Álvaro's intentions. And, after Beatriz is shunted off to the side to wait her turn, she speculates about how her lover and brother must be feeling at this moment.

The one pairing where ToM is still necessary involves Lisarda/o and Álvaro. In the first two acts, we have witnessed her perverse attraction to the man who killed her brother, as well as Álvaro's strong affection for the valiant stranger who took his side in a duel. In the final act, Álvaro declares that his attachment to his new friend is nearly as strong as his love for Jacinta; for this reason his most ardent wish is a match between boon companion and sibling, "que nos hagamos hermanos" (III.2949). In an aside, Lisarda/o employs Simulation Theory to project that this bond will prove strong enough to produce a marriage when her gender is revealed. This complex relationship seems to invite spectators to engage in their own Theory Theory, analyzing the uncanny similarities between homosocial friendship and heterosexual love as emotional and social forces. In addition, this unique relationship appears to fly in the face of neo-Platonic writings about the impossibility of true friendship between the sexes, and to demonstrate the possibility of a heterosexual variant of the "mirror" relationship based on mutual respect and virtue (Simerka, "Homosociality" 525).

This scene appears to offer a feminist realignment of gender relations. However, it was necessary for a woman to dress as a man to reveal those virtues; early modern society had not yet learned to recognize and reward the virtues available to women (Soufas, *Dramas* 130; Maroto Camino, "Transvestism"). In addition, this mirror friendship is somewhat distorted, for Álvaro has shown himself to be anything but virtuous in his behaviors with all other characters. In fact, as Lisarda/o noted in their first encounter, Álvaro had already marked himself as a bad friend by killing Clarindo. Clarindo further underlines this discrepancy during his long soliloquy, in which he notes that Jacinta has proven herself to be more loyal than his erstwhile best friend. However, this discovery does not seem to impact Clarindo's Theory Theory projections about males and females in general, for he characterizes Jacinta's virtue as a "milagro" (III.3577). And, the pain Clarindo caused Jacinta during his adventures as Clara is barely noted. These episodes of cognitive exploration thus highlight, but do not help the audience to resolve, the varied and contradictory codes of gender and deceptive courtship behavior. Still, it is worth noting that in this female-authored play, the most deceptive character is a male, and that the female characters employed Machiavellian strategies for more positive purposes. In addition, throughout the play, female characters are generally more skilled than males at performing Theory Theory and Simulation Theory to accurately project the thoughts and emotions of others.

The final scene of mutual reconciliation completely excludes references to cognitive activity. As each Machiavellian strategy is revealed and the perpetrators pardoned, all of the characters—parent, siblings, and lovers—accept each other's statements as being completely truthful and innocent of all guile. SI is thus depicted as a necessary but temporary practice, one that disappears as soon as the desired match is obtained. The comic convention of order restored requires that the characters and the audience focus on the final emergence of truth, rather than on the web of deceit that was necessary to arrive at this moment of closure. However, the *gracioso*'s final comment undermines such certainty, "Tal caso no ha sucedido, / pero como casos raros / suceden, también supongo / que ha sucedido este caso" (II.3805–09). This reference to a lack of verisimilitude could of course refer to the unusually complex emplotment, but also could be seen as alluding to the equally improbable happy ending and to a questioning of whether Machiavellian strategies that support patriarchal dominance are so easily undone in the real world. The third act of this play begins at line 2350 and continues for an additional 1400 verses; thus it is nearly 20 percent longer than a conventional comedia. The additional length is necessary in order to develop the complex courtship games of not one or two but three couples, as well as two characters who employ cross-dressing as part of their Machiavellian strategies.

In the third act, Azevedo appears to engage in ToM of her own audience, projecting that they may have difficulty in keeping track of all the different plot lines and Machiavellian schemes, for she provides several long soliloquies in which each of the main characters recapitulates his or her situation and stratagems. Lisa Zunshine has noted that modern readers and critics sometimes express negative reactions to experimental modernist fiction that pushes too many boundaries (*Why* 41–44). Azevedo appears to project a related concern that audiences may feel overly challenged rather than appreciative of the mental task she has set for them; this at any rate is one possible explanation for the numerous occasions that the *gracioso* Papagayo praises her intricate artistry, with comments such as "¿En qué comedia se han visto / más extrañas novedades, / ni enredos más excesivos?" (III.2863–65) and "¿qué Diablo de poeta / machinó tantos delirios" (III.3128–29). In addition, as quoted previously, his final speech emphasizes that this is a fantastic rather than realistic sequence of events. In this instance, Azevedo may be highlighting for her audience the variable nature of literary mimesis (Mujica, *Women* 238). Where many dramas openly seek to guide the ToM of characters and readers or viewers for the purpose of providing moral and ideological exempla concerning gender conventions, Azevedo's final act appears to guide her audience's analysis to different ends. In addition to overt praise and condemnation of particular aspects of gender and ideology, Azevedo also invites her audience to revel aesthetically in the highly complex but fictional situation that she has created.

Here, her projection of the audience's reaction seems to focus on assuring appreciation of woman-authored artistic innovation. In addition, Lisa Vollendorf notes that the play condemns conventional social structures and dramatic norms that "leave little room for nonviolent reconciliation" even as she creates a new narrative in which bloodshed is indeed averted (*Lives* 78–79). Christopher Gascón asserts that

> the motif of woman as mediator is more pervasive in Azevedo's extant plays than in the comedia in general … Azevedo does not treat female diplomacy in isolation, but consistently links it with a critique of male attempts at mediation: where man's impulsiveness, self-interest, arrogance, and violence fail, woman's ingenuity, justice, humility, and compassion triumph. (143)

It is in part due to Jacinta's ability to use SI for positive ends that she is able to manipulate characters and events to achieve the more just denouement that Vollendorf and Gascón highlight. Azevedo's courtship play, whose generic structure follows and develops that of a conventional comedy, presents a vastly different and more optimistic perspective on the intersection of gender and ToM than does her hagiographic play, *La margarita del Tajo que dio nombre a Santarén.*

An Insightful Martyr: *La margarita del Tajo*

In *La margarita del Tajo que dio nombre a Santarén,* Azevedo also explores patriarchal norms concerning the relative merit of female and male intellect through a reinscription of gender and mind reading. The plot does not emphasize but nonetheless requires an urban setting, which provides daily opportunities for men and women to encounter unknown members of the opposite sex as well as the geographic proximity and anonymity necessary for night time escapades. In this hagiography of Saint Irene, a nun who was killed because she resisted the advances of a married aristocrat, the male antagonist is quasi-autistic, so limited are his capacities to read the intents of other humans via their actions; his *gracioso* side kick is not much better. On the other hand, both his wife and the martyred nun are shown to excel at ToM. When Britaldo first reveals his secret passion for a nun—a flame that was ignited when he saw her in church on his wedding day—the *gracioso* Etc. infers that his master merely wants what he cannot have; thus, imagining that the nun wants him but his wife does not is the proposed cure. Here Etc.'s MR would appear to be a valid Theory Theory supposition that his master shares the common male characteristic of neophilia. Etc.'s assumption that Britaldo lost interest in what he had already won was not expressed in conjunction with any specific reference to previous instances of that behavior by his master; but rather, seems to be grounded in a Theory Theory truism about the neophilic mindset of males in that social class and era. The fact that Britaldo lost interest in his wife on the very day he gained legal possession would place him at the extreme edge of the novelty/honor continuum. Although early modern Spain had no knowledge of brain chemistry, Etc.'s ToM concerning Britaldo, like Aldora's reading of Rosaura, indicates an awareness of this trait as a psychosocial phenomenon.

Neophilia is shown here to be supported and stimulated by the urban setting; even in church and even on one's wedding day, new faces and new temptations are constantly encountered. Urban neophilia, both in its actual manifestation and in the fear characters express that their mates will succumb, supports the formation of Theory Theory paradigms of gender and cognition, in which each gender projects specific deceptive behaviors allied with betrayal upon the other. The application of such norms concerning mutable affections appears when Britaldo's wife tries to understand his disdain. While her first explanation concerning why her husband has lost interest is not correct, it is nonetheless valid for her society. She posits, "esto es sin duda recelos" and asserts that although she has done nothing to deserve reproach, "a veces contra razón / se arma una mala sospecha" (I.623, 635–36). This pattern of jealousy based upon unfounded doubt is rampant in the *comedia*; likewise, mistaken belief of a partner's infidelity is a dominant element of dramatic plotting. In both cases, an urban or court setting fosters fears, opportunities, and gossip. After Rosimunda spies her husband sneaking out of the house at night and incognito, she revises her earlier mind reading. This new behavior points to a different mental state, related to neophilia: a husband who is neglectful because he has fallen for another woman and is unhappy because of failing to conquer her. Like Etc., Rosimunda blames this infidelity on a Theory Theory of masculine group mentality, "más lo ajeno lisonjea / que siempre enfadó lo propio"

(I.1056–57). Her counselor Banán, upon confirming that Britaldo pursues Irene, weighs two sets of evidence for his projection of the nun's likely response. On the one hand, he notes that she has gained public fame for her exemplary faith and virtue; with an individualized Simulation Theory interpretation this would lead him to assume Irene would reject Britaldo. But he also notes "si es mujer y él es hombre / ¿para qué lo dificulto?" (I.1161–62). Banán follows the patriarchal norm in choosing an unflattering Theory Theory of all women rather than a more favorable Simulation Theory for a specific and well-regarded nun, and thus errs completely in his initial evaluation of Irene. By the next morning, as Rosimunda sets out to confront the woman she perceives as a rival, Banán offers some new caveats based on ST; first, he warns his mistress, "no son premisas éstas / para sacarse infalible / consecuencia de que Irene / tales lisonjas admite" (II.1241–44). He also engages in a revised Theory Theory of his master, suggesting that Britaldo's suffering is due to being scorned. However, Rosimunda offers a different, and this time incorrect projection: that his misery stems from the fact that the obstacle is posed by the nun's professed vows, rather than personal rejection. Because this is a drama of a martyred saint, the audience can be sure from the outset that every instance of a condemnatory Theory Theory concerning Irene is flawed, while in secular drama the truth about an individual mind is often not obvious until the final scene. Britaldo's father offers a related projection of his son that is also incorrect but conforms to religious and ethical norms of the era. He interprets his son's situation as a typical human spiritual quandary: "no os culpo vuestros deseos / porque no está en vuestra mano / no tenerlos, que es muy libre / la voluntad" (II.1952–55). Thus, he reads Britaldo's desire as theological and social rather than individual, a consequence of God granting free will and hence the freedom to desire to all humans. However, he is incorrect in assuming that his son will be persuaded by the use of reason to cease his fruitless and immoral endeavor; whether this ToM is based on Simulation Theory of his son as an individual or Theory Theory for the likely response of an educated and moral male of his era, is unclear. What is clear is that the father's attempts to use MI to manipulate his son are unsuccessful. His lament that the son gives full sway to his lesser instincts, "que no queréis refrenerlos / haciendo gala del gusto" falls on deaf ears as Britaldo replies, "viva mi gusto" (II.2013). Considering this scene in the context of failures by other reproachful fathers to reform wayward sons, such as Don García and Don Juan Tenorio, it may be a genre-specific or epochal norm that *comedia* parents cannot use MI correctly to reform their own offspring, that the resolution of plot conflicts must come from another source. Here also, the urban setting is relevant, for it is easier to impose surveillance and control in a rural ambience where anonymity vanishes, social inferiors will not risk opprobrium, and social equals have a vested interest in supporting the morality and reputations of young people who are likely to be—or to become—their relatives.

When Irene finally appears in person in the second act, she is the first in the play to openly discuss her use of ToM. In an aside, she ponders which of several responses will best achieve the mind-set she wishes to elicit: to convince the enraged Rosimunda of her innocence, "si aquí de culpa / me eximo, ésta mi disculpa / ha de pensar que la engaña … así ablandarla procuro" (II.1570–73, 1579). Irene is also the first character in the play whose Simulation Theory is completely successful, for she infers rightly that humble behavior will completely disarm Rosimunda's anger. Her cognitive skill is not surprising but merely adds to the litany of the future saint's superior character traits and to Azevedo's hagiographic goals. Still, it is noteworthy that Azevedo emphasizes the nun's mentalistic ability as well as her spiritual gifts. Gascón notes that Irene, like Jacinta, is a skilled mediator who knows the value of humility; ToM is crucial to choosing successful mediation strategies (132). This competence in worldly relations also points to the conditions of life in the urban convent, whose permeable membrane permits numerous interactions between the secular and the sacred.

Irene's success with SI continues in her encounter with her besotted suitor. However, before analyzing her successful reading, let us look first at Britaldo's spectacularly flawed reading of how to persuade a nun to have sex with him. First, he uses a Theory Theory paradigm of what moves all women, and devotes fifty lines to conventional courtly love explanations of his undying passion for her. Then he moves to a more nuanced projection for a woman who is a nun and hence more spiritual; he begs for satisfaction as an act of Christian kindness, deploying the terms "caridad" and "dar alivio" on numerous occasions (II.2480–2545). Irene's use of Simulation Theory is similar to that offered by his father, appealing to Britaldo's better instincts. She gives him a theological lesson on the distinction between "querer bien" and "querer mucho" (II.2550–2660). She also emphasizes her status as the bride of a jealous and dangerous divine spouse, one who has already sent down an angel on a previous occasion to protect her (DiPuccio 384). This combined appeal to logic, spirit—and basic mortal fear—is successful, as Britaldo declares, "mis ojos de las tinieblas / se van abriendo" (2692–93). However, this epiphany is accompanied by the caveat that what she will not give to him, no other human male may receive. Although Irene's insightful projection and manipulation win her a short-term reprieve, Britaldo's ultimatum also sets the stage for Irene's ultimate martyrdom (DiPuccio 393).

For a literary moment in which *desengaño* plays a key role both for emplotment and for epistemology, the phenomenon of *flawed* mind reading is especially important. Ellen Spolsky points to the many reinscriptions of the Rape of Lucretia legend as evidence of early modern Europe's obsession with the cognitive difficulties posed by trying to ascertain not merely the physical chastity but also the mental virtue of women—their thoughts and, more importantly, their desires ("Women's Work" 51–54). Spanish honor drama is littered with the bodies of female characters who were not fortunate enough to have a dea-ex-machina at their disposal. The Spanish *comedia* and *novela ejemplar*, as created both by men and women authors, offer many examples of incorrect mind reading concerning false suspicions of infidelity as a source of dramatic conflict and even tragedy (see Chapter 7 for a complete exploration of cognition and honor). In Azevedo's play, when Britaldo learns of the false rumor that Irene's mentor Remigio now enjoys her favors, he immediately uses Theory Theory to remember the previous conversation in the worst possible light, employing all the conventional epithets that a cuckolded mate projects upon the thoughts of his spouse, "engañosa, traidora, falsa, fingida," and "hipocresía" (III.3380–81). He reinterprets Irene's tale of a heavenly defender as "todo embuste y falsedad" employed to hide the existence of a rival earthly suitor (III.3405–40). In a hagiographic drama, such erroneous accusations mark him as mind blind, on a par with the autistic mind as portrayed in current cognitive study. In this instance, an innocent woman's death is presented as both heroic and glorious, for an Angel appears to inform Irene that her most ardent wish, holy martyrdom, is about to be fulfilled. In this unique circumstance, the murder of a blameless woman due to flawed mind reading leads to apotheosis. In Azevedo's play, women's excellence in ToM, juxtaposed with the mind blindness that pervades masculine thought, reveals that patriarchal conventions concerning gender and intellect are not only incorrect but also a major source of social injustice. Like Caro, Azevedo fuses dramatic and narrative genres, in this case tragedy and hagiography, to produce a unique hybrid. However, this exception may even be said to prove the general rule, as audiences compare Irene's situation to the unhappy marriages of Mencía, Camila, Desdemona, and the many tortured brides in Zayas's novellas (see Chapter 5). Soufas views this play as a condemnation of patriarchal codes that view the female body as a battleground where men compete with one another for dominance; in this hagiography of a female martyr, God is simply the most powerful of the many male "rivals" (*Dramas* 102). In the normal course of human events of that era, as represented textually and theatrically, a tragic miscarriage of justice without redemption is the most common result in cases of false accusations of female sexual transgression. Where Caro and Azevedo's comic dramas had emphasized female ToM as a redemptive force, Azevedo uses hagiography to decry conventional masculine ToM, demonstrating the toxicity of social conventions and patriarchal gender codes that foster mis-Mind-Reading of women.

Machinations of a Female Don Juan: *La traición en la amistad*

María de Zayas's *La traición en la amistad* is a play that incorporates and reinscribes many of the key epistemological quandaries that underlie plot conflict in early modern courtship drama; for this reason application of MI precepts is particularly relevant. The *gracioso* León specifically links early modern tropes about a lost Golden Age to deceptive courtship behavior in urban settings. He begins by describing the courtship practices of the moment as corrupt and deceptive, then delivers a conventional evocation of a lost paradise with abundant natural beauty and resources. This lament is accompanied by nostalgia for the passing of an era of innocence and truth, "y la gente entonces / sin malicia estaba / en esta de hierro / tan pobre y tan falta /de amistad, pues vive / la traición malvada" (III.2543–48). Although complaints about social dishonesty are common to all *beatus ille* texts, León enumerates forms of deception that are specific to male-female interaction, instead of the more typical condemnations of flattery and rivalry among courtiers. Here, the hallmark of a fallen era is the distortion found in the social world of courtship rather than the political world of palace intrigue. León's unique formulation of the marriage mart as an example of a fallen age reinforces my contention that early modern urban and court life provides the material circumstances that foster a specific type of courtship comedy, in terms of character and plot development. As Raymond Williams has noted, nostalgic Golden Age rhetoric often arises at moments of transition from rural to urban society, dating back to classical times and continuing through the industrial age of nineteenth-century Britain (*Country* 9–11). It is ironic that even as scholarship of recent centuries has labeled the age of Cervantes and Lope as *aurea* or *dorada*, the authors themselves depicted their period as one of moral and spiritual as well as political decline, and focused much of their iron age discourse around *engaño* as a malevolent force. In urban marriage drama, reliance on MI to manipulate potential mates appears to be an inevitable byproduct of negotiating a complex social world. The link between easy deception and urban life is emphasized throughout this play; for example, it is the anonymity of the public garden at the Prado that provides Fenisa with a site for encountering her many suitors without detection.

As a comedy that veers toward the satiric, *La traición en la amistad* foregrounds a *figurona*, a character who destabilizes society and must be punished (Bayliss 11). The specific generic attributes of the early modern satire, in which social dishonesty is imbricated with MI, focuses on the unique mental qualities of the satiric antagonist. Indeed, Fenisa states explicitly that she is "extremo de las mujeres" and so conventional Theory Theory attempts to understand her would not be valid (II.1598). Robert Bayliss, Catherine Larson ("Gender"), and Matthew Stroud ("Love") concur that Zayas portrays Fenisa as a female Don Juan. The resemblance is obvious from the very first scene, in which she employs MI in an attempt to dissuade her friend Marcia from accepting the attentions of Liseo, because Fenisa is herself interested in him. She tries various approaches that incorporate both Simulation Theory and Theory Theory: condemning masculine preference for wealth over love, lauding the devotion of Marcia's suitor Gerardo, and describing that relationship as an "obligación," so that Marcia will stay with this ever-faithful *galán*; she also provides a litany of mythical female characters who were deceived in love (I.55–68). When these strategies prove fruitless, Zayas gives the audience direct access to Fenisa's mental machinations and Simulation Theory projections, in the first of many asides: "Fuerza será que le diga / mal de él, porque le aborrezca" (I.124–25).

In this play, most of the major characters will use MI and all will engage in ToM. For example, when confronted with Fenisa's lack of enthusiasm for her new choice of beau, Marcia performs a Simulation Theory reading of her own, deducing correctly that Fenisa is motivated by jealousy rather than true concern (I.144–52). Of course, the norms of plot development, as well as Fenisa's skill in Machiavellian behaviors, prevent Marcia from realizing immediately that this projection is accurate. From the opening lines, the play emphasizes the prevalence of deception purveyed through MI and the need for skills in ToM in order to survive and triumph in the courtship game. As even this first scene indicates, it is worthwhile to scrutinize the Machiavellian aspects of male and female characters as a point of departure for evaluating the gender ideologies at work in this play. This Machiavellian mind reading stands in direct contrast to the use of ToM by Aldora, Rosaura, Jacinta, and Saint Irene as described above, which correspond more closely to Shirley Strum's model of Social Intelligence as a positive force (74).

The next scene dramatizes the Machiavellian aspects of courtship rituals as they are mediated and regulated by early modern social codes. As Juan complains of Fenisa's disdain, he characterizes her as "sirena" and indicates that he is applying ToM, "Ya sé tus tretas" (I.210). Although the previous scene has confirmed that Fenisa is indeed unfaithful, his accusations are consistent with Theory Theory and generic courtly love norms in which all women are assumed to have a mentality marked by falsehood; he appears to have no specific grounds for jealousy—yet. Fenisa once again speaks of deception in two asides, before voicing a perfectly Machiavellian and baroque lie "Tu engaño don Juan, me obliga / a descubrirte el secreto" (I.249–50). Here she feigns concern for Marcia in order to get Juan to investigate Liseo for her, turning the tables so that his jealousy is condemned as unfounded and this task characterized as the service he is obligated to perform as penance. This entire scene conforms to standard *comedia* plotting, except that the *dama* is normally innocent and the purpose of plot development is to lead toward eventual recognition and reconciliation. Here, Fenisa's MI is a key component of the generic strangeness of this play, and an integral component of its satiric dimension.

Once Fenisa begins to pursue him, Liseo is very open with his companion León about his Machiavellian intentions: without abandoning his plan to marry Marcia, he will take whatever side benefit he can get, "a Fenisa voy a ver / y aun a engañarla si puedo" (I.612–13). In accordance with cultural norms for female virtue, he uses Theory Theory to project that he will have to declare (feign) an honorable love with implications of future marriage to win her favors—the scheme he had already used successfully with the now forgotten Laura. As the relationship progresses, he confirms the success of this strategy, "si yo a Fenisa galanteo / es con engaños, burlas y mentiras, no mas de por cumplir con mi deseo. / A sola Marcia mi nobleza aspira, / ella ha de ser mi esposa, que Fenisa / es burla" (II.1298–1303). Although he and Fenisa are in some senses kindred spirits, the social codes of the era prevent mutual understanding and dictate elaborate Machiavellian schemes in order to pursue nonmonogamous relationships. Use of Simulation Theory would not be successful because social codes require Fenisa to perform a charade that conceals her true nature.

Up to this point, MI has been used to pursue goals that violate social norms, which is also customary in the literature that describes primate use of MI and deception. However, when Laura seeks out Marcia, we are able to see that deception can be used for purposes that are not self-serving and that promote social cohesion; this is an example where the term "social" rather than "Machiavellian" Intelligence is appropriate. Marcia does indeed use her cognitive skills to create a successful deceptive strategy, but with the goal of tricking Liseo into fulfilling his promise to Laura. She must put aside her own desire in order to achieve social justice, using SI for altruistic reasons even though the term Machiavellian is normally seen as the incarnation of selfishness. In looking for feminist aspects of Zayas's reinscription of courtship drama, Marcia is a pivotal figure, putting in motion the duplicitous but ultimately virtuous schema that will enable Laura to salvage her honor. She is the only character in the play who is proficient at ToM and also selfless enough to use SI for communal rather than personal benefit. In this aspect, she functions as a comic dea-ex-machina, much like Caro's *maga* Aldora. Through Marcia, Zayas portrays a single woman whose function goes far beyond finding an appropriate mate in order to propagate her elite bloodlines; this *dama* is capable of using wisdom and wile to restore order within her entire social group. In this sense, Marcia serves as a feminist foil to the devious Fenisa; the contradictory scenes that incorporate beneficent and nefarious acts of ToM underline the problematic and contradictory nature of early modern gender and courtship norms, in addition to serving as the springboard for Machiavellian activity.

The elusive nature of MR is highlighted in the next scene; when Juan discontinues his pursuit of Fenisa and seeks the forgiveness of his former love Belisa, she reiterates all of the tropes associated with a standard *desengaño* scenario. Initially she uses Theory Theory to reject all his words as typical masculine "engaños" and "hechicerías" (II.1207–08). After further explanations, Belisa begins to waiver concerning her interpretation of his intent, using Simulation Theory to observe that "parece que es verdad / tus palabras y es mentira" (II.1223–24). An additional speech full of adoration and protestations fuels her uncertainty concerning her cognitive abilities, "¿cómo te puedo creer, / quien teme que tu malicia / como primero, me engaña?" (II.1245–47). Although Belisa eventually gives in to Juan's blandishments and is rewarded by faithfulness throughout the rest of the drama, the very next scene is the one described previously in which Liseo tells his valet of his plans to cheat on Marcia. In the following scene, Fenisa confronts Liseo about the rumors concerning his engagement to Marcia. Liseo follows up his declarations of love for her with inquiries that seek to measure his skill at MI and her ToM ability: "no merezco que me creas? ... No basta lo que he jurado?" (II.1409, 1413). Of course, the audience has been forewarned that Liseo is lying to her. These brief scenes epitomize the plight of male and female *comedia* characters: because early modern courtship norms dictate highly ritualized and unnatural behaviors that often do not reflect actual thoughts and emotions, characters of both genders are hesitant about trusting their ToM capabilities. This sequence thus reinforces both personal and societal uncertainty concerning the reliability of SI in a world that so often rewards deception.

The final act of the play is brought to a close, and social cohesion restored, as Marcia and Laura's Machiavellian strategies bear fruit. The revelation of Fenisa's multiple affairs causes all of her swains to lose interest, and the two women successfully lead Liseo to make a written commitment to the woman he pursued at Marcia's window. Their use of Theory Theory had correctly predicted that even males who themselves were pursuing two women simultaneously would not forgive Fenisa for that same behavior, and that Liseo would not renege upon his vow once he discovered that it was Laura at the window. The final scene provides a form of Machiavellian resolution that is echoed in Caro's *Valor, agravio y mujer*. The resolutions of these two plays provide a feminist reinscription because it is females rather than males who are in charge of saving an innocent woman from dishonor at the hands of a faithless suitor. Cognitive theory enriches this analysis by shedding light on MR, and Machiavellian or Social Intelligence, as the epistemological operations that characters of both genders employ. Both Zayas and Caro redefine the functions of male and female dishonesty, revealing that male characters are at least as guilty as females of using strategic deceptions in order to enjoy multiple partners, and are perhaps even more prone to neophilia, or *mudanza*. In addition, they assert that women are more likely than males to use Social Intelligence for honorable and even altruistic purposes. Cognitive theory thus enables us to more deeply scrutinize social and literary conventions concerning gender and deception, and to tease out the strategies that women writers pursue in order to defend their gender's intellect and honesty. However, the aspects of the ending that have been discussed up to this point do not help us to resolve the critical quandary of how Zayas wished her readers to view Fenisa.

Fenisa is a character who straddles interpretive categories. On the one hand, she is a primary character of noble status and marriageable age involved in courtship activity—in other words, a comic protagonist. On the other hand she engages in antisocial behaviors that are more typical of *figurón* antagonists such as Alarcón's Don García: either the blocking figure in a comedy or the negative example in a dramatic satire (Bayliss 11). This liminal status cannot be rewarded by a happy marriage; thus García is forced to marry a woman he does not prefer, while Fenisa finds herself alone as the curtain falls. Yet, she also displays highly attractive attributes that lead to critical consternation concerning her ultimate status. The liminal status of such figures leads to a heightened need to evaluate the characters' true mental and emotional states, and invites critics to engage in our own ToM. Of course, we must not fall into a naïve sort of reading in which we lose sight of the fact that they are characters rather than human beings and begin to posit childhood traumas or other psychological issues that the text does not provide (and that early modern Spanish culture did not use to explain character flaws). Zunzhine observes that "literature pervasively capitalizes on and stimulates ToM mechanisms that had evolved to deal with real people, even as on some level readers do remain aware that fictive characters are not real people at all" ("Richardson" 131). Here, the quandary of how to analyze complex characters gives rise to the even more complex "paradox of fiction." Jerrold Levinson describes this paradox as the tendency of readers to feel emotions for characters they know to be unreal (22). Cognitive theorists have suggested several forms of resolution; Levinson asserts that because the emotional response to art lies at the cognitive end of the emotion/reason continuum, the paradox is only apparent (22). Kendall Walton notes that humans engage in many forms of emotional response to events that are not present; for him, "regret, remorse, and nostalgia" concerning real life experiences are on the same mental plane of imaginative engagement with human response to literary situations and beings (44–46). For literary scholars, the paradox entails intellectual as well as or instead of emotional engagement; although the studies cited here seem to indicate that strong intellectual engagement is not as problematic as emotional responses, nonetheless both forms of affective response entail granting significant attention to fictional beings. As noted above, theories of cognition and character have tended to focus on narrative rather than drama. It is true that the sort of ToM that an audience engages in with a theatrical character on the stage is quite different from the reading act; the resources of stage, lighting, props, and physical embodiment provide radically different types of cues (Zunshine, *Why* 23). But we do not often have access even to modern productions of these plays, and cannot even be sure if female-authored plays were ever fully performed in their own era or were merely given dramatic readings in private salons. Thus, despite certain limitations and obvious differences, I feel that the model for cognitive analysis Zunshine employs with novelistic characters closely approximates the scholarly task of analyzing the ToM of early modern dramatic characters.

La traición en la amistad is rife with moments that invite ToM both from intratextual characters and extratextual scholars. Fenisa's initial aside, quoted above, is an important first indicator of this tendency. The dramatic technique of providing asides in which a character describes plans to deceive others is generally associated with revealing the true nature of the antagonist, because of negative cultural connotations for the use of MI. Often, such an aside is a metacognitive cue to categorize the character as a villain. Nieves Romero Díaz views these asides as a key component in Zayas's questioning of dramatic as well as social conventions of gender and in particular as an effective tactic for inviting direct audience engagement with the ideological implications of female transgression ("En los límites" 479). In addition, Fenisa sometimes uses these asides to present herself as truthful and sincere. On many occasions, she declares that she loves all of her many suitors; for example, right after deploying MI to dupe Juan, and before pursuing Liseo, she declares that "aunque a mi don Juan adoro / quiero también a Liseo, / porque en mi alma hay lugar / para amar a cuantos veo" (I.432–35). Later, she affirms, "Diez amantes me adoran, y a todos / los adoro, los quiero, los estimo, / y todos en un alma caben" (II.1518–20). Although she also refers to "tan loco embuste" in this speech, the deception lies not in the sincerity of her feelings but in the fact that she must induce each one to believe he is her only love (II.1517). And, as she herself points out, the proof of her sincere love is the sorrow and jealousy she feels over each of the rejections or defections that punctuate the second and third acts (III.2316, 2360). If the audience or critic decides as a result of Simulation Theory analysis that Fenisa truly does love each and every one of the men, then our interpretation of her fate will be vastly different than if we judge her to be an immoral hypocrite. Thus, we must weigh her declarations of sincerity against such observations as "no hay gloria / como andar engañando pisaverdes" (II.1593–94).

In addition, our MR must incorporate the evaluations of other characters. While every one of the key male figures denounces her in hostile and highly negative terms, Belisa does not approve of

Juan's harsh treatment (Vollendorf, "Future" 269). Even though Fenisa had stolen her *galán*, Belisa suggests that, in dealing with loose women, "les basta para castigo / no hacer, don Juan, caso de ellas" (III.1742–43). This observation also subtly places some of the blame on the men who generally do pay attention to and take advantage of such women, only to condemn them afterwards—even while expecting pardon for their own sins. Belisa expresses regret for women who do not follow moral guidelines, but voices none of the epithets so common to male-authored or male-uttered condemnations of unchaste females. The most blatant critique occurs after the last of her suitors abandons Fenisa, as her maid Lucia addresses the audience, "Señoras, que las entretienen / tomen ejemplo en Fenisa, / huyan de estos pisaverdes" (III.2473–75).

In the closing scene, Marcia delivers the judgment that Fenisa's greatest error has not been her infidelity to the men, but rather, that she has been "amig[a] deslea[l]" (III.2901–02). This sentiment is of course reflected in the title of the play. It is also important to note that Marcia concludes on a slightly hopeful note, "consuélate y ten paciencia," implying that Fenisa's solitary state may be a temporary punishment. Where patriarchal honor drama often punished women with convent enclosure or even death for such transgressions, Zayas implies that an involuntary cooling off period suffices. Scholarly interpretation of this unconventional closure is decidedly mixed. As indicated above, Fenisa can be seen as a Don Juan figure and thus as a *pharmakos* in need of punishment and exile. In addition, Bayliss cautions against the dangers of mechanically applying to this early drama the ToM we have formed concerning Zayas's unwavering rejection of patriarchal codes as found in her later novellas. However, just as scholars have wrestled with the paradoxical appeal of Tirso's *pharmakos*, many scholars also view Fenisa's Don Juanesque transgressions in a dual or even positive light. Feminist analyses of this play interpret Fenisa as a sympathetic character whose rebellion is a form of ideological subversion against gender codes (see Campbell; Gorfkle; Hegstrom Oakey; Leoni; Soufas, *Dramas*; Vollendorf, "Future"; Wilkins). Romero Díaz believes that the final lines are open-ended, inviting the audience to make a final determination based upon the intimate relationship they have formed with the protagonist though her asides ("En los límites" 492–93). The contradictory clues that Zayas provides serve to guide—and to complicate—the MR powers of respondents off-stage as well as of her *dramatis personae*.

The Deceiver Deceived: *La verdad sospechosa*

Although the cognitive model of ToM does not necessarily enable us to *resolve* quandaries about complex characters, it does serve to illuminate the parameters of our critical contemplation. Like Zayas's drama, Juan Ruíz de Alarcón's *La verdad sospechosa* provides a protagonist that elicits both admiration and contempt. The play also serves an obvious test case for the viability of cognitive approaches to early modern theater, both because Don García's lies constitute a clear-cut example of MI in action, and because both MR—and mis-Mind-Reading of the other characters—is crucial to the plot development. The title leaves no doubts concerning the moral message the play seeks to convey concerning the dangers that lies present for the honor and dignity of the court and its denizens; the use of cognitive approaches enables us to delve more deeply into exactly how and why liars succeed in duping those around them. The first scene establishes the gravity but also the ubiquity of García's sole vice. The tutor who delivers to the court the young scholar, who has now been elevated to the role of eldest son and heir, tries to reassure the outraged father that his son will outgrow his bad habit. He theorizes that García had no incentive to reform himself in Salamanca, where "hacen donaire del vicio" but that he will surely mend his ways at court, where "tan validas vemos / las escuelas de honor" (I.173, 179–80). Don Beltrán quickly disabuses the tutor of his naïve idealism, informing him that at court, "hay quien le dé cada día / mil mentiras de partido" (I.187–88). This admission of the prevalence of deceit is followed up by a tirade in which the distressed father declares that he would prefer his son practice any other vice, have married poorly, or even be dead, rather than be a liar.

The opening scene presents an immediate paradox: García indulges in a terrible vice, but a vice that is rampant at court. Although no character in the play makes a reference to the virtues of the countryside, the "menosprecio de corte y alabanza de aldea" *topos* is clearly relevant to this depiction of courtier decadence (see Chapter 4 for a related exploration of ToM and courtier literature). Throughout the play, deliberate lies as well as innocent misunderstandings flourish because of the complex nature of urban culture. On a metaphorical level, García could be conceptualized as a young primate from an exogamous species who has been adopted into a complex new troop, and who uses Machiavellian tactics in order to establish a place in the new system of hierarchy and dominance as well as to obtain a mate (see Chapter 3 for an extended comparison of youthful pícaros and primates).

García's propensity to lie has been the subject of numerous critical studies; in particular, several generations of critics have addressed the thorny issue of this protagonist's character as both appealing and appalling, without coming to a satisfactory conclusion. Many essays highlight the connection to the moral treatises of the period that condemn dishonesty (Parr, *After* 13–15; DiLillo 255; Morton 53–55; Riley 288–90). Frederick de Armas and Geoffrey Ribbans trace the more grandiose lies to Renaissance discourses concerning the desire for fame as both heroic and vainglorious, and link Don García to Herostratus as negative exemplars (De Armas, "Burning" 33–36; Ribbans 146). On a more positive note, many essays depict the lies as a form of creativity, so that García can be seen as a quasi-poet (Riley 290). Alan Paterson emphasizes this verbal skill as a form of virtuosity that inspires (reluctant) admiration (362–65). Similarly, Michael Jones notes the link between lying and metatheater in order to present the lies as a form of dramaturgy (204–06). Another defensive tactic is to study the liar in the context of an equally corrupt society (Simerka, "Dramatic" 197–98; Concha 145). Ribbans observes that "the individual story of a vain youth precipitately launched into the *corte y villa* is not at odds with what is happening in the society of the time" (153). Jonathan Thacker astutely asserts that García "is comparable to many of the women of the Golden-Age stage who, in fighting for justice for themselves, send a message to other women about the injustice of their allotted roles" (61). Psychological explanations for García's lying also abound: Louise Fothergill-Payne offers a potential excuse for the lies as perhaps deriving from an inferiority complex (591). Robert Fiore concurs, depicting the lies as a "compensatory" mechanism (20). Mary Malcolm Gaylord points out that García's psyche is marked by an ironic combination: "his insight into the desires of others is matched by a near-perfect blindness with respect to his own" (236). She characterizes the protagonist as "both a liar and a bungler, the duper and the duped, the villain and the victim. In his conflicted psyche he joins both meanings of the word error" (226). Eduardo Urbina offers a comprehensive analysis of the lies as both creative flourishes and the product of a psychologically compromised social outsider, "los embustes son expresión vital de sus deseos de adquirir identidad propia" (724). The models of ToM and MI cannot resolve the difficulties in pinning down a definitive interpretation; however, explorations of mentalistic moments enrich these readings by providing deeper insight into the cognitive strategies that García employs in order to weave (and become entrapped in) his web of deceit—and into the ways that we as critics employ ToM to evaluate complex literary characters.

García's initial attempts to carry out Machiavellian strategies confirm the primate and outsider analogies. First, under the influence of his new valet, who uses Theory Theory to deduce that all marriageable aristocratic women are gold-diggers, García presents himself to Jacinta and Lucrecia as a wealthy *indiano*, and offers, "Las joyas que gusto os dan, / tomad de este aparador" (I.525–26). Because of the anonymity of urban culture, this deceit is not immediately noticed. In misrepresenting his status, García actually follows the most common deceptive strategy of male primates as noted above. Of course this tactic can succeed only because his deception was one of degree; if he were poor or a commoner such a lie would be a "deal breaker." The related lie, in which he declares that he has been devoted to her for a year, would appear to follow the norms of courtly love poetry, where the ideal suitor is endlessly faithful. As we have seen throughout this chapter, courtly love literature provides Theory Theory norms for many forms of gendered behavior—which are often erroneous. García's next major lie, in which he regales his erstwhile companion from Salamanca with a long and lyrical speech about a party he held the previous night, is related to social politics rather than love: the desire to establish a strong position in the urban *galán* hierarchy, to avoid occupying the lowly rung of the newly arrived "hick." The desire to hide his nonprestigious newcomer status could also be a factor in the story he concocted for Jacinta of a long-standing attraction. García provides some insights for both the valet and the audience member seeking to form a Simulation Theory of his cognitive processes; he justifies the lies about his wealth by explaining, "me pesa / que piense nadie que hay cosa / que mover mi pecho pueda /

a invidia o admiración"—in other words, he wants to be envied for his status from a position of superiority rather than envy others from the position of inferiority he had hitherto occupied as *segundón* (I.838–40). And, when Tristán reminds him that the fabrication about his *indiano* status will be revealed if he does indeed seek marriage to the woman, García responds by indicating his own Theory Theory of why a woman would forgive him in that context, "cuando lo sepa, / habré ganado en su casa / o en su pecho y a las puertas / con ese medio, y después yo me entenderé con ellas" (I.822–25). In both cases, his primary concern is with the initial impression he will make upon people and making a positive entrée into court society; his Theory Theory for how others will respond to the truth entails projecting that the price he will pay later will be minimal and acceptable.

In large measure, García's fate will be determined by his skill (and lack of) at reading the minds of others. Because he is new to court he must reply on a Theory Theory that is formed on the basis of second-hand experiences and knowledge; he lacks both the education granted to primogenitors and the court experience that would allow for the more individualized Simulation Theory approach (Simerka, "Dramatic" 190; Concha 254). In these same initial scenes where deliberate lies provide one form of confusion, the audience sees that incorrect mind reading can also cause grave problems. When Tristán seeks out a servant and asks the name of the more beautiful of the two young women García saw, he takes at face value that the coachman names Lucrecia. Tristán commits a serious Theory Theory error when he assumes that all males would agree about who is the more compelling of two women who are both attractive, in particular by not considering that a servant would be more likely to give preference to his own mistress. Although he is never criticized by any character, the audience is aware that this miscalculation on Tristán's part contributes mightily to García's eventual disgrace. This error also sets the stage for several future misunderstandings that further perpetuate the dichotomy that García loves Jacinta's face and personality but under the name of Lucrecia.

The first conversation between García and Jacinta features a rapid-fire dialogue that displays the charm, wit, and verbal virtuosity of both; there are no asides in which either addresses his or her respective confidant in order to project a ToM for the other. In the initial encounter, as we have seen, García behaves in accordance with a generalized Theory Theory of courtier women, as guided by Tristán's cynical advice, and Jacinta does not seem to concern herself with MR. However, once Jacinta and Isabel retire to her room in order to contemplate what they conceive of as three suitors (her long-time love Don Juan, the *indiano*, and Beltrán's son) ToM does come into play. The advice that Isabel proffers is based on her Simulation Theory perspective of her mistress, whose actions at the *platería* have lead her to project that Jacinta has begun to forget Juan in favor of the new face, "si no me engaño yo, / hoy no te desagradá / el galán indiano" (I.906–08). Jacinta's feelings toward Juan are influenced by a variant of the evolutionary concern with male ranking and the survival of a woman's offspring, as refined in the early modern era by the patriarchal dictum that a daughter's partner is chosen in order to maintain or improve the family treasure and status. Jacinta is shown to be far more pragmatic than most *comedia* protagonists. Rather than clinging to the memory of a deceased love or to an informal vow, she acknowledges that "el hábito detenido / y no ha de ser mi marido" and begins to ponder the other two prospects, "en un imposible intento / no apruebo el morir de firme" (I.982–83, 989–90). Although Jacinta has agreed to look at Beltrán's son as he rides by her balcony, she does not believe that true knowledge of his character—in cognitive terms, an accurate ToM—can be formed based on physical presence alone. For this reason, she wants a better opportunity to evaluate him, although her criteria is voiced in the theological diction of the era rather than in cognitive terms, "el alma, que importa más, / quisiera ver con hablarle" (I.1010). Because patriarchal norms of male status and honor discourage the type of encounter Jacinta deems crucial (and also because she does not want to alienate Don Juan before being sure that the new candidate is acceptable), she is pushed to deploy her first Machiavellian strategy. Under normal circumstances, her plan to have him visit Lucrecia's balcony would be an ideal arrangement. However, because of the confusion concerning the names and identities of the two women, as well as García's dual identity, her use of SI collides with other levels of *engaño* and helps to drive the plot to its uncomfortable denouement. As Alarcón develops his portrait of courtier society, Machiavellian strategies are shown to have numerous potential negative consequences, due to competing deceptions, complex levels of intentionality, as well as the normal and accidental errors in human perception and ToM. In this context, deployment of Social Intelligence further muddies an already murky social pond, rather than advancing positive goals.

When García receives the invitation from Lucrecia to visit her at her balcony, he interprets this act as the ultimate confirmation that the coachman gave him the correct name, asserting "es cierto que quien me habló / es la que el papel me envía /... Que la otra, ¿qué ocasión / para escribirme tenía?" (II.1160–64). García deploys Theory Theory here; he cannot conceive of a reason why the woman who did not speak to him would summon him. Whatever the reality of such situations in real life, *comedia* heroines often use their friends as decoys, to avoid detection not only by jealous lovers but also by parents. Because García is a novice in the courtship games of the aristocracy, he is unaware that the restrictions placed on women cause them to resort to various types of stratagems. His MR is impaired because his upbringing did not prepare him for the forms of interaction he now encounters. García's ToM is again inadequate to the circumstance when he receives a challenge from Don Juan; he is totally mystified concerning the nature of the offense. A more experienced courtier—or a better practitioner of MR—could have reflected upon the previous day's encounter to conclude that the fanciful tale of the elaborate dinner party must in some way have impinged upon his friend's amorous concerns.

For scholars who are wary that any sort of embodied approach to literary characters may imply determinism, my analysis of these two misreadings highlights the fact that within cognitive cultural studies, ToM is not conceived of as deterministic. To the contrary, careful cognitive interpretation of these two errors on García's part reveals that such strategies are highly culture-bound, and people or characters learn and practice cognitive skills according to social groups norms. The relations between cognition and social power are reinforced when father and valet discuss García's first public forays; as Beltrán asks Tristán for a report, he emphasizes, "dímelo, por vida mía, sin lisonja" (II.1231–32). This plea reveals Beltrán's awareness that the Theory Theory that servants project concerning their masters is a desire to hear only good news, which gives rise to flattering lies. Beltrán must make very clear his desire for the truth, unpleasant as it may be, in order to enable Tristán to project that in this instance Beltrán sincerely wants an accurate evaluation and will not mete out the usual punishment inflicted on the bearer of bad news.

When Beltrán ponders his course of action concerning his son in the following soliloquy, a new form of ToM becomes visible, one that will dominate the rest of the play. Beltrán decides that his best course of action is to marry off his son as quickly as possible, before his reputation can be ruined. He disregards completely the possibility that parental intervention could eradicate "una costumbre tan fea"; rather, he projects, "es vano pensar que son / el reñir y aconsejar / bastantes para quitar / una fuerte inclinación" (II.1287, 1289–92). Here the father is the first to use Theory Theory to make the judgment that each of the other main characters will also come to believe, that a person who lies is beyond redemption and wholly untrustworthy. The gradual transformation of García's image across the play, from *galán* to pariah, is based on the era's shared cultural Theory Theory concerning the *embustero* as an unredeemable social type. This pejorative label, like the cultural myth of the boy who cried wolf, indicates that one universal concern of Western ToM is the difficulty in rearing children to be honest adults. Moving beyond this universal concern, Alarcón's drama provides a historically grounded and contextualized account of the particular challenges posed by early modern courtier society. Beltrán himself demonstrates an ambiguous attitude toward truth; as Fiore has noted, this *caballero* is not a good father and also does not live up to the social code he professes (16). His main concern is Tristán's warning that the lies are unconvincing; "son tales, que podrá / cogerle en ellas cualquiera" and that discovery of the lies could harm their chances to obtain for their family line a bride commensurate with their "calidad" (II.1254–55, 1284).

The very next scene, coming at the midpoint of the play, would seem to put all fears to rest. When Jacinta and Lucrecia see Beltrán's son ride by, they do of course realize that the *indiano* suitor was an imposter and *embustero* (II.1334). However, as García had projected, Jacinta is easily pacified after her maid Isabel uses Theory Theory to defend him. Her explanation echoes that of evolutionary psychology concerning males, deception, and courtship, "Los que intentan siempre dan / gran presunción al dinero / y con ese medio, hallar / entrada en tu pecho quiso" (II.1337–40). Jacinta voices further objections concerning his other lie about the year of devotion and the brief period of time between the first

encounter and the proposal; each time Isabel offers further discul-
patory mind readings to assuage Jacinta's anger, such as "¿qué te
admira, / que ... para creditar su amor / se valga de una mentira?"
(II.1354–58). Ultimately, Jacinta pardons him, as her swain had
predicted. Despite García's newcomer status, his readings of courtly love literature had provided adequate knowledge of the cultural
Theory Theory concerning young men in love, and thus he was
correct in projecting that the courtship lies would be excused.

This forgiveness shows the error and even naiveté of Beltrán's
conception of the social function of lies; he tells García that he
does not understand the mentality of the liar, for this vice is unlike
others that at least "dan gusto o dan provecho; / mas de mentir,
¿qué se saca / sino infamia y menosprecio?" (II.1461–63). The fact
that lies can foster certain types of social success is attested to by
Jacinta's willingness to overlook them. It is little wonder, then, that
when Beltrán warns his son, "estáis a la vista / de un Rey tan santo
y perfecto, / que vuestros yerros no pueden / hallar disculpa," such
advice falls on deaf ears (II.1477–79). Beltrán seems to possess an
inconsistent ToM concerning his son; he had indicated earlier that
he would not bother with homilies or warnings because someone
who is a liar by nature cannot be changed. Yet he does deliver
a lecture, and concludes his remonstrance to his son with the
confident prediction "y no he de deciros más / que esta sofrenada
espero / que baste para quien tiene / calidad y entendimiento"
(II.1488–91). His cognitive activities exaggerate both the vicious-
ness of the liar and the virtue of the blue-blooded heir. Beltrán's
Theory Theory for his society is also unstable. Here, he names
the King as ultimate arbiter, even though seventeenth-century
Spanish monarchs were not known to be particularly vigilant
about curbing such vices as dishonesty at court. To the contrary,
under the auspices of the Duke of Lerma, Philip III's court was
notoriously corrupt. Earlier, Beltrán had indirectly acknowledged
this problem, as he enlightened the Salamanca tutor concerning
the ubiquity of liars at court. In evaluating both his son and his
entire social milieu, Beltrán vacillates between an idealized Theory
Theory concerning how the noble mind should work, and a pragmatic Simulation Theory, conceding to the social benefit that can
accrue to the crafty or Machiavellian courtier.

When Beltrán informs García of the proposed marriage to
Jacinta, the young man seems to infer that his father would not

be willing to hear about his interest in Lucrecia, even though the woman is of exceptionally noble birth and has expressed interest in him. The text does not provide any basis for this ToM concerning his father, but the fact that García has spent many years at Salamanca may help to explain why he has no basis for an accurate projection of his father. Having lacked contact with a flesh-and-blood parent, García seems to base his Theory Theory on the *comedia* convention of the father as *figurón*—unaware that this particular father will accept any wedding that will give him an acceptable daughter-in-law in a timely fashion. The inaccuracy of García's projection is implicit already in his father's calm reaction to the story of his union with a noble but poor woman, but García does not adjust his initial projection. Ironically, the misreading of Beltrán is revealed only in the final scene, when he not only permits, but even compels, this very union at the end of the play. In exploring the many sources of social deceit in early modern Spain, Alarcón seems to indicate that the lack of intimate contact between parents and children contributes to an inability to use Simulation Theory within families and as a result forces fathers and sons to make ill-formed ToMs and to resort to Machiavellian tactics.

On the other hand, the needlessly elaborate lie that García constructs about his prior marriage, which parallels the grandiose banquet described in Act I, would seem to indicate that he does at times tell lies for the sheer pleasure of invention. Indeed, as he launches into the dramatic tale, García utters this aside, "agora es menester / sutilezas de mi ingenio" (II.1522–23). Alarcón encourages negative spectator MR of García; after Beltrán leaves the room, the son gloats about the "gusto" and "provecho," "es tan notorio gusto / el ver que me haya creído / y provecho haber huido / de casarme a mi disgusto" (II.1735–39). García performs a Theory Theory analysis that may be accurate concerning parental gullibility at a general level, "que fácil de persuadir / quien tiene amor" (II.1744–45). However, for the spectator who has seen that Beltrán actually chose the woman his son loves, and knows that this lie will hinder rather than help his cause, this self-congratulatory speech highlights the inadequacy of García's ToM and the absolute futility of his Machiavellian strategy. The audience may also share in García's amazement that the forewarned father would credit such an improbable tale from a known fabricator. Mutual mis-Mind-Reading between father and son, grounded in misleading cultural discourses and a lack of embodied familial interrelations, propels the drama toward its noncomic end.

Like Beltrán, Don Juan also faces the problem of idealized vs. pragmatic reality as he seeks to form a ToM concerning García. When he learns that the entire banquet narrative had been a lie, immediately after having engaged in swordplay and found García to be both brave and skilled, he cannot reconcile the contradictory characteristics, both "mentiroso" and a modern "Alcides" (II.1906, 1908). His friend offers an explanation that anticipates the contemporary controversies of nature vs. nurture (Mancing, "Embodied" 39). His companion uses both Simulation Theory and Theory Theory as he explains that the lying is the product of his social circumstances of "costumbre," while his courage is "herencia"—genetic (II.1910–11). The trajectory of this play demonstrates that human behavior is ineradicably and inextricably shaped by the constant interplay of both and that successful ToM must take this into account.

The weight of many different forms of social manipulation and deceit, deliberate and accidental, converge upon García when he arrives at Lucrecia's balcony. Here, the levels of intentionality are so complex that first time readers are often as befuddled as the suitor himself; he does not know that they know his true identity, and they do not know that he has lied to his father and mixed up their names and identities. The two women's asides to each other focus on constructing an accurate ToM for this elusive character; they constantly repeat that although other sources of information have given them what they believe to be the truth, his lies appear completely convincing from a Simulation Theory perspective, "que buena / la trazó, y que de repente" (II.2058–59). The spectator, who has been challenged to keep track of the many levels of truth and lie, is easily able to appreciate the characters' interpretive dilemma, knowing that each of the three is interacting within a mixture of truth, lie, and misperception that defies the best ToM in the world. This plight becomes particularly excruciating as the scene moves forward, for just at the moment when García finds out that they know he is both the *perulero* and the son of Beltrán and convinces them that he is not married, just at the moment when it seems as if all levels of truth will finally be revealed and accurate ToM will finally be possible, the coachman's error concerning whom

García had found most beautiful comes back to haunt them. As the confusion between name and face and prior encounters raises Lucrecia's hopes, Jacinta's ire, and García's despair, he is left to wonder "¿Verdades valen tan poco?" (II.2123).

Tristán's explanation of the cultural Theory Theory for liars sets the stage for all the events of the third act, "quien en las burlas miente, / pierde el crédito en las veras" (II.2150–51). Thus, although García's ToM had been correct in projecting that his lie about being an *indiano* would be forgiven within a Simulation Theory context, he did not project far enough ahead to see that being caught in one lie would lower his credibility in any other problematic circumstance, even when he was indeed truthful. In other words, he did not take into account the permanent negative impact that a lie would have upon the Theory Theory others would form of him as a falsifier. As the third act opens, Lucrecia seeks to use Simulation Theory to analyze García's behavior. After the disastrous encounter at the balcony, both women are highly suspicious of his motives and character. However, Lucrecia begins to reevaluate her reading of García in the face of his "porfía" and wonders, "¿éste puede ser fingido, / tan constante y desdeñado?" (II.2167). Where his erratic actions and statements at the balcony had lead her to condemn and reject him as unreliable, his unrelenting pursuit, in the face of total indifference, causes her to question her earlier ToM. Her rereading is based on Theory Theory norms for cognitive interpretation that equate true love precisely with this form of persistence. Camino concurs, providing a list of the many behaviors that their society uses to define the enamored male; for him, the most important piece of evidence is "me da dineros—que es hoy / la señal más verdadera" (III.2182–83). This judgment by the servant, like that of the coachman who drove Lucrecia and Jacinta, underscores the ways in which personal considerations can impact and even distort ToM.

Similarly, Lucrecia herself concedes that her optimism that García might have reformed himself, and her revised viewpoint, are influenced by "la esperanza / y el propio amor" (III.220–21). Desire for economic gain or the love of an attractive *galán* are thus shown to shape cognitive behavior, which turns out to be, not a simple and objective tool of measurement, but a product of two-way interactions. Here also, cultural norms play a role; even today some courtship discourses still propagate a Theory Theory model that attributes to young males the ability and desire to reform vices under the influence of a virtuous woman. Jacinta supports Lucrecia's new reading of García based on two other norms for the Theory Theory of young men as a group; first, she notes that even liars are truthful on some occasions, and also, his dedication is plausible because Lucrecia's beauty is sufficient to inspire love "en cualquiera que te viera" (II.2359).

Cognitive theory provides new frameworks and vocabularies for analyzing recurring early modern themes such as interpreting behavior via "señas." This "sign reading" activity is in fact the cultural metaphor that is used to describe what cognitivists now label ToM activity. Here, the interpretation of García is both valid and not, for it is indeed true that his perseverance is due to an unshakable love, but not toward Lucrecia. Once again, as in the previous act, accurate ToM is difficult not only because of deliberate Machiavellian strategies but also because of the complex social environment. In a rural, feudal society, such a mistake concerning names and identities would be unlikely to occur, or would be corrected quickly. In the following scenes, mis-Mind-Reading once again stems from the challenges of urban courtship. García has to contend with numerous different iterations of his beloved: the women to whom he spoke at the jewelry store and at the balcony, the woman deemed most beautiful by the coachman, and now the woman who holds the letter he wrote. When García addresses the woman reading his letter, who is Jacinta, as "Lucrecia," the audience is presented with the moment of a conventional comedy in which all errors could be resolved and a happy marriage could take place. However, in the context of mendacious urban courtier society (and also as a result of García's previous lies), both Simulation and Theory Theory projections lead her to infer the worst, "finge, por no enojarla, / que por ella me ha tenido" (III.2556–57). García misreads Jacinta's reaction as false modesty in the presence of a friend, and believing that he is helping her to play act, pretends to go along with the game. The mutual *engaño* reaches peak intensity as Jacinta declares of she and Lucrecia, "en mí y en ella / vive solo un corazón" and García responds "Si eres tú, bien claro está" (III.2601–03).

García reiterates his flawed ToM when he is alone with Tristán, using qualifiers like "sin duda" and "claro" as he praises "Lucrecia's" intellect; he exudes cognitive confidence precisely at the moment when nothing is at all clear to any of the characters. Tristán supports García with additional analysis of his own, first by projecting, incorrectly, that García's lie to his father about being married is the primary obstacle. Then, the proofs that he offers of mutual love crystallize the unwitting confusion of identities, for he cites both the woman who reads the letters and the woman García speaks to—not knowing that they are two separate persons. These two scenes once again demonstrate the value of Dennett's model of multiple levels of intentionality for analysis of complex *comedia* plots in which both the baroque aesthetic and epistème are developed across four and five levels—so that even the audience or reader who has access to the true thoughts of all characters sometimes has difficulty keeping track!

Just at the point when the problems caused by unwitting confusion might push the spectator to empathize with García, the protagonist once again reverts to lying for the sheer pleasure of invention. This time he regales Tristán with a sensationalized account of the brief duel with Don Juan from the first act. Upon seeing the supposedly bedridden Juan come striding toward them in perfect health, the valet applies Theory Theory to himself to excuse his gullibility, "¿a quién no engañarán / mentiras tan bien trobadas?" (III.2784–85). Here, we see one of two recurring themes concerning ToM; on the one hand, Lucrecia and Jacinta reiterate on several occasions that once a person is known to be a liar, the listener's reactions will be shaped such that all subsequent utterances are suspect—hence, the play's title. On the other hand, even for the forewarned listener, a well-told tale with convincing details can entice belief even when the story itself is fantastic and the speaker suspect. Tristán's ready acceptance of García's mendacious narrative highlights the power exerted on the human mind by a compelling narrative or a gifted raconteur, and the attendant temptation for those with such gifts to abuse their talent. However, at this point in the drama, the major point to be made is cautionary. When Beltrán bestows upon Juan his *hábito*, in thanks for his help in uncovering the truth about García's marital state, we see that one of his earliest lies has ultimately resulted in social promotion for his main rival.

The following scenes continue to emphasize García's complete lack of credibility, as the other characters feel compelled to double check each "fact" he offers prior to arranging the marriage to Lucrecia that he has requested. Similarly, when García finally becomes aware of the confusion about the women's names, his prior acts have so undermined his standing with the primary social arbiters that they barely bother to perform any sort of ToM. Lucrecia's father posits "inconstancia loca" but indicates that the accuracy of his Simulation Theory is now irrelevant; García has given his word and hand, and regardless of his mental state, must comply or die. Ultimately, García is made to pay the price for the lies that deceived and angered his entire social circle. In a sense, the crime for which he is punished is that his skillful lies made him totally inaccessible to the ToM of the other characters. The final reiteration of the title "en la boca / de quien mentir acostumbra, es *La verdad sospechosa*" confirms this "law" of urban social life: in a complex setting where the ability to form an accurate ToM is essential to social stability, those who seek to block or evade Mind Reading are anathema and must pay a price. A liar may be excluded, like Zayas's Fenisa, or denied his "gloria" like García, but cannot be allowed to triumph. Because of their excessive use of MI, both of these characters metamorphose from typical *comedia* protagonists in pursuit of marriage to satirical *figurones* who serve as negative *exempla*.

This play also reveals Alarcón's Theory Theory concerning women and love, and it is a unique reading. David Pasto has characterized Alarcón's heroines as unusually independent; their cognitive skills contribute to this force of character (227). Jacinta's behavior presents a direct repudiation of the courtly love variant of ToM as explored above in regards to *El muerto disimulado*. Although Jacinta had apparently been attracted enough to Juan to agree to marriage to him when and if his *hábito* were to be granted, she is equally willing to marry García, and passionate devotion does not seem to be a factor in either decision. She lets Isabel devise excuses for García's lies not for love, but because "de sus partes me contento; quiere el padre" (II.1380). Although from Juan's perspective Jacinta would appear to be a typical *mudable*, the reason for her change of affection is presented as legitimate rather than immoral from a patriarchal standpoint. How could anyone vilify a woman who abandons a secret, chaste courtship with a man who is noble but too poor, in order to accept the man her father chose for her? Of course, Juan *does* vilify her with the typical epithet of "livian[a]" and "falsa," but no other character supports this view, and in the end Juan is quite happy to marry her (I.1080, 1084). Alarcón presents a subtle and nuanced portrayal of a woman's mind, as she navigates the treacherous waters of early modern courtship. Even as she vacillates among the secret lover, the foreigner, and the approved suitor, Jacinta is depicted as a clever character who makes the most of the limited role allowed to her by her social milieu. She is alternately attracted to three (apparently) different but acceptable males, violates surface-level rules concerning unchaperoned contact but remains chaste, and her ultimate marriage is neither a reward nor a punishment, but rather the maintenance of her family status quo. In direct contrast to the *comedia's* usual affirmation for courtly love precepts of unquenchable and undying love for noble men and women alike, Alarcón portrays a female mind that is concerned primarily with assuring her marriage to a suitable and compatible male. It is noteworthy that her attitude is in concordance with the viewpoint normally attributed to match-making parents. For example, Jacinta is not satisfied with merely seeing Beltrán's son and making a choice based on physical attributes; rather, she seeks a chance to meet with him. Her desire to speak with any potential suitor underlines the play's emphasis on character over superficial attraction. Given Alarcón's well-known penchant for using theater to provide moral *exempla*, it could be argued that Jacinta functions to provide an alternative model of female mentality and behavior, as a corrective to the excesses of conventional courtship drama and courtly love literature. To reinforce this possible interpretation, it is relevant that García is made to look foolish in his heedless pursuit of love at first sight.

Mirror Neurons in *El desdén con el desdén*

Agustín Moreto's *El desdén con el desdén* is permeated with characters using MI upon each other, as the title indicates. William R. Blue has demonstrated convincingly that the *galán* Carlos's success is dependent on his ability to mirror the heroine Diana's behaviors; the model of ToM and MI allows us to probe more deeply into the cognitive mechanisms that support this tactic ("Echoing"). In particular, neurological findings concerning the engagement of mirror neurons during MR activity provide interesting—although not strictly necessary—empirical documentation to reinforce Blue's observations (Saxe and Baron-Cohen, "Introduction"; Gallese and Goldman 495). The initial scenes, like those of *El muerto disimulado*, focus on the MR skills of the men who seek in vain to persuade a young woman to marry. Carlos and his *gracioso* Polilla begin by describing Diana as excessively immune to his—and his rivals'—advances. They use Simulation Theory to describe her rejection as completely individual and unique because her lack of interest goes beyond standard indifference, "le extraña demasía / de su entereza pasaba / del decoro la medida, / y, excediendo de recato, / tocaba ya en grosería" (I.138–42). Carlos initially uses Theory Theory to infer that Diana might have formed a negative opinion of him because of a false rumor—a common dramatic plot device that seems to correspond to an endemic problem of urban life. However, he soon learns that her chilly reception toward all males is due to "excessive" reading and study, especially of classical mythology, which has led her to distrust men and avoid courtship. Elizabeth Howe compares Diana's comprehensive education to that of Queen Isabella; clearly, this is well beyond the norm for a woman who is not a future monarch (154). Due to her expansive study, Diana uses a Theory Theory based on information derived from elite literary sources, in contrast to characters from other plays who form their projections on the basis of popular courtly love texts.

The play's opening scene summarizes her father's failure to find the correct MI technique to convince his wayward daughter to accept matrimony; like Azevedo's Rodrigo, the Count of Barcelona employs persuasive tactics of "razón," "ruegos," and "furia"—all to no avail (I.212–14). Carlos has arrived in Barcelona because of a new tactic; her father has brought together a group of acceptable suitors to compete for her favor, with the assumption that over time she will come to recognize and overcome her own error: "no hay cosa / como dejar a quien lidia / con su misma sinrazón" (I.234–36). Carlos's first soliloquy thus delineates the outline of a plot in which men use ToM in order to convince a woman to occupy her proper place in the social order (Rissell 220).

At this point, Carlos detours from his focus on Diana, in order to evaluate—and condemn—his own mental processes. He uses Theory Theory to describe himself, and the typical lover, as a pathetic and paradoxical being, "solo por la privación / de más valor lo imagina, / y da el más precio a lo difícil. / que su mismo ser le quita" (I.267–70). Neophilia is once again shown to be a dominant cognitive force, compelling men and women alike to pursue disinterested people against the dictates of their logic. Diana herself will echo this lament in the final act. Carlos's long and intensive inquiry concludes with the assertion that this emotion is not actually love, but rather "sentimiento equivocado en caricia" (I.348–49). However, giving his urges a new label does not give him any power over them, "la razón discurre, / mas la voluntad, indigna / toda la razón me arrastra" (I.350–52). Although early modern characters do not know that they are influenced by their dopamine receptors, most courtship dramas devote significant attention to neophilia as a primary though detrimental component of the law of attraction. Polilla reinforces the notion that this is a universal human trait with his parallel story of a kitchen servant not wanting to eat grapes until the vine was moved out of his reach, a tale which in turn echoes a Sapphic poem.

Once the suitors arrive at court, the Count asks their aid in using Simulation Theory to determine a successful course of action for swaying this atypical female. Bearne suggests, and Gaston agrees, that the norms of decorum be transgressed slightly, because more direct interaction with the men could be more effective with Diana than the socially accepted, indirect approaches of sending musicians, letters, and gifts. Here, the father is willing to violate conventional segregationist precepts, which are based upon fear of familial dishonor due to the Theory Theory cultural projection of the female mind as too weak to withstand the temptations of a masculine physical presence. In this unique case, the projection of female vulnerability is seen as a potential benefit, because this inherent weakness can be used to lure Diana into the marriage she currently resists. There is an additional unspoken aspect of Theory Theory on the father's part in this scene; he projects that honor strictures, and the advantages of being married to a high-ranking female, will prevent the suitors from taking advantage of this unusual freedom. In this scenario, the father is successful in his use of Theory Theory to comprehend his male counterparts, who do indeed behave honorably. But his use of Simulation Theory toward his daughter fails, for it is not mere proximity that eventually wins over Diana.

Diana and her attendants also employ various forms of ToM in their discussions of love. While her ladies in waiting, Laura and

Cintia, appear to follow their mistress's lead in disdaining men, Diana uses Theory Theory to assert that women who enjoy being courted are already halfway down the path to falling in love. Although Cintia defends herself and friends, "la que agradecida es / no se infiere que es liviana," audience members are likely to push Diana's assessment even further and to use our own ToM to infer this is a Machiavellian strategy designed to allow her companions to pursue marriage without offending their patroness (I.581–82). Diana's conclusion, "quien no resiste a empezar, / no resiste a proseguir" is both a Theory Theory projection of the mindset of women in general in courtship, as well as a Simulation Theory explanation for her own apparent discourtesy in rejecting even the most innocuous demonstrations of male gallantry. It is clear that Diana acknowledges this as a general rule of human behavior and prefers to break social norms of courtesy in order to avoid falling into love's trap, because she does not consider foreknowledge to be sufficient. Diana's words and actions show a very keen awareness of the intricacies of human courtship mentalities; she is no mere "blue stocking" but also a perceptive social actor (I.621–22).

In order to persuade Diana to allow the men to court her more personally, the Count justifies his decision by referring to his ToM concerning the various suitors and the general public. He explains that the current circumstances could cause the men to make unflattering Simulation Theory readings of her mind—that they could accuse her of "desprecio" toward them and "resistencia" toward her father (I.799, 804). By allowing the courtship to move forward, she could show herself more appropriately amenable to them and to her father, and thus avoid the men spreading rumors that could cause a negative ToM concerning her within their social circle "que esto importa a tu decoro / y acredita mi respecto" (I.811–12). In both this play and Azevedo's comedy, as well as in *La verdad sospechosa*, it is the fathers who express concern about the ToM that court society could project upon their children and shape their behaviors accordingly. Characters of the younger generation are more likely to frame group Theory Theory projections in terms of cultural norms or stereotypes concerning how members of the opposite gender behave in courtship situations, in order to understand and shape their own circumstances.

This unusual courtship proceeds as all the suitors encounter Diana together and seek to wear down her resistance, each of them employing a different Simulation Theory reading of her resistance and thus pursuing a different tactic. The reader or spectator must infer, as it is not directly stated, that the Prince of Bearne's ToM indicates that appealing to Diana's pride in her rational powers is the best angle. He urges Diana to question her own epistemological process, telling her that her attitude is based on mere speculative "argumentos" and that she should allow personal experience to provide her with better "prueba" (I.899, 902). Bearne uses this lack of direct experience to assert that Diana violates "la razón natural" (I.907–08). Diana responds that precisely by allowing these courtship encounters she is going to be able to take experience into account; however, she is confident that the tests being employed will confirm her theory that "el desdén... es natural en mi pecho" (I.944–46). As the conversation concludes, the prince goes off to contemplate Diana's mind once more, in order to find "contra vos / el más agudo argumento" (I.960–61). Carlos is the last suitor to leave; before his departure he puts into action the plan that William R. Blue has deemed "mimetic"—that is to say, he imitates her disdain and feigns courtesy as the only reason for his pursuit. In this scene, Carlos's mimetic behavior is based entirely upon his Simulation Theory analysis concerning Diana; without a ToM no such Machiavellian or mimetic strategy could be conceptualized or enacted. My expansion upon Blue's reading of mimetic behaviors highlights the usefulness of cognitive theory, not only for permitting new modes of analysis but also for enriching existing interpretations.

The likely eventual success of Carlos's Machiavellian strategy is immediately apparent, as Diana confides to Cintia that she would enjoy overcoming his indifference in order to "enamorar a este loco" (I.1003). Cintia uses the same type of generalized human Theory Theory that Diana had employed earlier when warning of the dangers of wanting to be loved, to assert that in her pursuit of such a deception, Diana risks falling in love. Here, Cintia argues her case halfheartedly and in an aside announces her delight that she has failed to convince her mistress, for such a scheme actually promotes Cintia's own self-interest. This scene is exemplary of the crucial role played by MI in developing the complexity of multiple and interwoven levels of intentionality that drive the plots of early modern courtship drama.

As the first act closes, Carlos reveals to his valet Polilla the tremendous emotional toll extracted upon those who employ such complex MI schemes, "estoy muriendo; / todo mi valor ha habido / menester mi fingimiento" (I.1049–51). This plaint helps to explain why, in literature and life, from primates to modern humans, MI is used as sparingly as possible. This ability can be tremendously beneficial to success in certain types of situations, but it depletes significant cerebral resources that are then unavailable for other aspects of survival—at the literal or social level. The model of Social Intelligence emerged as scientists searched for adaptive capacities significant enough to justify the increased caloric needs imposed by a more complex brain; however, Carlos indicates that, in advanced *homo sapiens* culture, the price paid is emotional rather than caloric depletion (Milton 285). In early modern aristocratic society where the appropriate marriage is the key to passing on wealth and status to subsequent generations, courtship literature is the primary locus for MI. However, as the next chapter will demonstrate, in the picaresque literature depicting lower social classes, Social Intelligence is instead deployed for purposes of physical survival and class mobility. Thus, as both real life experience and literary tradition reveal, such strategies are reserved for only the most crucial human interactions.

In the second act, as Diana and Carlos put into play the mind games they have devised, the *gracioso* Polilla occupies a central role. He earns a place within Diana's entourage in order to be able to provide concrete feedback to Carlos concerning the impact of his strategy; thus, Carlos does not have to rely solely on his own ToM in order to evaluate and modify his game plan. In addition, Polilla's direct access to Diana's mindset enables him to give Carlos excellent advice concerning how best to use Simulation Theory tactics to engage the woman's affections, as well as letting him know about—and helping to shape—Diana's ToM concerning Carlos. It is for this reason that Polilla promotes the seemingly counter-productive strategy of Carlos becoming more and more inaccessible as Diana seeks to engage his affections, even to the point of appearing "grosero," if his ultimate goal is "que se pique esta mujer" (II.1118). Diana's initial Theory Theory reading of Carlos indicates that in order to win him over, "he de hacerle más favor" (II.1171). Here Diana is shown to be less skilled at ToM than Carlos; she does not equate his indifference with her own. If she had made that connection, she would certainly have realized that, just as the lavish attentions bestowed by her various suitors had failed to spark her own interest, granting favors to a truly disinterested swain would not be productive for her either. Diana's use of Theory Theory here seems to depend upon her understanding and projection of male mentality at a general level, where the granting of favor would be effective. Carlos's more insightful scheme was based upon his understanding of her mind as highly unique. In this case, it is the ability to use Simulation Theory to read and manipulate a specific mind, combined with the insider information that Polilla provides, that enables Carlos to begin to gain an advantage over Diana in the mind war they wage.

It is hardly necessary to point out that Moreto projects a more traditional gender ideology than the *dramaturgas* studied in this chapter; what is noteworthy is that cognitive theory enables us to see that masculine superiority is conveyed through the depiction of Carlos's more skillful use of MI. In the following scene, Polilla provides constant asides to both Diana and Carlos as each seeks to simultaneously mislead and entice the other and to use ToM to gauge his or her success. This charade intensifies as Carlos vows that he could never return Diana's devotion were she to fall for him, and insisting "no sé engañar" even at this moment of greatest deception (II.1284). The initial verbal duel is followed up by two long soliloquies in which each character describes his or her vision of what Love is; both incorporate their own Theory Theory concerning what conventional lovers think and feel. After this bravura performance, Carlos once again emphasizes the emotional price he pays, "lo que finjo, / toda una vida me cuesta" (II.1394–95) and laments "la violencia / que me hace la obligación / de haber de fingir finezas" (II.1505–07). Once the masked ball begins, Carlos takes advantage of the social norms associated with pairing off couples by color to openly declare his love to Diana. The context of the ball provides him with both a pretext for this emotional release and also a strategic retreat, should Diana fail to respond. Then, after Diana rejects him, he uses MI both to defend his own actions and to shield himself from correct ToM on her part. He defends his seemingly intense pursuit as pride in performing well at his appointed role, "¿Tan necio queréis que sea / que cuando a fingir me ponga, / lo finja sin apariencia?" (II.1617–19). He also chides her for deficient Simulation Theory capacities in not detecting the pretense, "Pues vos, siendo tan discreta, / ¿ no conocéis que es fingida?" (II.1610–11). Throughout the second act, as Diana and Carlos go to ever greater lengths to hide their true feelings, they begin to display the ultimate form of MI, which Miller terms "proteanism" (after the shape-shifting mythical figure), consisting of behaviors that combine both deception and unpredictability, designed to frustrate the cognitive abilities of the most skilled opponent (312–14). Carlos continues his protean approach as he expresses surface appreciation for her courtesy in a way that in reality chides her for having believed him, "Cortesanía fue vuestra /el fingiros engañada" (II.1641–42). Diana's scrutiny of the underlying insult is absolutely correct, as she fumes in an aside, "Bien agudo ha sido el modo /de motejarme de necia" (II.1652–53). Carlos then offers the same type of Theory Theory observation to Diana that she herself had performed on Cintia in the first act, warning that the person who seeks to be courted and desired is in extreme danger of allowing gratitude to metamorphose into love.

At the midpoint of the play, it becomes ever more clear that Carlos's Social Intelligence IQ is higher than Diana's and that for this reason he will triumph. Diana's susceptibility is manifest as her anger leads her to abandon him at the ball, despite the "sospecha" that such an act may cause, and as she declares herself willing to risk all for this conquest, "aunque ... a costa de mi decoro" (II.1704–06). Although the public courtship was set up by Diana and her father precisely in order to prevent gossip, she is now willing to endanger her *fama* to assuage the pain that she attributes to damaged pride. Even as she continues to view herself as a "peña" in her disdain, Polilla's interpretation reflects the Theory Theory of early modern culture— that the man or woman who protests too much is on the verge of capitulation. Or, in the *gracioso*'s vulgar analogy, "Aún es verde la breva; / mas ella madurará / como hay muchachos y piedras" (II.1741–43). At this point, the audience's own ToM is likely to mirror that of Polilla, so for the second half of the play the audience can take for granted that Carlos will succeed in manipulating Diana into declaring her passion first, and that the intrigue will derive from the increasingly daring moves each will make to obtain his or her objective. Thus, throughout the final two acts, Social Intelligence is crucial to plot and character development, and monitoring the competing ToMs is likely to be the central focus of audience attention.

As Diana increases the stakes in her Machiavellian strategy, the levels of intentionality become more and more complex. Thus, when she makes a plan to gather with her ladies in waiting for a musical evening in the garden, and tells Polilla to make sure Carlos passes by, "sin que el sepa / que es cuidado" Diana believes she is at the second level, where Carlos won't know that she knows that he is present. However, because of Polilla's dual identity as her doctor Caniqui and as Carlos's valet, the audience sees an additional level where Carlos pretends that he isn't aware of her machinations and also will continue to pretend indifference in order to further fan the flames of her growing interest. As always, once he is in her presence, Carlos emphasizes that this strategy is incredibly difficult, declaring "yo muero" and "no podré emprenderlo" (II.1805, 1813). This level of suffering occurs merely at the sound of the women's voices; once Carlos enters the garden and sees Diana in "traje doméstico" he is so moved that he is able to restrain himself only because Polilla threatens him with a dagger (II.1854–55). He is forced by that dagger to feign an interest in the garden's flowers and décor, even as Diana sends her ladies to summon him. In the face of Carlos's continued lack of interest, Cintia uses her ToM to declare, "es un tronco" (II.1965). Although the act closes as Diana declares her intention to conquer him no matter the cost, there is no indication that her MI ability will enable her to formulate a new and more successful plan.

The third act opens as the two other suitors approach Carlos to suggest the very same plan that he has already been executing. Their Theory Theory projection derives from the dictum that because women as a group are vain, Diana's pride will suffer if all three men ignore her and court the other ladies, "porque en viendo perdida la fineza / la dama, aun de aquel mismo que aborrece, / sentirlo es natural en la belleza" (III.2044–46). Although Carlos and his two rivals use different criteria to evaluate Diana's ToM, all agree that feigned disinterest is the best strategy, based on the cultural precept that vanity is the determining factor in the psychological make-up of marriageable women. This projected vanity, a love of being chased rather than chasing, actually bears a close resemblance to the neophilia associated with masculine courtship behavior by ethologists. It bears repeating that I do not seek to explain in a cause-and-effect manner the behavior of early modern literary characters through evolutionary biological determinism. In this context, references to the neurological basis for neophilia can help us to understand the persistent representation of this behavior in amorous literatures of many different eras, and more concretely to analyze the early modern cultural Theory Theory that projects a form of this attitude onto female beings and literary characters. When Polilla describes Diana's current mental state to Carlos in the next scene, he explains her behavior with another masculinist projection: that when a woman expresses intense dislike it is because she does not recognize her true feelings, "lo que ira le parece / es quinta esencia de amor" (III.2085–86). Indeed, the entire plot trajectory reinforces the patriarchal ToM that encourages males to pursue women who appear to disdain them, that defines male persistence in such instances as a virtue, and that explains rejection by different but related negative projections of the female mind as, at worst duplicitous (feigning a lack of interest when she in truth enjoys being pursued) or at best naïve and unaware of her true emotions. This Theory Theory of women's dishonest response to pursuit remains ubiquitous in contemporary media culture three centuries later, and prompted one of the women's movement's most catchy cultural reinscriptions: "What part of 'NO' don't you understand?"

The concluding scenes validate all of these patriarchal assumptions concerning the female mind. As Bearne and Gastón laud the other women, Diana nags Polilla about Carlos's failure to compose songs for her, and laments "nadie se acuerda de mi" (II.2218). At this point, Diana employs MI one last time to capture Carlos's interest, telling him that she has used logic to reconcile herself to marriage, and has decided upon the Prince as her future spouse. Once again she chooses a Theory Theory strategy rather than an individualist Simulation Theory approach; projecting the male mentality as inherently jealous, she determines, "se ha de abrasar, o no es hombre" (III.2323). At this moment Diana appears to regain the upper hand, she uses the courtly love norms to infer the signs of success, "Bien he logrado la herida, / que del semblante lo infiero, / todo el color ha perdido" (III.2378–80). However, when Carlos regains his wits and informs her that he too has decided to marry, Polilla compliments his master's MI in an aside, "como diestro / herir con los mismos filos" (III.2428–19). Diana's lack of self-awareness is emphasized in the following scene; as she rages about the anger Carlos's decision has aroused in her, it is left to Caniqui to use Simulation Theory to read her mind correctly and enlighten her concerning the true nature of her feelings. In a soliloquy, Diana finally concedes the truth, "quien quiere encender un edificio / suele ser el primero que se abrasa" (III.2574–75). Her strategy of feigning desire for the Prince immediately backfires, as the happy suitor immediately shows up to claim his prize. Diana focuses her SI upon Carlos rather than the man in the room; not worrying at all about what sort of impression she may make upon her prospective fiancé, she instead contemplates Carlos's motivations for telling the Prince. Her Simulation Theory reading leads to the unhappy conclusion, "el nunca lo hiciera, no, / si a mi me quisiera bien" (III.2620–21). At the same moment, the Prince ponders Diana's unexpected reaction, and uses his never very accurate ToM to project that she is unhappy about his direct approach and that she would prefer that he seek out her father first.

Diana provides the most extended speech of the entire play as she explains to her two companions, Cintia and Laura, her new understanding of her own mental state and the functioning of love in the female mind. Diana confirms all of the most negative Theory Theory stereotypes concerning women's cognition in her speech, and takes all of the blame for her failed schemes and lack of self-awareness. However, Laura completely disregards Diana's analysis and instead resorts to an alternate but equally patriarchal neophilic reading of the situation, "viendo prohibido el plato, / Diana se ahitó de amor" (III.2809–10). In order to salvage a comic closure within the last one hundred lines, Moreto's play requires unlikely self-sacrifice from every character except the two protagonists. Although Laura had warned Cintia to say nothing to Carlos unless she had a promise from another suitor, Cintia unselfishly enlightens Carlos about Diana's true feelings. Then, once Carlos publicly declares his love for Diana, it is necessary that both the jilted suitor and her father accept this new state of affairs and allow Diana to make her own choice, despite the possible negative social repercussions.

In Moreto's play, both of the characters who engage in Machiavellian behavior are ultimately rewarded with the desired marriage. This success constitutes a radical departure from the fates meted out to Fenisa and García. Furthermore, in the process of working out this complex and convoluted plot, Moreto's depiction of gender and MI also differs markedly from the other dramatists. Even though Diana ultimately gains the husband she desired, she must first suffer public humiliation and the loss of her *fama* as a highly intelligent woman, within a plot structure that condemns female intellect as inferior. So, even though Zayas's play offers a conclusion in which a primary female character is denied the marriage she desires, the *dramaturga* does not present the same level of misogynist discourse about female deception as Moreto. Moreto's negative depiction of women and MI present the flip side of the critique of masculine deception offered in Azevedo and Caro's dramas. As we have seen throughout this chapter, dramatists can represent the use—and misuse—of Mind Reading to explore a vast terrain of deceptive social interactions, condemning men and women alike for the havoc wrought, as well as highlighting situations where deception is a *pharmakos*, a necessary evil that promotes a greater social good. These readings of a wide variety of dramaturgical tactics demonstrate the benefits of cognitive research and the models of ToM, MI, and levels of intentionality for new modes of analysis of gender ideology, emplotment, and character in courtship drama.

Social Intelligence and Foraging

Primates and Early Modern Pícaros

Theory of Mind (ToM) and Mind Reading (MR) refer to cognitive activities that entail projecting the mental activities of another sentient being, for social purposes that include producing a positive impression, currying favor, and social advancement (Chapter 1). The form of ToM that is used to deceive and manipulate others is called Machiavellian Intelligence (MI) or Social Intelligence (SI) (Byrne and Whiten, "Machiavellian" 1). Cognitive theorists have posited two forms of MR: Theory Theory advocates postulate that human beings form an internalized set of rules, like a grammar, in order to associate observed human behaviors with non-observable internal states. The rival, Simulation Theory, postulates that we come to understand how other minds function based on attempting to simulate how they will react—"placing yourself in their shoes." This chapter will explore the applicability of both Simulation Theory and Theory Theory and will demonstrate that picaresque characters use each paradigm in specific circumstances. The ToM paradigm and its related subcategories provide a new way to approach the deceptive cognitive activities that are the hallmark of the picaresque universe. Although this *topos* has been explored in many studies, most recently by Donald Gilbert-Santamaría, who discusses a "poetics of engaño," such analyses have tended to present this topic from a perspective that is dehistorized and abstract (108). This chapter and the next will provide an exploration of the function of ToM, Social Intelligence (SI), and Machiavellian Intelligence (MI) in *Lazarillo de Tormes*, *Guzmán de Alfarache*, and *La vida del Buscón*. In this chapter, I will focus on the opening sections of each novel, where the protagonists learn the cognitive skills necessary to survival in the early modern urban jungle. I will provide an introduction to and overview of the ways that cognitive approaches can shed new light on picaresque narrative but do not

pretend to be all-inclusive; a comprehensive treatment of the cognitive dimensions of the picaresque novel would require an entire
book-length treatment.

The Pícaro's Cognitive Epiphany

In studies of children, the mentally challenged, and apes, ToM
research often focuses on the gradual development of awareness
of how other minds function. The minimal threshold of cognitive
sophistication for normal children is equated with understanding
that another can hold a "false belief" (Whiten 153–57; Wimmer
and Perner 103–04). In picaresque literature, mental maturation
is defined by very different criteria, coinciding with a moment
when the protagonist becomes aware that humans often seek to
use awareness of false beliefs in order to deceive others—and that
for this reason he needs to develop a ToM as a self-defense mechanism. Thus, a key moment in the trajectory of nearly all picaresque
narrative is the initial moment of illumination when an innocent
youth realizes that the social world is a game of wits in which MR,
the ability to anticipate and avert the machinations of others, is
the minimum requirement for survival. The pícaro realizes that to
survive and prosper he must always assume that those he meets are
using their ToM against him, and devise ways not only to avoid
their traps but also to create his own scams. All three of the major
picaresque protagonists, Lazarillo, Guzmán, and Pablos, experience this perverse form of epiphany within the initial chapters of
their respective narratives. Most major studies of the picaresque
refer to this moment; it is generally not a major focal point but
rather is used to set the stage for a particular reading (see Blackburn 38; H. Reed 46; Rico 11; Castillo 44–45; Dunn 87; Parker
64; Deyermond 15–25; and Alter, *Rogue* 12). In my reading, this
awakening is a decisive event—analogous to the "false belief" test
for children—because it is the moment when an innocent youth
makes the initial cognitive leap that is a precursor to all of the ToM
activity that makes possible future deceptions and scams.

Lazarillo's intuitive leap concerning the need for a ToM arises in
reaction to his blind master's mistreatment:

> "Necio, aprende que el mozo del ciego un punto ha de saber
> más que el diablo," y rió mucho la burla.

> Parecióme que en aquel instante *desperté de la simpleza en* que como niño dormido estaba. Dije entre mí:
> "Verdad dice éste, que me cumple *avivar el ojo y avisar*, pues solo soy, y pensar cómo me sepa valer." (Tratado primero; emphasis added)

Employing cognitive vocabulary, Lazarillo's "simpleza" can be characterized as the initial, quasi-virginal—or even autistic—lack of awareness concerning the normal (deceptive) operations of other minds in his society. The ToM model also enables us to identify and analyze far more specifically the attributes that Lazarillo and other poor youth must develop to survive. Although the phrase "avivar el ojo" implies careful visual perception, it is in actuality the cerebral ability to predict how others might think, and thus anticipate and evade their detrimental actions, that will enable Lazarillo and his progeny to feed and clothe themselves, and eventually embark upon social advancement. Lazarillo's new perception provides him with cognitive ammunition that will enable him to survive the less-than-tender mercies of his first three masters, but it is not until he is old enough for true employment that his SI begins to provide substantial benefits.

Guzmán's cognitive shift entails a more gradual process. Like Lazarillo, it is physical suffering, in this case the regurgitation of rotten food, that sets the process in motion. However, it is only when he is offered bad food again by the next innkeeper—twice—that his ToM finally awakens:

> Y entonces *me vino a la memoria* el juramento tan fuera de tiempo que hizo la noche antes, afirmando que era ternera. *Parecióme* mal y que por sólo haberlo jurado mentía, porque la verdad no hay necesidad que se jure, fuera del juicio y habiendo necesidad. Demás que toda satisfacción prevenida sin queja es en todo tiempo *sospechosa*. (1.I.vi; emphasis added)

Guzmán would appear to be a slower learner than Lazarillo; despite the initial misadventure at the first inn, the second innkeeper's excessive protestations concerning the high quality of the meat served at dinner had not kept him from eating mule the previous evening. But the digestive discomfort from the suspicious meat, coupled with the completely disgusting appearance of the breakfast offered the next morning, "tan tiesa y de mal sabor, que no hay quien hinque los dientes en ella," eventually jolts his MR skills to manifest themselves so that he is saved from consuming a third unwholesome meal. Although Lazarillo and Pablos are the picaresque characters whose initial travails focus on starvation, it is Guzmán whose SI awakening occurs due to negative eating experiences. However, he does not immediately extrapolate that ToM is necessary in *all* facets of urban life, and not only in scrutinizing the food sold at bad inns.

Pablos's ToM is also somewhat slow to manifest itself and is in fact prompted by other people. After the economic fleecing that he and his master suffer at the inn where they spend the night on their way to Alcalá, the innkeeper advises, "Señor nuevo, a pocas estrenas como ésta, envejecerá" (4). Similarly, when Pablos cries to Don Diego about the humiliations perpetrated by the other servants, he is told to wake up, "Pablos, abre el ojo que asan carne. Mira por ti, que aquí no tienes otro padre ni madre" (5). However, it is not until he finds excrement placed in his bedclothes that Pablos at long last experiences his own moment of clarity, "dije entre mí: —«Avisón, Pablos, *alerta*». Propuse de hacer nueva vida" (5; emphasis added). Like Lazarillo, Pablos uses metaphors of awakening and of vision to express the acquisition of SI. When Pablos loses his innocence and begins to use ToM, his life improves immediately, both because he uses this skill to eat well and also because once he uses MR in his interactions with other students, he ceases to be the unwitting victim of *burlas* by his peers. It is likely that Pablos's initial successes are easier to attain than Lazarillo's because he is dealing with people his own age rather than with cognitively sophisticated adults.

All three protagonists experience a moment in which they re-weigh society as a whole, in many ways a parallel to the cognitive act early modern culture labeled *desengaño*. This term was often used for awakenings of a spiritual nature, but the meditative musings of Guzmán as he reflects back on his earlier experience demonstrate the gulf that lies between abstract forms of philosophical or spiritual enlightenment and the materially grounded, socially oriented ToM of cognitive theory:

> Cuando determiné mi partida, ¡qué de contento se me representó, que aun me lo daba el pensarla! Vía con la imaginación el abril y la hermosura de los campos, no considerando sus agostos o como si en ellos hubiera de habitar impasible … No pensé que había tantos trabajos y miserias. Mas, ¡oh, cómo es

el «no pensé» de casta de tontos y proprio de necios, escusa de bárbaros y acogida de imprudentes! Que el cuerdo y sabio siempre debe *pensar, prevenir y cautelar.* Hice como muchacho *simple,* sin *entendimiento* ni *gobierno.* (1.I.vii; emphasis added)

Like Lazarillo, Guzmán contrasts a prior state of simplicity or thoughtlessness with a new awareness of the need to employ advanced mental capabilities; the italicized series of verbs and nouns in the final lines above indicate an intense focus on the importance of MR. Guzmán had baptized himself with a new last name when he left Sevilla; however, this is the moment when he is truly reborn. In all three cases, ToM emerges as a new and keen awareness that other people are prone to deception. I would label this awareness an example of Theory Theory in the sense that each protagonist establishes a generalized theory of mind for all new acquaintances, anticipating that each one is likely to try to deceive, rob, or cheat him. This initial phase of ToM is an extrapolation from a series of experiences to a general rule concerning the cognitive activities of strangers in the cut-throat urban setting.

Once the pícaro realizes that he needs to become adept at MR in order to detect the scams of others, the related development of his own ability to deceive others is never far behind. Thus, it is not surprising that Lazarillo begins to steal from his master soon after he develops a ToM, and that in the heading to the chapter that immediately follows his *desengaño,* Guzmán describes himself as a pícaro. Likewise, Pablos immediately turns to petty crime, as he explains in an aside to his readers, "«Haz como viere» dice el refrán, y dice bien. De puro considerar en él, vine a resolverme de ser bellaco con los bellacos, y más, si pudiese, que todos" (6). Pablos enjoys immediate reinforcement for his new path; after his first successful prank, his fellow servants reward him with laughter and Don Diego praises him, "—A fe, Pablos, que os hacéis a las armas" (6). As his exploits increase in sophistication and become well known, Pablos enjoys both basic material comfort and the respect of students and servants alike. For each pícaro, the moment of awakening and the turn to SI brings valuable although not permanent rewards.

Machiavellian Intelligence, Foraging, and Famine

Studies of primate SI in natural environments reveal that a significant portion of time and cognitive activity is related to food gathering. When the living environment does not provide a substantial and predictable supply of calories, feeding is a primary focus of social organization. Foraging entails an individualistic or selfish struggle for resources, replete with many forms of deception that enable some primates to eat better than others—for example, by directing a troop member's attention away from a food source, in order to return to eat it alone at a later time. But even among primates, it is also a communal enterprise with significant amounts of interaction for hunting, gathering, creating extraction tools, and equitable distribution (Milton 285). The invention of agriculture, leading to a more predictable food supply and the accumulation of reserves, freed many early humans from foraging and redirected social energies. However, in historical moments of great social upheaval, when stable patterns of food production and distribution are disrupted, foraging returns to the forefront. The historical record and the representations of medieval literature indicate an era of relative stability, in which literary concerns about food centered upon gluttonous clergy rather than nutritional scarcity. However, as Robert Jütte has shown, across the entire European continent, the combination of decreased food production, drought, plague, and urban mercantilism greatly reduced access to food for the poorer classes in the early modern era (21–36). Michel Cavillac has traced the particulars for the Iberian peninsula; as the rural peasantry flocked to urban areas, either to escape from rural food shortages or to pursue social mobility, hunger emerged as a social, economic, and artistic concern. In the first picaresque novel, *Lazarillo de Tormes,* the earliest adventures of the young protagonist emphasize foraging as the primary daily concern; he first learns how to deceive in order to avoid starvation, converting his autobiography into a conduct manual on "the art of survival" and a "discourse of poverty" (Maiorino 16; Cruz 8). The depictions of Social Intelligence used for purposes of foraging within the early chapters of this picaresque novel mirror in many ways the cognitive activities of primate society. For this reason, I would like to argue that the social transformation Lazarillo undergoes could be compared to that of a primate evolving into a human (Maiorino 28). His escapades involving food can of course be compared to adventures found in *Guzmán de Alfarache* and *La vida del Buscón,* such as the above-cited reference to the inn that served mule meat. However, Lazarillo's life narrative offers the most extreme case of a subhuman, foraging-oriented existence.

For all primates, from vervets to humans, foraging entails the pursuit of a variety of food sources. Every ecological niche necessarily includes one primary food that provides the majority of calories, supplemented by rarer items that have higher nutritive values in terms of protein or sugar content and that involve more elaborate foraging or hunting protocols (Milton 285–88). For human beings at the lowest levels of the social order, some form of grain-based carbohydrate is the pre-eminent dietary component. Bread constituted the main source of calories in pre-industrial peasant societies, wheat or rye being the cheapest and most plentiful agricultural commodities. For this reason, even when he is denied easy access to food, bread is the item that is most often within Lazarillo's reach. Even the poorest or most miserly masters usually had bread on a daily basis, offered crumbs and crust to their servants, and kept reserve quantities at hand. More valuable food items, such as meat or wine, were rarely given to the poor as alms, were guarded zealously by vendors, had little in the way of an undesirable byproduct such as a crust to be shared with social inferiors, and were often consumed immediately upon purchase; these were therefore harder for a servant to forage (Maiorino 15–40; Cruz 5; Jütte 72–74).

The scant difference between poor urban humanity and the animal world is made clear at the outset of *Lazarillo de Tormes*; the objects that his stepfather steals from his employer to provision his family are taken from a stable—where they were intended to benefit the horses belonging to a more privileged class of human. Lazarillo emphasizes (or exaggerates) the stinginess of the blind master, who forces him to follow in Zaide's footsteps, "jamás tan avariento ni mezquino hombre no vi, tanto que me mataba a mí de hambre, y así no me demediaba de lo necesario. Digo verdad: si con mi sutileza y buenas mañas no me supiera remediar, muchas veces me finara de hambre." There emerges an ironic form of poetic justice in that the very same man who starves his servant also teaches him the mind set that allows the young boy to successfully steal food or coins from him without detection. In this first *tratado*, we see that a society plagued by food shortages, combined with inadequate support from an employer, reduces a human to a primate whose every thought and action is directed to survival levels of foraging.

Lazarillo employs his ToM for complex con games, which entail not only stealing from his master, but also avoiding being named as the culprit when items are missed. Lazarillo manages to steal both food and coins without detection because of his emerging SI skills:

> por un poco de costura, que muchas veces [de] un lado del fardel descosía y tornaba a coser, sangraba el avariento fardel, sacando no por tasa pan, mas buenos pedazos, torreznos y longaniza; y ansí buscaba conveniente tiempo para rehacer, no la chaza, sino la endiablada falta que el mal ciego me faltaba … Todo lo que podía sisar y hurtar, traía en medias blancas; y cuando le mandaban rezar y le daban blancas, como él carecía de vista, no había el que se la daba amagado con ella, cuando yo la tenía lanzada en la boca y la media aparejada, que por presto que él echaba la mano, ya iba de mi cambio aniquilada en la mitad del justo precio. Quejábaseme el mal ciego, porque al tiento luego conocía y sentía que no era blanca entera, y decía: ¿ … de antes una blanca y un maravedí hartas veces me pagaban? En ti debe estar esta desdicha. (Tratado primero)

Ironically, although the beggar does attribute "blame" to the young servant, it is for being a bad luck charm rather than a nimble thief. In this instance, Lazarillo employs Simulation Theory in that he projects what this particular person, his blind master, will think in specific situations in order to determine the best ways to deceive him. Yet, as advanced as Lazarillo's SI is at this point, it is not sufficient to enable him to move beyond sneaking food out of the provisions bag, or gaining the coins necessary for his next meal. Lazarillo cannot even advance to the simplest level of hunter-gatherer existence, characterized by collecting some form of reserve as insurance against ill fortune. Lazarillo's tactics for obtaining wine also resemble primate foraging; lacking any sort of sophisticated tool, he uses a straw to siphon off the prized beverage, much as primates use a twig to uncover insects and increase access to scarce protein.

The final pages of the first episode highlight the precarious state of picaresque foraging tactics; as Lazarillo grows bolder, he is caught more frequently. This is due in large part to the blind man's own highly developed SI, which allows him to use Simulation Theory to infer Lazarillo's theft of grapes and also to devise tests that prove his guilt in the matters of the wine and sausage thefts. The blind man's SI is such that he even finds a way to depict himself publicly as a victim when he creates narratives to enhance his begging technique,

> Contaba el mal ciego a todos cuantos allí se allegaban mis desastres, y dábales cuenta una y otra vez, así de la del jarro como de la del racimo, y agora de lo presente. Era la risa de todos tan grande que toda la gente que por la calle pasaba entraba a ver la fiesta; mas con tanta gracia y donaire recontaba el ciego mis hazañas que, aunque yo estaba tan maltratado y llorando, me parecía que hacía sinjusticia en no se las reír. (Tratado primero)

Although Lazarillo does not elaborate, the recounting of these tales was surely beneficial to the alms-gathering process, enabling the old man to move some listeners due to the entertainment value of the story, as well as eliciting sympathy gifts from others. As Lazarillo indicates, this master uses MR in an adroit fashion to shape his "pitch" according to the ToM formed for each prospective donor. The blind man appears to use a combination of Simulation Theory and Theory Theory tactics; he first uses simulation to determine which subgroup of humans a particular target belongs to, then deploys the specific begging tactic that his Theory Theory has designated as most effective for that specific group. The fact that he recounts the tales repeatedly indicates that, ironically, his servant's SI and foraging can be manipulated as a source of profit for a master who knows how to make the most of the materials at hand. And, although the final trick against his new master provides the pícaro with the temporary pleasure of revenge for protagonist and reader, his escape from this master does not lead to an improved existence.

With his second master, the quantity and quality of Lazarillo's food supply decreases, even as his SI schemes grow more sophisticated. He reiterates his ever-increasing hunger throughout the second *tratado* as he serves an even stingier master, "Los sábados cómense en esta tierra cabezas de carnero, y enviábame por una que costaba tres maravedís. Aquélla le cocía y comía los ojos y la lengua y el cogote y sesos y la carne que en las quijadas tenía, y dábame todos los huesos roídos." At this point, even bread has become a luxury and his ordinary meals consist of onions or well-picked bones—the latter reminiscent of the leavings that a scavenger species consumes, that which is abandoned after a predator has eaten all of the most desirable and nutritious parts. He emphasizes the extreme consequences of privation, "A cabo de tres semanas que estuve con él, vine a tanta flaqueza que no me podía tener en las piernas de pura hambre. Vime claramente ir a la sepultura, si Dios y mi saber no me remediaran" (Tratado segundo).

In an urban locale, under the watchful eye of a rapacious and clever master, even the most basic opportunities for foraging are few and far between. Lazarillo cannot take advantage of the SI and tricks he developed with the blind man because of the cleric's highly developed ToM; his Theory Theory model presumes the intent of theft on the part of all servants and thus the cleric is ever vigilant,

> Para usar de mis *mañas* no tenía aparejo, por no tener en qué dalle salto; y aunque algo hubiera, no podía cegalle, como hacía al que Dios perdone, si de aquella calabazada feneció, que todavía, aunque astuto, con faltalle aquel preciado sentido no me sentía; más estotro, ninguno hay que tan aguda vista tuviese como él tenía. Cuando al ofertorio estábamos, ninguna blanca en la concha caía que no era dél registrada: el un ojo tenía en la gente y el otro en mis manos. Bailábanle los ojos en el caxco como si fueran de azogue. (Tratado segundo)

For this reason, Lazarillo devises new tactics to obtain calories via cleverly plotted pilferage (the italicized phrases highlight his use of SI):

> "Este arquetón es viejo y grande y roto por algunas partes, aunque pequeños agujeros. *Puédese pensar* que ratones, entrando en él, hacen daño a este pan. Sacarlo entero no es cosa conveniente, porque verá la falta el que en tanta me hace vivir. Esto bien se sufre."
>
> Y comienzo a desmigajar el pan sobre unos no muy costosos manteles que allí estaban; y tomo uno y dejo otro, *de manera que* en cada cual de tres o cuatro desmigajé su poco; después, como quien toma gragea, lo comí, y algo me consolé. Mas él, como viniese a comer y abriese el arca, vio el mal pesar, y *sin dubda creyó ser ratones* los que el daño habían hecho, porque estaba *muy al propio* contrahecho de como ellos lo suelen hacer. (Tratado segundo; emphasis added)

As with the blind man, Lazarillo's level of ToM is measured not only by the food he manages to obtain but also by his ability to displace the blame for his actions; the simplistic nature of the openings and the way the food is taken lead the cleric to suspect a mouse here (and a snake later in the chapter) rather than a human culprit. In this instance Lazarillo employs the simulation variant of ToM; as the italicized phrases indicate, he imagines how his master would interpret various types of evidence in order to choose types of food attrition that will not be attributed to him. Lazarillo displays considerable ingenuity in his use of Simulation Theory for misdirection; however, the necessity of this level of SI is a reflection of the harsh material reality of the urban poor. Although Lazarillo does have human cultural knowledge of advanced tools and their functions, his social position is of such complete marginalization that he has no better access to those tools than does a rodent or serpent. In evaluating Lazarillo's progress on an evolutionary scale, it is noteworthy that the cleric grants Lazarillo access to the bread only after he believes it has been contaminated by (another) animal. In other words, only when food has become garbage does Lazarillo receive an adequate share. And, as with his first master, it is inevitable that the thefts are eventually uncovered and severely punished. His status with both employers, as the lowest level of live-in servant, leaves him continually vulnerable to the surveillance of masters with strong MR skills.

The vast differences between Lazarillo's life and Guzmán's can be measured by analyzing two somewhat parallel episodes involving food that is locked up. Like his predecessor, Guzmán uses primitive tools to gain access to food kept in a locked chest,

> Alzaba un poquito el un canto de la tapa, cuanto podía meter una cuña de madera y, alzaprimando un poco más, metía un palo rollizo torneado, como cabo de marrillo. Este iba poco a poco cazando con él, dando vueltas hacia la chapa y, cuanto más a ella lo llegaba, tanto la dejaba del canto más levantada. De manera que, como era mozuelo y tenía delgado el brazo, sacaba lo que se me antojaba, de que poblaba las faltriqueras. (1.III.vii)

And like Lazarillo he initially escapes detection by using Simulation Theory in order to assure that a different culprit will be suspected, "Mas nunca se entendió que se hubiera sacado menos que con llave contrahecha" (1.III.vii). However, in his role as a page Guzmán receives adequate nutrition, clothing, and shelter and never mentions hunger; rather, it is the pursuit of a dessert item, candied fruit, that obsesses him. Here, Guzmán does not use SI for survival, but for pursuit of pleasure (Davis 83).

Quevedo offers a third perspective on hunger and the use of SI among the poor. Even though the second chapter of the *Buscón* narrates an extreme level of hunger at Dr. Cabra's school, Pablos suffers his fate passively and does not turn to foraging or theft to improve his circumstances. At Alcalá, Pablos does engage in food theft, but with no indication that this is necessary to avoid starvation. He rarely describes the food he steals or the act of eating; rather, he emphasizes the pleasure of being admired for the scams used to obtain the food, "Yo, como era muchacho y oía que me alababan el ingenio con que salía de estas travesuras, animábame para hacer muchas más" (6). Unlike Lazarillo, Pablos uses Theory Theory in these exploits, whose goal is to make an impression upon a large and homogenous social subculture, for whom he has identified a respect for pranksters as a shared cognitive response. Pablos describes his SI and foraging skill most extensively in the chapters that take place in Madrid. There, his goal was to piece together enough scraps and rags of clothing to present the appearance of a well-garbed gentleman, as a prelude to more advanced swindles (Maiorino 70). It is the gulf between primate-like foraging for basic survival that entail use of simulation tactics to deceive a specific master, and the more "human" uses of Theory Theory to obtain luxuries or elevated status, that separates the first three *tratados* of *Lazarillo* from the forms of SI deployed in the rest of that novel and in subsequent picaresque tales.

Over the course of the first three *tratados*, Lazarillo's physical misery increases, even as his SI improves, because each successive master has less and less food or coin available for appropriation. As he enters service with the impoverished squire, he is reduced to using his SI to feign indifference to food, and even to competing with his master for the few crumbs of bread that remain from the cleric's wooden chest. In this case, his initial use of Theory Theory led Lazarillo to infer that he would fare better as the servant for a man who owned a cape and sword. When this approach let him down, Lazarillo moved to Simulation Theory in order to understand the specific and unique aspects of this master's deceptions. Despite the projections that confirm this master's lack of malice or greed, Lazarillo is closer than ever to starvation and must create new forms of deception to survive. It is this drastic state that induces Lazarillo to put his previous training in ToM from the blind man to good use and resort to begging.

Charity, Poor Laws, and Social Intelligence

Begging, which in its most successful manifestations requires significant use of ToM, is an important form of foraging in primate society. Anne Russon writes that advanced ape cultures possess "ritual gestures to beg, which suggest that food scrounging is a species-typical social negotiation" (192). In the wild, begging is tolerated in specifically circumscribed ways that reflect the perceived capabilities of the supplicant: a mother will share a food item that is difficult for a youth to process or to obtain, but not one that is easy. In addition, apes will respond to begging gestures from adults to share food items that are rare or that require coordinated effort to obtain, perhaps to assure that the recipient will return the favor in the future (Russon 193). Begging is also a primary mode of foraging in the urban milieu of the picaresque novel; however, as in the forest, charitable giving occurs under specific conditions. In recent years, studies by Michel Cavillac, Anne Cruz, and Giancarlo Maiorino have shed new light on the historical context from which picaresque representations of destitution and charitable relief emerge. The year of this novel's publication is precisely the historical crossroad at which the influx of poor peasants and the decrease in harvests produced unprecedented hunger and begging in urban locales all across Europe and led to a major reconsideration of how to provide for indigent people. The poverty relief debates of this decade pitted those who favored maintaining or increasing the role of the church and private charity against secular reformers who sought to create new, tax-supported secular institutions to feed, clothe, house and provide vocational training for the destitute (see Jütte 100–67; Cruz 40–56; Maiorino 110–15; Cavillac 423–25; Dunn 130–32; Castillo 23–25; and Tierno Galván 27).

Many of the major theologians of the age, especially Juan de Robles and Domingo de Soto, were involved in this debate, which led to new Poor Laws in 1565. In the 1590s, the decimation of the Spanish economy and a steep decline in agricultural production spurred a new influx of vagrants; Cristóbal Pérez de Herrera emerged as the primary voice for a new generation of political rather than religious reformers (Cavillac 413; Cruz 62). The discovery of a substantial correspondence between Alemán and Herrera has been used to support reconsiderations of the ideological dimension of *Guzmán* (Cavillac 414).

One pivotal point in the debates about charity involved concerns about deception; great attention was paid to using MR to distinguish those whose infirmities or age would make them legitimate recipients of charitable aid from social parasites who were mentally and physically capable of labor but who were conceptualized as precursors to "welfare cheats." Many discourses of poverty, from the early modern age to the present, have denied the reality of insufficient employment opportunities and instead depicted a nefarious social group that disdained labor and feigned disability in order to enjoy a life of relative ease. Goffman cites nineteenth-century research by Henry Mayhew, in order to describe several different common dramatizations of poverty: the very clean but poor family, the person dressed in tatters who is too weak to eat the bread people throw to him, and the "ashamed" beggar who appeals with sad eyes and never utters a word (40–41). These roles confirm the two-way nature of ToM, which prosperous people deploy in order to distinguish beggars who "deserve" charitable support from those who don't, and which the indigent must deploy in order to appear worthy rather than criminal. Writing at the mid-point of the twentieth century, Goffman notes an almost complete disappearance of such performances; perhaps, in the wake of governmental social safety nets, Western cultures no longer believed in any form of destitution that would merit individual charity (41). In recent decades, as the net has begun to unravel in the US, performances that use ToM to deduce which sort of destitution will elicit material manifestations of sympathy are once again common. Some common tactics include "Will work for food" signs, which indicate a ToM that beggars must not appear unwilling to labor, as well as poor people with pets at their sides whose signs request funds for dog or cat food. The ToM for this latter performance implies the conviction that in a heartless modern society, people will support a hungry animal more readily than a human. In all eras, performances of a meritorious beggar require that a poor person be skilled at ToM in order to choose the persona that will open the greatest number of wallets. As we have seen, the early modern pícaro deploys similar types of deception. In modern times, false presentation of a sacred or elevated role is considered a far more serious transgression than impersonation of a low-level identity, such as a "hobo"—but this was not the case in the era of the Poor Laws (Goffman 60). During the interlude between the first and second drafts of this book, the double dip recession in the US has resulted in a large group of people exhausting the limits of unemployment benefits. Conservative pundits have attacked this group as lazy or overly picky; the accusations that they prefer to stay home and collect benefits, rather than accept any job available, appear as a distant echo of the early modern critiques. Because of deeply held cultural suspicions concerning unemployment, successful panhandlers of all eras have used ToM to determine which forms of indigence are viewed as legitimate, and then to perform the approved social state in order to receive alms. It is thus not surprising that all of the pícaros depict their begging as a form of performance (Burningham, *Radical* 101; see Chapter 4 for an extended study of picaresque performance in other contexts).

Lazarillo emphasizes the new level of ToM he develops during his apprenticeship with the blind beggar as a highly valuable skill that he can use to support himself via cleverly scripted self-presentations,

> en muy pocos días me mostró jerigonza, y como me viese de buen ingenio, holgábase mucho, y decía: Yo oro ni plata no te lo puedo dar, mas avisos para vivir muchos te mostraré. Y fue ansí, que después de Dios éste me dio la vida, y siendo ciego me alumbró y adestró en la carrera de vivir. (Tratado primero)

As this master is truly blind, he does not use SI to mislead people concerning his legitimacy as a recipient of alms; instead he employs a skilled ToM to wring every cent possible out of as many supporters as he can rather than trusting to people's charitable impulses for sustenance. Lazarillo describes the blind man's tactics as steeped in a keen understanding of the primary concerns of many different social groups,

> tenía otras mil formas y maneras para sacar el dinero. Decía saber oraciones para muchos y diversos efectos: para mujeres que no parían, para las que estaban de parto, para las que eran malcasadas, que sus maridos las quisiesen bien; echaba pronósticos a las preñadas, si traía hijo o hija. Pues en caso de medicina, decía que Galeno no supo la mitad que él para muela, desmayos, males de madre. Finalmente, nadie le decía padecer alguna pasión, que luego no le decía: "Haced esto, haréis estotro, cosed tal yerba, tomad tal raíz." (Tratado primero)

The blind man's relative prosperity derives from a highly evolved SI that allows him both to intuit or elicit admissions about his victims' problems as well as to feign a vast repertoire of knowledge, convincing people he can cure all of their ills. As indicated above, this level of SI derives from a sophisticated combination of Simulation and Theory Theory approaches to MR. To fully appreciate the unusual level of success he enjoys, we must keep in mind that this beggar is able to eat meat and drink wine on a regular basis, which most guild members of that period could not afford (Jütte 93–96). Even though the blind man is in one sense a "worthy" beneficiary, he also employs many of the deceptive strategies of fraudulent beggars. His performance thus reinforces many of the negative social stereotypes addressed by the poverty relief debate.

The text explores in depth the validity of social and legal limitations placed upon charitable aid. In Lazarillo's case, it is considered legitimate for a young boy to aid a blind man in his begging, and his neighbors are happy to feed and tend to him as he recovers from the cleric's physical abuse, because an injured youth is not expected to work. However, once he is healed, charity is no longer an option,

> con ayuda de las buenas gentes di comigo en esta insigne ciudad de Toledo, adonde con la merced de Dios dende a quince días se me cerró la herida; y mientras estaba malo, siempre me daban alguna limosna, mas después que estuve sano, todos me decían: "Tú, bellaco y gallofero eres. Busca, busca un amo a quien sirvas." (Tratado segundo)

At this point, the destitute boy would have to feign some form of disability in order to continue to seek charity—an option that he does not choose right away but that his picaresque descendent Pablos will not hesitate to exercise. As he is still too young for any sort of truly gainful employment, taking his chances with another master seems to be his only option. Lazarillo does attempt to use ToM to gain a better employer; as he examines the squire he notes, "me parecía, según su hábito y continente, ser el que yo había menester." He uses Theory Theory to make a generalization based upon the supposed cognitive and economic characteristics of a group, rather than the specific qualities of a unique individual. It is interesting that most cognitivists describe Theory Theory as the more basic and primary form of MR, and the one that young children learn first. Simulation Theory is depicted as a more "fine grained" approach that is learned when generalizations proves inadequate (see Chapter 1). However, the unique nature of Lazarillo's severely reduced circumstances resulted in the need for very targeted insights into the specific details of each miserly master's cognitive processes. Sadly, just as Lazarillo's use of Simulation Theory enables him to achieve only the most basic level of subsistence, his initial foray into Theory Theory also meets with limited success. The cognitive models that Lazarillo has internalized up to this moment are not sufficient either to fool his first two masters in a sustained fashion, or to penetrate the advanced form of SI that the squire deploys, which entails displaying misleading markers of economic prosperity. Apparently, no amount of SI is sufficient to enable a servant boy to achieve food security. Society's strict interpretation of Poor Laws thus condemns young boys to wretched conditions of service and can be said to compel varied forms of deception in order to avoid starvation.

The social opprobrium associated with illegitimate begging is such that Lazarillo prefers to steal from his masters until he finally lands with a master who has nothing to offer. However, once it is clear that charity is the only option, Lazarillo employs his SI to assure that his endeavors are successful. His efforts produce plentiful quantities of bread as well as some meat,

> Con *baja y enferma voz* e inclinadas mis manos en los senos, puesto Dios ante mis ojos y la lengua en su nombre, comienzo a pedir pan por las puertas y casas más grandes que me parecía. Mas como yo este oficio le h[u]biese mamado en la leche, quiero decir que con el gran maestro el ciego lo aprendí, tan suficiente discípulo salí que, aunque en este pueblo no había caridad ni el año fuese muy abundante, *tan buena maña me di* que, antes que el reloj diese las cuatro, ya yo tenía otras tantas libras de pan ensiladas en el cuerpo y más de otras dos en las mangas y senos. Volvíme a la posada y al pasar por la tripería pedí a una de aquellas mujeres, y diome un pedazo de uña de vaca con otras pocas de tripas cocidas. (Tratado tercero)

Lazarillo's abstract reference to "wiles" allows the reader to infer that he is feigning some sort of disability that allows him to be viewed as a legitimate recipient of charity according to the new discourses of poverty relief. Here, Lazarillo employs Theory Theory again, in that he assumes a form of deception that is designed to appeal to the entire class of servants who give scraps to worthy beggars. This episode marks the nadir of Lazarillo's suffering; the rest of the novel documents the means by which he uses his

ever-increasing store of *mañas* and a developing competence with
both forms of SI to achieve economic security.

In its representation of the protagonist's begging, *Guzmán de
Alfarache* fleshes out what is only hinted at in the earlier tome.
Although not mentioned directly, the influence of the Poor Laws
is implied in the fact that Guzmán creates a wound in order to
begin this new phase in his life, eliciting sympathy through his
ability to devise a truly pathetic leg ulcer. Alemán provides a
detailed explanation of how such an ailment may be feigned; the
ubiquity of such scams is highlighted when one of the three doctors summoned by the Cardinal to cure Guzmán recognizes the
ruse and delineates the exact process for creating—and destroy-
ing—the illusion. Guzmán's begging is successful because of his
multifaceted use of ToM, which goes beyond inventing a malady.
He uses Simulation Theory to correctly single out the Cardinal
as a patron prone to charitable acts, and then employs the cultural Theory Theory of doctors as greedy charlatans to choose the
strategy most likely to induce the physicians to go along with his
scam. He appeals to their desire to continue receiving payment for
tending to his wound, "En lo de la ganancia no se repare: mejor es
acertarla que perderla. Juguemos tres al mohíno, que más vale algo
que nada. Estas plegarias y prerrogativas fueron bastantes a que
tuviesen por acertado mi consejo" (1.III.vi). Guzmán cleverly em-
broils the three professionals in his charity scheme, to the mutual
benefit of all concerned. Guzmán does not resort to fraudulent
begging to avoid starvation, but rather to gain entrée to a noble
household in which he hopes to rise to prominence. In his case,
begging serves as a stepping stone to forms of social advancement
that are generally out of the reach of low-born or fallen youths.

In Quevedo's *Buscón*, Pablos turns to begging with little explanation, presenting this decision as merely another of the many
deception-based career options available to those gifted in SI. He
describes this career as a new form of theater, complete with a new
costume, "un coleto de cordobán viejo y un jubonazo de estopa fa-
moso, mi gabán de pobre, remendado y largo, mis polainas y zapa-
tos grandes, la capilla del gabán en la cabeza, un Cristo de bronce
traía colgando del cuello, y un Rosario" (III.viii). Like Lazarillo's
blind master, Pablos emphasizes that an accurate ToM, composed
of both Simulation and Theory Theory, is the key to success at this
enterprise. For it is the beggar who knows how to present many

fronts, and to correctly choose the one most likely to impress each individual donor, that will prosper. Pablos describes in detail the dualistic SI of his role model:

> Estaba riquísimo, y era como nuestro retor; ganaba más que todos; tenía una potra muy grande, y atábase con un cordel el brazo por arriba, y *parecía que* tenía hinchada la mano y manca, y calentura, todo junto. Poníase echado boca arriba en su puesto, y con la potra defuera, tan grande como una bola de puente, y decía: «¡Miren la pobreza y el regalo que hace el Señor al cristiano!» Si pasaba mujer decía: «¡Ah, señora hermosa, sea Dios en su ánima!» Y las más, *porque las llamase* así, le daban limosna y pasaban por allí aunque no fuese camino para sus visitas. Si pasaba un soldadico: «¡Ah, señor capitán!», decía; y si otro hombre cualquiera: «¡Ah, señor caballero!» Si iba alguno en coche, luego le llamaba señoría, y si clérigo en mula, señor arcediano. En fin, él *adulaba* terriblemente. *Tenía modo diferente* para pedir los días de los santos; y vine a tener tanta amistad con él, que me descubrió un secreto con que en dos días estuvimos ricos. (III.viii; emphasis added)

This paragon of deception employs a multifaceted ToM in order to appeal to the specific weaknesses of a wide variety of social types. Like the other two pícaros and this mentor, Pablos's ruse includes the pretense of an infirmity that will allow him to evade the strictures of the Poor Laws, "Llevaba metidas entrambas piernas en una bolsa de cuero, y liadas, y mis dos muletas" (III.viii). In the sections that focus upon begging, each novel emphasizes the necessity of correctly gauging the cognitive tendencies of potential benefactors in a social milieu that not only penalizes illegitimate begging but also offers fierce competition (Davis 67). In addition, these adventures provide an opportunity for the protagonist to use his ToM to engage the sympathy of his intradiegetic and extradiegetic readers, as the final section of the next chapter will demonstrate.

Beyond Beef: Social Intelligence and Swindling

As a complement to MR, pícaros soon deduce that to move beyond mere subsistence to any form of social stability or prestige requires cultivation not only of MR to detect the machinations of others, but also of their own SI, in order to metamorphose from victim to culprit (Davis 20). Due perhaps to the rather abbreviated nature of Lazarillo's tale, this protagonist moves directly from small scale thievery associated with foraging to pursuit of social advancement via legitimate employment. However, Alemán's extended narrative provides opportunity for an intermediate stage between destitution and stability that features more advanced forms of larceny.

In the first two books of Part One, Guzmán's thefts are generally minor in scale, reminiscent of Lazarillo's, although propagated neither from such dire need nor with much use of SI. For example, he cheats the clients whose horses he cares for at the stable where he is employed, even though he receives sufficient food and drink. But this endeavor does not require any significant mental exertion on his part; he merely falls in line with the practices his fellow stable boys demonstrate. Shirley Strum refers to similar examples of coordinated SI among the lower ranking members of ape troops as "distributed cognition" and claims that this model of group action proves that SI is not as individualistic or selfish as the original studies of MI indicated (74). Later, Guzmán engages in more complex thefts that require minor uses of ToM while employed as a cook's helper. These episodes arise out of a financial desperation whose source is gambling debts rather than hunger. His most profitable early theft actually falls into his lap, when he steals the substantial amount of coin he is asked to carry for a client who trusted him because of previous services. This scam requires a bare minimum of initiative and no SI; he merely takes advantage of the chance to dodge into a house he is familiar with and escape by a back door. I do not provide direct citations here because there are no moments of SI comparable even to the first *tratado* of *Lazarillo*.

Guzmán uses his first significant sum of money to purchase respectable clothing, as a replacement for the garb he had sold or lost after leaving home. However, he does not use SI to put this capital to work for him in a profitable way. Although he had asserted earlier that if he had suitable clothing he would seek to serve in a great lord's house, like Lazarillo's squire (explored in the next chapter), he instead embarks on affairs with two different women simultaneously. Perhaps because this money is so easily gotten, it is easily taken from him as well. When Guzmán finally realizes that both women were cheats, he derides himself in disgust, "Ves aquí mis dos buenos empleos y si me hubiera sido mejor comprar cincuenta borregos" (1.II.viii). This series of petty triumphs and misadventures is typical of the first part of *Guzmán*; which, despite being far longer than the entirety of *Lazarillo*, offers far less cognitive development. This episode also establishes a trend concerning the representation of female characters and Guzmán's use of MR with women: the text offers its own Theory Theory of lower class women as always and inherently deceitful, but Guzmán fails, here and throughout the novel, to use ToM correctly to evaluate the honesty and virtue of the women he meets. It is unclear whether he believes all women are virtuous, or is simply unaware that that both sexes possess the capacity for MI against which he must defend himself.

In the second volume, Guzmán's adventures in Italy depict the ultimate possibilities and limitations of SI. In the two major economic swindles, with the merchant and with his own relatives, he takes a great leap forward in terms of the sophistication of his con games. The combination of a strong ToM and sufficient resources to produce a temporary appearance of prosperity enable him to carry off swindles on a grand scale. For Guzmán as for Lazarillo, the key to a successful theft is not merely to obtain the necessary goods, but also to escape with no fear of future repercussion. Thus, although Sayavedra's friend Aguilera is able to devise a simple strategy to rob the Milanese merchant he serves as a clerk, Guzmán realizes that this would result in suspicion and likely incarceration. And, Guzmán's crafty MI goes far beyond conceptualizing the plot to mark the money and falsify the ledgers to make it seem that he has made a large deposit; he makes sure that his landlords view him as a man of means and that they will serve as witnesses to the wealth he feigns depositing (Davis 113). In addition, he cries out his accusation in a loud voice to attract witnesses at the moment he presents his phony evidence, knowing that "el vulgo" will be on his side,

> Cuantos estaban presentes quedaron con esto que vieron y oyeron tan admirados, cuanto enfadados de ver semejante bellaquería, satisfechos de que yo tenía razón y justicia. Eran en mi favor la voz común, las evidencias y experiencias vistas y su mala fama, que concluía, y decían todos: —Mirad si había de hacer de las suyas. No es nuevo en el bellaco logrero robar haciendas ajenas. ¿No veis como a este pobre caballero se le quería levantar con lo que le dio en confianza? Que, si no fuera por su buena diligencia, para siempre se le quedara con ello. (2.II.vi)

Guzmán succeeds in deceiving the public and legal officials because he uses both Simulation and Theory Theory forms of ToM to create a preponderance of evidence that appeals to different mentalities: he combines falsified evidence, duped witnesses, the prior bad reputation of the merchant (no doubt based in part on a Theory Theory awareness of generalized anti-Semitic sentiment) and his own air of injured innocence to manipulate specific individuals as well as unknown groups—legal officials and witnesses. Further, Simulation Theory indicates that it would undermine his credibility with the police to appear too eager to reclaim his treasure, so even though he could walk off with it on the spot, he goes through a formal judicial procedure

> Yo, como sabía que no bastaba decirlo el vulgo para dármelos, que sólo el juez era parte para podérmelos adjudicar, preveníme de cautela para lo de adelante y, cuando todos a voces decían: «Suyo es el dinero, dénselo, dénselo», respondía yo: «No lo quiero, no lo quiero; deposítense, deposítense.» (2.II.vi)

Guzmán uses his highly advanced and multivalent SI to devise a complex scam that permits him to claim the merchant's wealth publicly and legally. Given the lack of mass media to communicate public events quickly, he could undoubtedly have perpetuated several more schemes of this type across the Spanish empire to amass a substantial fortune. However, because his ultimate goal is to reclaim and even improve upon the gentrified position his father had once occupied, Guzmán uses his capital to pursue social ends—as well as petty revenge.

Guzmán employs the fruit of this *burla* for yet another con game, both to avenge himself on the relatives who had scorned him previously when he was destitute and to further increase his fortune. This scam requires clever deployment of his capital to put forth the appearance of an even more impressive fortune, such as will impress his prosperous family,

> Salimos de Milán yo y Sayavedra bien abrigados y mejor acomodados de lo necesario, que cualquiera *me juzgara* por hombre rico y de buenas prendas ... Ya no se *juzgan* almas ni más de aquello que ven los ojos. Ninguno se pone a *considerar* lo que sabes, sino lo que tienes; no tu virtud, sino la de tu bolsa; y de tu bolsa no lo que tienes, sino lo que gastas. (2.II.vii; emphasis added)

Here, Guzmán begins to describe the strategy of leveraging his small bonanzas to create a false impression of extreme prosperity. A week of lavish entertainment, with fine food served in luxurious (rented) dishware, confirms the initial impression. As Guzmán anticipated, this display of wealth completely lulls any suspicions his relatives might have; rather than question him, they seek ways to gain his favor (Davis 122). Guzmán does not single out his relatives as especially greedy; the citation above indicates the use of Theory Theory because he views the cognitive processes of the entire aristocracy as identical (and he has had no significant contact that would enable him to form a more personalized Simulation Theory). As the swindle progresses to its conclusion, it is clear that Guzmán's ToM is accurate and that he will be successful precisely because people do not expect and protect themselves against MI scams from those that they perceive as being wealthier. Instead, their ToM appears to be completely focused upon finding ways to use this new relative and his wealth to their own benefit. Guzmán correctly projected that his performance of prosperity would lure his relatives into depending on the falsely reassuring projections of Theory Theory as applied to persons perceived to belong to one's own in-group.

In both of these economic swindles, Guzmán displays a high level of general intelligence in devising the complex plots and the convoluted bait-and-switch tactics; Nina Cox Davis emphasizes the significance of his ability to deceive with the truth (113–24). More importantly, Guzmán deploys both MR theories in a manner that enables him to manipulate large numbers of people from many different social strata in order to set in motion and bring to fruition his deceptions, as well as to escape unharmed with his ill-gotten treasure. At this point in the narrative, readers could reasonably expect Guzmán to embark upon a carefully delineated path of social advancement, employing his large economic reserves (as well as the forms of socially directed SI on display in his service to the Cardinal and the Ambassador, addressed in Chapter 4). The narrative arc of *Lazarillo* would also prepare readers for this outcome. However, this chapter marks the high-water point of the continuation of *Guzmán*. Unlike Lazarillo, Guzmán manages to fritter away his fortune on ill-advised, unsuccessful, or unfinished scams and a disastrous marriage. In addition, Guzmán's ToM proves to be less reliable than Lazarillo's, in that he is duped nearly as often as he scams others. This change in success appears to derive in part from Guzmán's faulty uses of simulation ToM on specific individuals, especially women. Pablos has no better luck with either his fortune or his courtship pursuits. The next chapter will trace the second phase of picaresque cognitive development in the area of SI, as the three protagonists seek to use economic gains to obtain upward mobility. The three men meet with very different ends that are directly related to the vast differences in their skills at employing SI for purposes other than basic survival and economic swindles.

Chapter Four

Social Intelligence and Social Climbing
Pícaros and Cortesanos

In Chapter 3, this study traced the initial development of Social Intelligence skills among young picaresque protagonists. The cognitive skills include Mind Reading (MR)—also known as formation of a Theory of Mind (ToM)—for projecting the thoughts of other people who seek to deceive unwary youths, including Simulation Theory and Theory Theory approaches. Over time, the young pícaro will learn to emulate his deceivers, developing the cognitive traits of Machiavellian Intelligence (MI) and Social Intelligence (SI) in order to ascertain the most appropriate modes of deception (see Chapter 1 for a comprehensive survey of this branch of cognitive theory). Once the pícaro achieves a certain level of economic stability, he can use the combination of ill-gotten gains and precocious SI in order to achieve a second metamorphosis: from mere survivor to bureaucrat or page. The creation of a substantial bureaucracy in the early modern Spanish court, especially under Philip II, gave rise to the emergence of the *letrado* class. This development allowed literate and witty men of nearly any background to escape humble status and obtain secretarial positions within the early modern court, providing another avenue of advancement. It is precisely this rung of gentrified society that the pícaro aspires to reach; however, all three of the picaresque novels indicate that such mobility is possible only via extensive and sustained use of ToM and MI (Ruan, *Pícaro*; F. Sánchez, *Bourgeois*). The SI required for this type of social advancement is far more sophisticated than that associated with foraging or thievery; it is precisely at the point where Lazarillo achieves food security and begins to pursue new forms of identity that he moves beyond primate status and appears fully human (Maiorino 28). The narratives of Guzmán and Pablos emphasize this more abstract pursuit of status; although extreme hunger does mark certain stages of the lives of all three youths, the most vivid adventures in the seventeenth-century novels revolve around SI deployed for the acquisition of elevated status.

Studies of early modern social advancement must take into account the rise of courtier conduct manuals, beginning with Castiglione's *The Courtier*, which circulated in Spain via numerous editions and translations throughout the latter half of the sixteenth century. The Italian text waned in popularity in the following century, but was replaced by home-grown variants such as Lucas Gracián Dantisco's *Galateo español* and Baltasar Gracián's manuals (Burke 82, 123; F. Sánchez, *Bourgeois* 103–15; Ruan, "Taste" 315). In a series of essays and books, Francisco Sánchez and Felipe Ruan have shown that picaresque fiction shares many features with courtier conduct manuals, and characterize the novels as an alternate form of handbook for those who aspired to *letrado* status. In recent years, scholars have paid new attention to the social anxieties produced by courtesy books; although such guides fostered a new level of surface civility at court, they also elicited concern about rampant deception and the (im)possibility of authentic selfhood and true knowledge of others in the wake of intensive "self-fashioning" (Burke 2–3, 31; Greenblatt 2–3). Picaresque con games designed to facilitate social advancement often depended upon the ability to amass enough monetary and cultural capital to put on a temporary front, designed to convince a superior that the pretender merits a court or government position—or even a prosperous or blue-blooded bride (F. Sánchez, *Bourgeois* 50; Ruan, *Pícaro*). Conduct manuals and picaresque novels could be seen as problematic precisely because they provided the type of social knowledge or capital that would permit class or caste "passing" (Ruan, "Taste" 320; Fuchs 9). In cognitive terms, then, the courtesy manuals taught dangerous SI skills, so that aspiring courtiers could better use ToM and MI to deceive and manipulate their social superiors.

By juxtaposing the functions of SI in the picaresque novel and in early modern courtier manuals, I am interested in developing the model Felipe Ruan has put forth in the recent study *Pícaro and Cortesano: Identity and the Forms of Capital in Early Modern Spanish Picaresque Narrative and Courtesy Literature*, which explores the representation of cultural capital. I will highlight instead the homologies between picaresque cognitive modalities and the types of cognitive behavior that Gracián represents as necessary for survival and advancement at court in his collection of maxims, *Oráculo manual y arte de prudencia*. Like the SI activities that were analyzed in regards to the picaresque novel and courtship drama, these cognitive functions are characterized as giving rise to new modes of thought and manner. In all three genres, SI is depicted in a paradoxical manner, both as a skill that virtuous protagonists use to their benefit, but also as a form of dishonesty or lack of authenticity. Each genre explores, albeit from a different perspective, the concerns that arise at this specific historical moment in response to a new type of court structure and new modes of urban life.

Gracián, Goffman, and Self-Fashioning

Stephen Greenblatt's model of "Renaissance Self-Fashioning" has been used to illuminate many aspects of early modern cultural production. Greenblatt writes that during the Renaissance, there arises "an increased self-consciousness about the fashioning of human identity as a manipulable, artful process" accompanied by "a change in the intellectual, social, psychological, and aesthetic structures that govern the generation of identities" (1–2). He notes that this new presentation of the self was found primarily among the elite, and in particular among the ambitious offspring of the emergent middle class comprised of prosperous lawyers, merchants and yeoman farmers (3, 7). The fashioning and performance of a new form of courtier identity functions in many ways as a mirror of the elaborate spectacles of early modern monarchy (Greenblatt 12–13; Brown and Elliott 38–40; Orgel 37–58). This chapter will enrich the model of self-fashioning by exploring the ways in which cognitive activities, such as ToM and MI, play a vital role in designing a new self for purposes of social advancement. Greenblatt identifies the rise to power of Sir Thomas More as a prime example of self-fashioning. His chapter on the career of this highly complex historical figure would seem to provide an ideal point of departure for analysis of Gracián's conduct manuals; however, there have been relatively few such projects undertaken. There were two dissertations from the 1990s that point in this direction, but the book and journal articles derived from those studies do not emphasize self-fashioning for class identity (Rico-Ferrer; Romano). I have found only a few passing references to self-fashioning in studies that address other Gracián texts (Ruan,

"Taste"; F. Sánchez, "Symbolic") or Castiglione (Burke 2–3). Similarly, critical attention to Baltasar Gracián's *Oráculo* has been minimal in recent decades. There are a few essays dedicated to this work in the Spadaccini and Talens anthology, *Rhetoric and Politics: Baltasar Gracián and the New World Order* (1987); Egginton's contribution analyzes Gracián's creation of a "persona" as a mode for separating oneself from the masses ("Gracián" 153–54). Apart from this anthology and a special issue of *Ínsula* in 2001, fewer than a dozen titles are listed in the *MLA Bibliography*. This is indeed surprising given the text's great popularity in its own day, and also considering current interest in other conduct manuals, especially Castiglione's *Courtier*. The cognitive model of SI offers a new paradigm for illuminating the intersections between modern theories of performative identity and the picaresque novel and courtesy manual as performative texts, and helps us to see the *Oráculo* in a new light.

Greenblatt's analysis of the way in which Sir Thomas More lays bare the norms of courtier deception offers many parallels to Gracián's scrutiny of SI in his conduct manual. Greenblatt characterizes More's self-fashioning as "the invention of a disturbingly unfamiliar form of consciousness, tense, ironic, witty, poised between engagement and detachment, and above all, fully aware of its own status as invention" (31). This self-consciousness is particularly noteworthy in *Utopia,* a text in which More dramatizes himself as the courtier Morus, and then proceeds to use an outsider protagonist to criticize the protocols of courtier performances of self and status (Greenblatt 35–42). Greenblatt carefully traces the paradoxes and inconsistencies between More's lived experience and his writings concerning the self-fashioning necessary for success as a courtier who serves an unreasonable monarch within an artificial and superficial court; the passages Greenblatt cites highlight More's careful use of SI and MI in order to survive at court. He observes that self-fashioning constitutes a secularized version of the medieval tradition of *imitatio christi*, and that this secularization aroused considerable anxiety concerning the high potential for hypocrisy and deception (Greenblatt 3). This ambivalent attitude is given voice in More's paradoxical treatment of the perfect society, and also in Gracián's *Oráculo,* which offers a subtle presentation of the schism between the norms for courtier behavior and the requirements of true virtue. Concerns about the cognitive practices currently referred to as Machiavellian or Social Intelligence lie at the very heart of these anxieties.

Greenblatt's theory of a self that is deliberately constructed and presented for the purpose of social mobility has interesting correlations to Erving Goffman's work of the 1950s and 60s, particularly *The Performance of the Self in Everyday Life* (Burke 31; Egginton, *World* 19–21). Of particular relevance is Goffman's model of "impression management," which may be considered a homology to self-fashioning (208). Goffman delineates several different strategies that are used in *modern* society to "stage a character" (208). Nearly all of these tactics entail the use of MR to discern what others are thinking, and of SI to present and conceal oneself—to evade MR and to enhance one's own status. Goffman's book is a varied (though not deep) sociological study of the performance norms of many different types of mid twentieth-century social groups, particularly those that are placed at the joints where social mobility occurs. His purpose is to document, as an outsider, a wide variety of performance norms—and the primary performance disruptors—practiced among the upwardly mobile of the early postwar era. Recent advances in cognitive studies offer a new way to view Goffman's insights, by enabling us to see the MR activities that facilitate such social theatrics. Early modern courtier manuals also described performance norms for a group seeking social mobility, but were written from an insider's perspective, in order to convey the details of the front required for success in one specific social milieu. In both eras, the public presentation of a manufactured self is completely dependent on using cognitive skills: ToM (both Simulation Theory and Theory Theory) in order to infer both the manner of being and the moment-to-moment actions that eventually lead to social advancement. In many instances, SI or MI—or both—are needed if the particular identity desired does not correspond well to the actual qualities and achievements of the aspirant. In this section, I will trace the web of connections among the cognitive paradigm of ToM, Greenblatt, and Goffman's models of fashioned and performed identity, and Gracián's collection of aphorisms. The manual provides a plethora of aphorisms that depict SI and performance as key elements of courtier success.

Goffman notes that performance becomes particularly complex—and particularly necessary—when delineation of a

particular status is not clear-cut, when there is no "formal ratification" (60). The need to use ToM well increases at such transitional historical moments. The shift in what constituted status
ratification, as the medieval markers such as large land holdings or
significant military achievement receded in significance and new
hierarchies emerged at urban courts, served to complicate early
modern social categorization. Since early modernity, the widen-
ing gap between inherited status and monetary wealth has given
rise to ever more sophisticated self-fashioning; Goffman analyzes
what may be the final phase of the trend that More's generation
initiated. Goffman points to the extreme degree of performativ-
ity required of the elite in twentieth-century Britain and characterizes the post-war aristocracy as unique in its requirement of
continual performance of a specific persona in all situations, not
only with intimates, but also with servants and even shop keepers
and strangers (30). This highly ritualized set of mannerisms has
come to constitute the only marker of "blue blood" in a society
where people from many different backgrounds can acquire and
display the luxury consumption items that had once served as
a simultaneous sign of birth and wealth (note, for example, the
many country estates now owned by rock stars or media moguls).
Courtier handbooks arose in tandem with the initial emergence
in Europe of this type of transitional social group, guiding the
upwardly mobile in the *social* management of their *economic* as-
sets. The advances in cognitive study provide a new framework
for analysis of the mental processes that underlie self-fashioning
and performance, and refocus our attention toward the complex
cognitive interactions between performer and audience.

Like Greenblatt, Goffman emphasizes performance of the self
as a strategy for social advancement, asserting that

> upward mobility involves the presentation of proper perfor-
> mance ... expressed in terms of sacrifices made for the main-
> tenance of front. Once the proper sign-equipment has been
> obtained and familiarity gained in the management of it, then
> this equipment can be used to embellish and illume one's daily
> performances. (36)

Goffman notes that in order for a person's self-fashioning or performance to be meaningful to others, "the individual typically
infuses his activity with signs which dramatically highlight and

portray confirmatory facts that might otherwise remain unapparent or obscure" (30). Such performance often requires that a significant amount of one's energy be devoted to *subtly* flaunting that identity (320). The genre of courtesy manuals, which flourished throughout the early modern era, can be seen as a guide to such sign management. The difficulty in properly calibrating the display of one's status, in order to elicit recognition but not contempt or envy, is a frequent theme in *Oráculo*. The cognitive activities that Goffman and Gracián describe in connection with this balancing act are clearly related to ToM and SI, requiring intensive effort to anticipate and manipulate the attention of one's fellow courtiers. In addition, Goffman's emphasis upon the "sacrifices made for the maintenance of front" are relevant to the third and concluding *tratados* of *Lazarillo* as well as to many episodes found in Quevedo and Alemán (36). Strong ToM skills are crucial to projecting which signs will serve to make a particular impression without annoying the beholder.

Goffman points out that there is often a disconnect between the effort and skill needed for an actual activity and the performance or front: for some roles, it is necessary to conceal diligence; for others, acclaim or respect derive from the ability to make visible hidden difficulties (32–33). According to Peter Burke, *sprezzatura*, which he describes as a careless grace manifested in the ability to achieve a high level of performance while appearing not to perform at all, is presented in Castiglione's *Courtier* as the highest virtue (30–31). Harry Berger also emphasizes the importance of this nonchalant grace in Castiglione's text, "the ability to show that one is not showing all the effort one obviously put into learning how to show that one is not showing effort" (9). The link between *sprezzatura* and SI is made manifest in the multiple levels of intentionality indicated by Berger's definition, which he also describes as "the display of the ability to deceive" (10). Daniel Dennett's model of levels of intentionality are crucial to *sprezzatura*: one person seeks to convince another person that he has done nothing special to win admiration that he pretends not to notice that he has won. Gracián's *Oráculo* likewise highlights the ability to impress others with the ease and naturalness of one's achievements as an important attribute for court success, which he deems "realce de los mismos realces" (#127; throughout this section I will cite the aphorism number rather than the page of a specific text).

He observes,

> todo lo natural fue siempre más grato que lo artificial. Los afectados *son tenidos* por estrangeros en lo que afectan; quanto mejor se haze una cosa se ha de desmentir la industria, porque *se vea* que se cae de su natural la perfección. Ni por huir la afectación se ha de dar en ella afectando el no afectar. Nunca el Discreto se ha de dar por entendido de sus méritos, que el mismo descuido *despierta en los otros la atención.* (#123; emphasis added)

Here, the strong positive impact that effortless grace has upon others is repeatedly emphasized. Later, he reiterates this point,

> *Reservarse* siempre las últimas tretas del arte. Es de grandes maestros, que se valen de su *sutileza* en el mismo enseñarla. Con esso se conserva la reputación y la dependencia. En el agradar y en el enseñar se ha de observar aquella gran lición de ir siempre zevando la admiración y adelantando la perfección. (#212; emphasis added)

However, he also highlights the contradiction that performance is absolutely necessary for success and yet is deprecated as dishonesty,

> No ser tenido por hombre de artificio. Aunque no se puede ya vivir sin él. ... El mayor artificio sea encubrirlo, que se tiene por engaño. ... El crédito de hombre que sabe lo que ha de hazer es honroso y causa confiança, pero el de artificioso es sofístico y engendra rezelo. (#219)

In the early modern age of performance and self-fashioning, there arises the paradox that performance is compulsory for success at court; and yet, the most glory accrues to those who appear not to employ artifice (Hafter 93). In all of these examples the courtier's pretense of lack of effort also entails concealing the cognitive efforts of ToM and SI.

In these four aphorisms, Gracián makes clear that *sprezzatura* is the king and queen of social graces. The courtier who is able to feign this natural grace is in a unique position; because his actions appear natural and hence transparent, he does not elicit SI on the part of others—and thus has less need to constantly employ MR and SI to defend himself. For this reason, *sprezzatura* can be considered the ultimate form of Social Intelligence, a rare and difficult performance tactic that places the successful practitioner so high above the rest of the court that he is relatively safe from the SI of others. Goffman describes a related phenomenon in modern social performance; he observes that because so many signs of status and self can be manipulated, audiences pay special attention to certain cues, "features of the performance that cannot be readily manipulated" (58). In other words, humans must trust their ToM to inform them accurately about which activities are truly natural and authentic. *Sprezzatura* can be placed in this category; because seemingly effortless grace is so difficult to perform, it is most often interpreted as natural rather than manipulated and hence as authentic. This precise management of one's self-presentation is a highly elusive goal; the limits concerning how far a pícaro may advance in the *letrado* class may be due, in addition to lack of economic capital, to an insufficient stock of this form of "social capital" (Ruan, "Taste" 320).

If *sprezzatura* is the pinnacle of successful SI and impression management, then ostentation may be seen as its polar opposite. According to Gracián, flaunting one's success is a major faux pas, condemned in no fewer than five aphorisms (## 106, 107, 117, 123, 278). Those who are brazen about their success risk immediate loss of status for failing to recognize the negative reactions they will provoke—such negligence implies weak ToM skills or, even worse, a failure to employ MR. Gracián warns, "La estimación se consigue menos quanto se busca más" (#106); and counsels, "No mostrar satisfación de sí. ... Nace la satisfación en los más de ignorancia y para en una felicidad necia, que, aunque entretiene el gusto, no mantiene el crédito" (#107). Further, he advises, "Nunca hablar de sí. O se ha de alabar, que es desvanecimiento, o se ha de vituperar, que es poquedad; y, siendo culpa de cordura en el que dize, es pena de los que oyen" (#117). Gracián emphasizes the relation between excess displays of the self and faulty SI; he condemns the failure to use ToM to anticipate how others will respond to such displays. The resultant ostentation

> Es tan enfadosa a los demás quan penosa al que la sustenta, porque vive mártir del cuidado, y se atormenta con la puntualidad. Pierden su mérito las mismas eminencias con ella, porque se juzgan nacidas antes de la artificiosa violencia que de la libre naturaleza. (#123)

Even the highest virtues will not redound to one's credit if displayed improperly, "Huir la nota en todo. Que en siendo notados, serán defectos los mismos realces. Nace esto de singularidad, que siempre fue censurada; quédase solo el singular. Aun lo lindo, si sobresale, es descrédito ..." (#278). In all of these observations, Gracián makes clear that insightful and beneficial self-fashioning crosses the border into ostentation at the point where the performance becomes more noticed than the attribute. Such faulty calibrations of display invite others to use their ToM upon an actor and his performance, and to draw unfavorable conclusions. Successful SI entails gaining positive notice in situations that do not encourage others to ponder one's own ToM. In fact, the biggest drawback to ostentation may simply be that it lays bare *all* court behavior as grounded in MR and SI, and as inherently theatrical. In the courtesy manual and the picaresque novels studied here, ostentation plays very different roles, yet in all four improper ostentation is shown to be a root cause of social instability.

In his analysis of the impact of *The Courtier* and subsequent generations of conduct manuals, Burke notes that the Protestant reformation gave rise to a new "culture of sincerity" (108). This produced a backlash against courtesy books, which were accused of fostering the sorts of deceptive and hypocritical behaviors that are associated with negative views of MI (108). In Elizabethan England, *sprezzatura* was critiqued as an exceptionally offensive form of dissimulation. In addition, Berger indicates that *sprezzatura* was considered to be a compensatory virtue, taking the place of the true and innate—superior—form of grace displayed by high-born nobility of previous eras (12). There arose a new genre of satires of courtier manuals, focusing upon performance as a negative aspect (Burke 110–13; Greenblatt 160–63). Guevara's *Menosprecio de corte* can be seen as this type of anticourtier manual, emphasizing such performances as a key flaw. Although the cult of authenticity as the secular and personal phenomenon by which we currently know it was first codified by Romantic thinkers, these critiques indicate an earlier period of rejection for the self as a construct, created and modified through a process of social interaction. ToM serves as the basis for nonauthentic or performed identity, providing the continuous feedback loop that a performer must use to gauge and modify the impact of impression management. As the paradox of seemingly effortless mastery is transformed from a virtue to a vice, by the seventeenth century SI itself appears to be under attack as a socially toxic cognitive activity (Burke 109).

Some parts of Gracián's text can be seen as participating in this backlash trend. He emphasizes the value of an uncommon use of ToM: that the wise man must use that ability to truly look inside of himself (## 34, 161, 194, 225, 238). These aphorisms suggest a schism between the courtier and the virtuous man, similar to the split that Greenblatt describes between More as courtier and as theologian, defender of the Catholic church who had constructed a quasi-monastery at his Chelsea country home, to which he retreated every week for a day of prayer and meditation. This same ambiguity concerning the results of self-fashioning and impression management can be found in the conclusion of the three picaresque novels. The later chapters of each of the picaresque novels can be viewed both as an adaptation and as a parody of the functions of SI in the upper reaches of urban society.

Impression Management among Pícaros

Although Goffman's paradigm of identity as a theatrical mode took as its object of analysis the performance of the shifting social class identities of the *modern* world, many of his insights are also pertinent to Greenblatt's paradigm of early modern self-fashioning as well as to representations of class mobility in the picaresque ambience. Bruce Burningham characterizes the picaresque role as inherently performative in nature; with the main difference between rogue and actor lying not in the quality of the performance played but in audience reception—whether or not a viewer is aware that he or she is watching an enactment (*Radical* 101). He points to the pardoner as the master who teaches Lazarillo the most important lessons about staging and "the power of performance" in the complex charade where pardoner and constable perform roles that are both authentic and theatrical at the same time (99–100). He astutely notes that this episode crystallizes a prominent theme of the picaresque as a genre, which "demonstrates that even seemingly 'real life' performances can often mask a deeper theatrical reality" (100). The Poor Laws reforms attempted to codify a set of norms and practices to identify worthy recipients of charity; Burningham's observations help to explain why the laws failed—and why picaresque literature's explorations of performative impoverishment were so popular. Burningham also views the process of self-naming each of the major pícaros undertakes as a form of self-fashioning (*Tilting* 140). Carroll Johnson also alludes briefly to self-fashioning in picaresque works, but his essay emphasizes imposed rather than self-determined forms of identity ("Defining" 161). Goffman noted that in modern times, different types of scams, known as "grifts, dodges and capers" have replaced theatricalized begging; it is precisely the change from performances of destitution to performances of scams that this chapter will explore (41).

Lazarillo's education in the manipulation of appearances, closely connected to the use of ToM and SI, is greatly enhanced during his tenure with the impoverished squire, who both models and demystifies the fine points of "impression management" (Goffman 208). Goffman cites a study of rural Scottish nobility who dined on oatmeal on a regular basis, so that, when noble peers came to stay for hunting parties, they could afford to serve ostentatious meals with numerous courses and an abundance of fine liquors (37–38). Here, as in the squire's judicious use of a toothpick and crumbs to present a façade of dining, and his refusal to sell the cape and sword that mark his class status in order to feed and lodge himself, SI is used to convey the false impression that a person of noble blood who still owns appropriate landholdings also retains the monetary resources associated with the gentry. Goffman's study does not specify any particular purpose to the Scottish use of SI; however, in the case of Lazarillo's squire and many pícaro situations, the false front is deployed for both social and economic gain. The squire is quite specific about the end goal of his current sacrifice: he is willing to starve in order to maintain the false front of nobility because his Theory Theory projects that such a display is necessary to win a position in the household of any great lord (see Chapter 1 for an exploration of Theory Theory and Simulation Theory as two variants of ToM). Although steady meals would be a surety in such circumstances, he could have subsisted equally well in his hometown. The major benefit is increased prestige, and an escape from the petty social humiliations suffered in his village. However, ascension to such a post would mark the prelude rather than the conclusion to his role-playing. The squire elaborates in great detail his mastery of the forms of ToM and MI that would be necessary to flourish in the type of courtier position he seeks,

Ya cuando asienta un hombre con un señor de título, todavía pasa su lacería. ¿Pues por ventura no hay en mi *habilidad* para servir y contestar a éstos? Por Dios, si con él topase, muy gran su privado pienso que fuese y que mil servicios le hiciese, porque yo sabría *mentille* tan bien como otro, y *agradalle* a las mil maravillas: *reílle* ya mucho sus donaires y costumbres, *aunque* no fuesen las mejores del mundo; nunca decirle cosa con que le pesase, *aunque* mucho le cumpliese; ser muy *diligente* en su persona en dicho y hecho; no me matar por no hacer bien las cosas que él no había de ver, y ponerme a reñir, donde lo oyese, con la gente de servicio, porque *pareciese* tener gran cuidado de lo que a él tocaba; si riñese con algún su criado, dar unos puntillos agudos para la encender la ira y que *pareciesen* en favor del culpado; *decirle bien* de lo que bien le estuviese …. (Tratado tercero; emphasis added)

The italicized words lay bare the squire's understanding of how SI would guide him in manipulating deeds, words, and appearances in order to gain and keep the favor of an illustrious master. His plan of action echoes in an ironic way many of the tips found in courtesy handbooks. This passage also demonstrates the utility of additional connections to be drawn using early and postmodern models for the performance of the self and cognitive models of MI. The squire repeatedly emphasizes the importance of using Simulation Theory to form an accurate ToM concerning his hypothetical lord and how he would use that knowledge to shape his own behavior according to the dictates of SI—with no concern at all for truth or authenticity. It is noteworthy that, despite his thorough explication of the tools needed for social success, the squire never does succeed in implementing this strategy for his own benefit and must instead flee when his rent comes due. We do not know if this failure is due to the harsh economic environment and the ever-increasing competition for positions in urban noble households, or if he fails to gain a position because his SI abilities are not as developed as his harangue would indicate.

The final *tratados* of *Lazarillo* provide further illumination concerning the high price that social climbers must pay to obtain and maintain a "false front" of gentility, as well as the limits of SI. Lazarillo explains that accumulating sufficient capital to dress like the squire marks a major turning point in his life. He describes this new costume with a level of detail previously reserved for recounting clever pranks,

> Fueme tan bien en el oficio que al cabo de cuatro años que lo
> usé, con poner en la ganancia buen recaudo, ahorré para me
> vestir muy honradamente de la ropa vieja, de la cual compré
> un jubón de fustán viejo y un sayo raído de manga tranzada y
> puerta, y una capa que había sido frisada, y una espada de las
> viejas primeras de Cuéllar. Desque me vi en hábito de hombre
> de bien, dije a mi amo se tomase su asno, que no quería más
> seguir aquel oficio. (Tratado sexto)

He then explains his supposed motivation for abandoning the
highly profitable but ignoble physical labor of water sales, "pensando en qué modo de vivir haría mi asiento por tener descanso
y ganar algo para la vejez." He foregrounds a desire for greater
financial security, but his obvious pride in the sword and cape ensemble indicates additional priorities—the very same type of social
pretensions that he had previously mocked when contemplating
the squire's life choices.

Although the squire did not succeed in improving his life
with his performance of nobility, the reader may extrapolate that
Lazarillo used such discussions as his own conduct manual. Active
reading is necessary because he is surprisingly vague about how he
comes to win the favor of those who aid him in his economic and
social advancement. He had conveyed conversations with previous
masters in great detail, yet we are not shown why or how it happens that a chaplain takes such a shine to him in the sixth *tratado*,
"me recibió por suyo, y púsome en poder un asno y cuatro cánta-
ros y un azote, y comencé a echar agua por la ciudad." Similarly,
we are told nothing beyond these few words in the Prologue about
the undoubtedly delicate process through which, "con favor que
tuve de amigos y señores, todos mis trabajos y fatigas hasta entonces pasados fueron pagados con alcanzar lo que procuré, que fue
un oficio real, viendo que no hay nadie que medre sino los que le
tienen." The reader is given similarly scant information about how
Lazarillo attracts the support of the Archpriest, the merest indication in the Prologue asserting "viendo mi habilidad y buen vivir,
t[uvo] noticia de mi persona el señor arcipreste de Sant Salvador,
mi señor." It is probably not coincidental that the term *habilidad*
echoes the first line of the squire's description of how to use ToM
and SI; this parallel indicates that after learning how to steal and
survive from his first two masters, Lazarillo learns to use ToM and
SI for purposes of flattery and social advancement from the squire.

It is also not surprising that, even though Lazarillo described in elaborate detail his use of SI to facilitate an amusing array of witty, petty thefts, he chooses to remain silent concerning his mastery of the more nuanced art of "impression management." We must consider the strong disdain he had initially expressed when he became fully aware of the squire's value system and the privation he endured for the sake of his false front, and his contempt for this particular mode of MI, "¡Oh Señor, y cuántos de aquéstos debéis vos tener por el mundo derramados, que *padecen* por la negra que llaman honra lo que por vos no sufrirían!" (Tratado tercero). As Goffman indicates, significant sacrifice is often required to perform social roles. In the final section of this chapter, I will examine in further detail the way that Lazarillo's reticence on this aspect of his life reflects his use of ToM to shape the extradiegetic impressions of his readers—relevant both to Vuestra Merced and ourselves.

Like Lazarillo's squire, Guzmán abandons a stable but lackluster existence in order to pursue social mobility. Like Lazarillo, he is at first completely lacking in ToM and SI; his deficiencies in this area cause an initial social descent, as he is forced to sell, or loses by theft, all of the clothing items that mark his original social category. As described in the previous chapter, the first two books of the first part convey a series of adventures in which Guzmán's SI develops at a slow and uneven pace, with plenty of amusing adventure but minimal cognitive advancement. The third book of part one depicts a youth who at last begins to get ahead in life because he has finally developed a ToM. SI is even more useful to Guzmán than to Lazarillo, because it serves as a complement to the superior education and manners that derive from Guzmán's much more propitious childhood. Guzmán is able to use this set of resources to attain far more prestige and social power than Lazarillo could ever have dreamed of, in the courts of the Cardinal and the French Ambassador. Unlike Lazarillo, Guzmán openly describes the tactics he used to win favor with these great lords, which are quite similar to those that the squire had enumerated for his protégé (Davis 67). Guzmán initially uses his ToM to gain entrée to the Cardinal's residence with a feigned leg wound, using his cognitive skills to select a target who was both wealthy enough to take him in with no inconvenience and also one who was publicly known to be very sympathetic to charity cases. He is less forthcoming about how he managed to charm his new master during visits to his sickbed; Guzmán merely comments in an offhand way, "venía todos los días a visitarme, y algunos tardaba comigo, hablando de cosas que gustaba oírme" (1.III.vi). The ability to charm such an important official implies successful employment of both Theory Theory, to infer the tactics most likely to appeal to great courtiers, as well as Simulation Theory in order to "fine tune" his performance for an audience of one.

The chapters that present Guzmán's rising stature among the Cardinal's various levels of servants portray a clear relationship between the clever use of SI and the general atmosphere of dishonesty and decadence in noble households (Davis 73). Although Guzmán was punished when he used MI to steal his master's candy, many other pranks win favor—or at least wary respect (Davis 81). When Guzmán tricks the chamberlain into attracting rather than repelling mosquitoes, the Cardinal is highly amused at his favorite's discomfort,

> viéndolo monseñor de aquella manera, que parecía leproso, y que yo de miedo no parecía, se descompuso riendo de la burla que le hice y, mandándome llamar, me preguntó que por qué había hecho aquella travesura.
>
> Respondíle:
>
> —Vuestra Señoría Ilustrísima me mandó dar una docena cabal de azotes por lo de las conservas, y se acuerda bien cuánto se recatearon uno a uno; demás desto, no habían de ser azotes de muerte, sino de los que pudieran llevar mis años. El dómine Nicolao me dio más de veinte por su cuenta, siendo los postreros los más crueles. Y así vengué mis ronchas con las suyas. (1.III.viii)

This cleverly staged revenge so diverts the Cardinal that Guzmán is allowed to return to the page position he had held before the theft; although Guzmán repeatedly refers to this master as unusually kind, he nonetheless sanctions *burlas* that humiliate and even harm other servants. In these ruses, Guzmán uses simple machinations rather than ToM to lure his peers into disgrace; the true target of his SI is the Cardinal whom he seeks to amuse. It is likely that he uses Theory Theory to deduce that this master will be entertained by this cruelty, for such enacted humiliations are described as a commonplace form of diversion in noble households. After a second successful deception against the chamberlain,

Guzmán observes that his prowess in SI has an additional social benefit—for it greatly impacted the ToM of the other pages toward him, "La burla se solenizó más que la primera, porque escoció más. Desta vez quedé confirmado por quien era: todos huían de mis burlas como del pecado" (1.III.viii). Thus, MI not only helps him to impress and amuse his superiors, it also facilitates his life among his peers, who fear his retribution and thus cease their own pranks against him. Guzmán's success here parallels that of Pablos at the student residence. His use of Simulation Theory also enables him to use his wiles to continue to break all of the household rules; he knows that his master is too tender-hearted to throw him out, "Era generalmente caritativo, por ser la caridad el primer fruto del Espíritu Santo y fuego suyo, primero bien de todos los bienes, primer principio del fin dichoso. … Deseaba tanto mi remedio como si dél resultara el suyo" (1.III.ix).

However, Guzmán's Simulation Theory concerning the Cardinal's cognitive processes fails him at a crucial moment, because he does not realize the extent to which his master feels concern for the state of his sin-blackened soul. If it is true that Simulation Theory deploys empathetic projections based on one's own mental states, then we can extrapolate that Guzmán's own lack of faith and scruples prevented him from simulating this aspect of his master's psyche. Thus, he is temporarily expelled from the palace because of his unwillingness to publicly renounce and repent his misdeeds, and his master dies before amends can be made and before Guzmán can regain his place in the Cardinal's will. Here, one single miscalculation undoes all the success Guzmán had achieved through many months of careful planning. With this rise and fall, the final pages of the first part of *Guzmán* lay the groundwork for the new narrative structure of the second part, providing a multifaceted exploration of a social world in which advancement obtained through SI is extremely precarious. In all subsequent scams, Guzmán fails either because he lacks sufficient data for successful Theory Theory projections or due to insufficient skill at simulation.

To close the first part, Guzmán recovers quickly from his first major error, taking advantage of the reputation for SI that he had achieved among the Cardinal's peers. His standing with his new master, the French Ambassador, derives from his success as a sort of court jester—one whose scams against others are a source of pride and prestige for his employer (Davis 80–82).

> Hacíame buen tratamiento, pero con diferente fin; que mon-
> señor guiaba las cosas al aprovechamiento de mi persona y, el
> embajador al gusto de la suya, porque lo recebía de donaires
> que le decía, cuentos que le contaba ... Y hablando claro, yo
> era su gracioso, aunque otros me llamaban truhán chocarrero.
> Cuando teníamos convidados, que nunca faltaban, a los de
> cumplimiento servíamos con gran puntualidad, desvelando los
> ojos en los suyos; mas a otros importunos, necios, enfadosos,
> que sin ser llamados venían, a los tales hacíamos mil burlas ...
> Buscábamos invención para que les hiciese mal provecho, por
> aventarlos de casa. (1.III.ix)

With the Cardinal, Guzmán's *burlas* had been a source of amusement that mitigated his many failings, a sort of "get out of jail free"
card. The Cardinal's reaction sets the stage for the Ambassador's
more direct involvement. At the Ambassador's court, Guzmán's
no longer uses SI to gain material goods or direct social power
for himself; rather, its deployment is sanctioned by an authority
figure and treated as a form of entertainment that gives credit to
the patron rather than the pícaro. The use of plural verbs, implying complicity between Guzmán and the Ambassador, makes clear
that MI is no longer a tactic that he uses covertly; rather, it is now
the very essence of his job description. In this frank depiction of
impression management and upper-class existence, Alemán goes
well beyond Lazarillo as an indictment of the deceptive nature of
the entire seigneurial caste. Here, Guzmán's persistent use of MI
is presented as the norm for "everyday life" among the aristocracy.

Social Intelligence and Gender Relations

Chapter 2 explored the ways in which SI is used to guide courtship strategies among those born into the gentry, as represented
in comic drama. In those plays, the relationship between gender
and SI is at the forefront. As this chapter has established, SI is
employed for a wide variety of purposes among the social climbers of the pícaro world. But, that is not to say that marriage is
unimportant among *arrivistes*; on the contrary, all three picaresque
protagonists seek an advantageous marriage as one component of
advancement. However, as a realistic rather than idealistic genre,
the picaresque novel approaches marital union from a highly
pragmatic vantage point. For example, Lazarillo entirely omits
narration of the courtship phase of his union to focus upon the

less-than-ideal outcome, while the courtship segments of *Guzmán* and *Buscón* emphasize the pursuit of economic benefit rather than the aestheticized sentimentality found in early modern poetry and drama.

Among the many important plot developments that are not narrated, the events that lead up to Lazarillo's marriage are perhaps the most significant in their absence. As a first-person narrative, there is of course no possibility of representing the scenes in which the Archpriest and his concubine would discuss the MI strategies they could devise to ensnare Lazarillo. Because the novel has had a trajectory of ever more astute and successful deployment of cognitive skills, it would have gone against the narrative arc for Lazarillo to describe the complete failure of his ToM at this key moment, if he did indeed enter the marriage naïvely. On the other hand, a frank description of being deceived by two expert con artists would have brought the plot full circle, reminding readers of his initial state of innocence and the necessity of a superior ToM capacity for survival in the urban jungle. A confession of this sort could have thus reinforced a sympathetic MR for his readers, right before the key moment of reweighing. The absence of such a statement renders the formation of a definitive ToM for Lazarillo even more difficult, as readers are left to draw their own conclusions concerning "what did he know and when did he know it?"

Lazarillo's strong condemnation of "negra honra" in the third *tratado* serves as a sort of foreshadowing of the plot twist in the final pages of the novel. Life has taught him to value security and a steady diet above all else and to use ToM toward achieving that goal. He cannot empathize with the squire's approach to MI, and would not perform a masquerade that entailed abandoning a secure if declining existence and undergoing starvation for the sake of mere social advancement. To a large extent, the false front that Lazarillo adopts at the end of the book, and which he must maintain for the rest of his life, is donned precisely to avoid that fate. In his recital of the telltale conversation with the Archpriest, we can see how his ToM guides him concerning when to take notice of an issue and when to look away. Repeating the pattern established with the third master, Lazarillo and his final master engage in a duel of mutual MI in order to come to terms with the conditions for the Archpriest's support and marital peace, without ever voicing the true state of affairs. Lazarillo thus reports, mi señor me ha prometido lo que pienso cumplirá. Que él me habló un día muy largo delante della, y me dijo: "Lázaro de Tormes, quien ha de mirar a dichos de malas lenguas, nunca medrará. Digo esto porque no me maravillaría alguno, viendo entrar en mi casa a tu mujer y salir della. Ella entra muy a tu honra y suya, y esto te lo prometo. Por tanto, no mires a lo que pueden decir, sino a lo que te toca, digo a tu provecho.

«Señor —le dije—, yo determiné de arrimarme a los buenos. Verdad es que algunos de mis amigos me han dicho algo deso, y aun, por más de tres veces me han certificado que, antes que comigo casase, había parido tres veces, hablando con reverencia de V.M., porque está ella delante.»

Entonces mi mujer echó juramentos sobre sí ... Mas yo de un cabo y mi señor de otro, tanto le dijimos y otorgamos que cesó su llanto, con juramento que le hice de nunca más en mi vida mentalle nada de aquello, y que yo holgaba y había por bien de que ella entrase y saliese, de noche y de día, pues estaba bien seguro de su bondad. Y así quedamos todos tres bien conformes. (Tratado séptimo)

This marriage, which leads to the culminating moment of Lazarillo's financial prosperity, is also the pinnacle of his MI—as we see in his achingly careful report of the conversational dance among the three members of this unholy trio. Mancing analyzes this scene as a perfect example of how characters navigate multiple levels of intentionality as they deploy MI against each other ("Sancho" 128). This passage is of central import both for appreciating the final stage of development of Lazarillo's ToM as well as for gauging his reliability as narrator of his own life and adventures.

In part one of *Guzmán*, as described above, we found the first indications that his ToM is not very reliable when it comes to evaluating women. In the initial part, as Guzmán pursues other concerns, his "mind blindness" in this area is of little consequence. However, this failure will have significant impact in the forthcoming part, as Guzmán himself alerts us in the final lines of the first: "Yo di mil gracias a Dios, que no me hizo enamorado; pero si no jugué los dados, hice otros peores baratos, como verás en la segunda parte de mi vida. ..." Once he arrives in Spain with the fruits of all his swindles, Guzmán becomes easy prey for a variety of women whose MI skills are superior to his. In fact, Guzmán seems for a long time to be unaware that he needs to use ToM to protect himself when he encounters the fair sex. On the streets of Zaragoza, for example, a woman manages to raid his pockets during a flirtatious encounter. Guzmán's ToM is not at all alerted when the woman allows easy and rapid familiarity, but instead seeks to turn the encounter to his advantage,

> Comencéme a querer desvolverme de manos, y como a lo melindroso hacía la hembra que se defendía; empero de tal manera, con tal industria, buena maña y grande sutileza que, cuanto en muy breve espacio truje ocupadas las manos por su rostro y pechos, ella con las suyas no holgaba. Que, metiéndolas por mis faltriqueras, me sacó lo poco que llevaba en ellas. Con aquel encendimiento no lo sentí ni me fuera posible, aun en caso que fuera con cuidado. (2.III.i)

Her rapid departure after the brief embrace and her promise of a future encounter does not spur his SI; rather, he notes, "Creíla todo cuanto me dijo; por tan cierto lo tuve, como en las manos." In retrospect, Guzmán explains his own deficient ToM as hormonal, "Porque nunca en tales tiempos hay memoria ni entendimiento; sólo se ocupa la voluntad" (2.III.i). However, this fleecing does seem to awaken him temporarily, for the next day he decides to abandon his pursuit of another woman, a wealthy widow. He realizes that an important component of SI is an understanding of the local culture and its inhabitants, and that he does not have enough information to form accurate Theory Theory projections, "Yo soy forastero ... Yo no sé quién son o lo que pretenden" (2.III. ii). Guzmán's level of ToM was more than adequate for his previous con games and swindles, but he confesses to being over his head in this situation where as an outsider he cannot perform simulations nor form overarching Theory Theory paradigms. Although Guzmán had gradually accumulated awareness of urban and palace life and upper class cognitive norms concerning wealth acquisition and display, he never will acquire a similarly effective ToM for success at courtship—and after this one moment of prudence seems to forget that such a skill is needed. For example, he allows himself to be led into his first marriage, with a banker's daughter, with no indication that he had even tried to use MR to assess her true motivation or her father's. He also seems to have no idea concerning how to use ToM skills once it becomes clear that his wife is spending far more than he has or can earn. This failure or inability to develop either simulation skills for understanding his own wife, nor a Theory Theory to explain women in general, not only results in the dissipation of the entire fortune he had so painstakingly accumulated, but also lands him in debt.

Just as his first wife's spendthrift nature came as a surprise, Guzmán appears equally unprepared for the revelation that his second wife is not loyal or chaste. As indicated previously, many of his adventures appear to be a fleshing out of the comparatively sparse descriptions of Lazarillo's life and adventures. If readers are to judge Lazarillo's mostly unspoken attitudes toward wifely virtue by Guzmán's frank discussion of pimping his second wife, Gracia, then we can extract yet another example of the "lemonade from lemons" perspective that marks picaresque life. Guzmán describes the slippery slope that leads to the ultimate indignity of a husband who helps his wife place horns on his head; first, in order to survive until finishing his studies, he ignores small improprieties, "permití en mi casa juego, conversaciones y otras impertinencias, que todas me dañaron... A los principios disimulélo un poco, y poco basta consentir a una mujer para que se alargue mucho" (2.III.v). Next, he describes an insight that might be termed an anti-epiphany, which occurs when he realizes he cannot afford to finish his studies and should make the most of the capital he does have:

> Hice mi cuenta: «Ya no puede ser el cuervo más negro que sus alas. El daño está hecho y el mayor trago pasado; empeñada la honra, menos mal es que se venda. El provecho aquí es breve, la infamia larga, los estudiantes engañosos, la comida difícil... Yo sabía ya lo que pasaba en la corte. Había visto en ella muchos hombres que no tenían otro trato ni comían de otro juro que de una hermosa cara y aun la tomaban en dote; porque para ellos era una mina ...» (2.III.v)

Guzmán's elaborate and detailed description of the life of a husband/pimp provides illumination into both his and Lazarillo's daily existence, concerning the ways that such a man must use both Simulation and Theory Theory forms of ToM in order to avoid directly confronting embarrassing truths:

> Vía también las buenas trazas que tenían para no quedar obligados a lo que debieran, que, cuando estaba tomada la posada, o dejaban caer la celogía o ponían en la ventana un jarro, un chapín o cualquier otra cosa, en que supiesen los maridos que habían de pasarse de largo y no entrasen a embarazar. A medio-

día ya sabían que habían de tener el campo franco. Entraban en sus casas, hallaban las mesas puestas, la comida buena y bien prevenida y que no habían de calentar mucho la silla, porque quien la enviaba quería venirse a entretener un rato. Y a las noches, en dando las Avemarías, volvían otra vez, dábanles de cenar, íbanse a dormir solos, hasta que se les hiciese horas a sus mujeres de irse con ellos a la cama. Y acontecía detenerse hasta el día, porque iban a visitar a sus vecinas. En resolución, ellos y ellas vivían *con tal artificio que, sin darse por entendidos de palabra, sabían ya* lo que había cada uno de poner por la obra. (2.III.v; emphasis added)

Although only the last line employs cognitive terminology, the entire passage describes a lifestyle that is marked by a façade of deliberate unknowing. The situation that Guzmán describes here entails a life-long game of mutual MI involving husband, wife, and patrons, and which may be seen as Alemán's projection of Lazarillo's marital circumstances as well. Significantly, Guzmán first provides this analysis *before* embarking on such a course himself, based on what he has previously observed. In this way, Guzmán seeks to exculpate himself with his reader by presenting such a dishonorable life as merely another of the unpalatable but profitable options available to the pícaro. Guzmán appears to suffer few pangs of jealousy, instead focusing on the material comfort to be derived from the more prosperous suitors he helps Gracia to attract. Indeed, it would appear that his most profound unhappiness during this episode derives from the loss of this income when his wife abandons him for a wealthier rival, rather than from any sense of wounded honor. Lazarillo's tale similarly indicates little discomfort, because his *ménage à trois* is expected to result in permanent prosperity.

Reading these two episodes side by side raises two additional considerations; first, the way that Guzmán and Gracia flee Alcalá is an indication that public gossip about wifely errors can be too much for even a pícaro to withstand. Here, Alemán may be presenting his own ToM as a reader of Lazarillo's narrative, one who projects that the final cozy arrangement and the attendant comfort cannot last. This prophecy is reinforced by the way that Guzmán's marriage terminates; Gracia may be said to stand in for every wife of loose morals, ready to abandon both cuckolded husband and paramour if a better opportunity presents itself. Alemán thus offers us two readings that indicate different but equally unhappy resolutions to Lazarillo's situation. Beyond this pessimistic view of marriage, both novels depict women's cognitive activities as even more duplicitous and impenetrable than those of men in a highly corrupted urban society, such that even a normally perceptive male's ToM will fail him when it comes to penetrating women's MI. The first-person narrative structure hinders consideration of the social conditions that might compel women to employ MI; for this reason the picaresque novel presents a more uniformly negative portrayal of women and gender relations than urban drama. It is worth noting that *La pícara Justina* ostensibly gives voice to poor women; however, Edward Freidman's study of the feminine picaresque, *The Antiheroine's Voice,* offers important insights on the ventriloquism that male authors deploy to feign a female—but not feminist—voice.

In comparison to the decisive roles that female characters play in the lives of Lazarillo and Guzmán, courtship and marriage play a relatively minor role in Pablos's development. The middle of Book III describes a brief episode in which the young man tries to pass himself off as a wealthy nobleman in order to win a prosperous bride, sporting a fine outfit and financing a picnic that he can ill afford, but the main focus of the episode is the humiliation he suffers at the hands of the male courtiers whose superior ToM enable them to see through his ruse. When seeking marriage to a wealthy woman, SI is more important for impressing the male figures who control access to women than for winning women's hearts. Pablos has sufficient cognitive skill to obtain women's affections, but lacks the intimate knowledge of court society that would enable him to use either Theory Theory or Simulation Theory in order to deceive the fathers and brothers who also must be "seduced" to transfer ownership of the females to a husband. In direct contradiction to Alemán, Quevedo devotes almost no attention to female use of SI. Pablos's marriage to Grajales on the final page of the book does not entail social advancement, is not part of any larger scam, and involves no MI; thus, the entire relationship can be conveyed in two highly prosaic sentences. There is little place for women in a novel whose narrative arc emphasizes the humiliation that low-born men suffer when they try to use MI to deceive their male social superiors.

ToM and Consequences

When evaluating the representation of cognitive skills among picaresque figures, one important question arises: what benefits does each youth ultimately attain as a result of his use of ToM and MI? All three protagonists deploy the capital they obtain via fraud as an investment; acquiring clothing, servants, or furnishings that will enable them to use impression management to pursue social advancement. In many ways, *Lazarillo de Tormes* presents the most complex situation, due to the much-studied ambiguity of the denouement. On the surface, Lazarillo attains the most stable economic position of the three canonical pícaros. He does not reach as high as Guzmán and Pablos, and perhaps for that reason his creator feels comfortable in letting him enjoy some measure of financial security. The final outcome of Guzmán's life journey is indeterminate; it is uncertain whether or not he will regain his freedom, and even if he does, the repeated miscalculations and failures in the final book of part two would indicate that his ToM will never be sufficient for him to attain and keep the social position to which he aspires. Pablos's ending is even less optimistic; the reader is told quite bluntly, although without details, that his life in the Americas was even worse than in Spain.

From a purely pragmatic perspective, Lazarillo's use of various types of MR skills and of his capital to climb the social ladder provides him with a much better life than most men of his origins could hope for. By financial standards, his fate is superior to that of Guzmán and Pablos, and I would argue that this is due to the more judicious nature in which he uses ToM. However, the ultimate measure of his success is ambiguous, depending upon both the importance placed upon his tarnished honor and also the outcome of the *caso*. Unless Vuestra Merced's investigation has extremely negative repercussions, Lazarillo will continue to enjoy his relatively privileged position—at least for as long as his patron survives.

In a spectacular blunder that shifted the entire narrative arc, Guzmán had tested the Cardinal at precisely the wrong moment and was not included in the will when he died, thus losing out on a pension for life. The pattern established here is consistent throughout the rest of the novel: although Guzmán can use ToM and MI successfully enough to win the favor of great lords temporarily or to pull off a large scale swindle, his tendency to continually press his luck, as well as the failure of his ToM to evaluate women correctly, eventually undermines every advance he ever achieved. Although Guzmán seeks to enhance his social position by marrying for money, he is amazingly incurious when a seemingly prosperous banker encourages courtship of his daughter—and even more shockingly naïve about his new father-in-law's excuses concerning her dowry. Another primary example is Guzmán's abandonment of a long road of study just at the point where it was about to pay off with a stable and prestigious theological position—in order to marry the promiscuous Gracia. This is one of the most significant turning points for a life path that descends ever further both in terms of *fama* and prosperity, and the utter failure of his ToM to detect the flaws in his second wife is startling indeed. The final failure of his ToM, which leads Guzmán to the galleys, entails an imprudent level of theft and sexual treachery against the woman who is both his employer and lover. Guzmán appears not to use cognitive skills at all in this episode, even though vigilant application of ToM could have helped him to monitor and evade negative consequences from his transgressions. His use of MR is far less consistent than Lazarillo's; in fact, his cognitive acumen nearly disappears in the final book, where the trickster often falls victim to the MI machinations of others and the vocabulary of cognitive activity all but disappears. Once he finds himself a galley slave, Guzmán devolves to the initial primitive phase of using MI for self-defense and basic survival; his desperate situation is akin to that of Lazarillo in the earliest *tratados*. Despite the few and fleeting moments of material or social triumph, Guzmán's MR is not adequate to the task of providing a stable existence. The first-person narrative voice that repents prior misdeeds, and vows to mend his ways in the future, is silent concerning exactly how he will manage to live a life that is both morally righteous and also materially secure.

Pablos, whose cognitive abilities were never as highly developed or creative as the other pícaros, is also very inconsistent in his use of MR. His failure to thrive may be attributed in part to insufficiently developed mentalistic skills. The ramifications of these differences for the reader's ToM concerning the three characters will be explored in the final section of this chapter.

(Un)Reliable Picaresque Narrators

As indicated in Chapter 1, when we apply cognitive theory to literary texts, it is likely that reconsideration of key academic paradigms will ensue. Analysis of the ToM skills of a protagonist stimulates new way of thinking about the paradox of fiction, because we address the mind of a literary character who does not actually exist. In most studies of the picaresque, no matter the ultimate verdict concerning the character of the protagonist, or the aesthetic or ideological nature of the text, an implicit assumption concerning the ToM of character, narrator, or author is central to the analysis. The unique nature of the picaresque text, with its overlap of narratological categories, is a fertile ground for metacognitive analysis—more so than most early modern genres. As an introduction to the metacognitive approach, this section will provide analysis of a small but representative sample of recent academic studies, rather than a comprehensive survey of the entire body of picaresque criticism.

The critical paradigm concerning how to judge the criminal and "immoral" actions of Lazarillo and Guzmán has undergone a 180-degree reversal in recent decades. For most of the last century, there was a critical consensus that the ideological thrust of the picaresque (and of "Golden Age" literature as a whole) was ideologically conservative (Dunn 144; Johnson, *Inside* 46; Castillo 2–5). If the ToM model had been available it would have been used mostly to support a condemnatory view of low-born characters and their uses of SI, in order to affirm that picaresque texts reinforce the tenets of Counter Reformation hierarchy. The debate concerning the sincerity of Guzmán's reform indicates the ways that assumptions about ToM would have functioned within those moralistic approaches. However, over the past quarter century, we have witnessed a paradigm shift. As cultural studies and neo-Marxist models began to gain currency, and interest in "contradictory subjectivities" developed, a new space opened for a reconsideration of social mobility in the era now renamed as early modernity (Mariscal 31–32, 99–104; Castillo 20–70). Substantial research on sixteenth-century discourses of economic reform and poor relief, as described above, has provided the contextualization necessary for a new ideological perspective on the picaresque to emerge and take hold. It is probably not an accident that critics in the US discovered an interest in researching sixteenth-century poor-relief debates in the wake of President Lyndon Johnson's "Great Society" movement, which sought to gain a new understanding of America's urban poor in order to put forth new social programs. A shared though unstated ToM supports the progressive viewpoint in the ideological studies.

A brief review of a few commonly cited passages will suffice to characterize the tactics that Lazarillo and Guzmán as first-person narrators employ to induce readers (and scholars) to form a favorable or at least indulgent ToM concerning these protagonists and their deficiencies. Apart from the few passages directed to Vuestra Merced, Lazarillo manipulates his readers indirectly for the most part, through condemnations of the masters he is forced to serve because the new laws deny charity to able-bodied youth:

> Escapé del trueno y di en el relámpago, porque era el ciego para con éste un Alejandro Magno, con ser la mesma avaricia, como he contado. No digo más sino que toda la laceria del mundo estaba encerrada en éste. (Tratado 1)

> «Tú, bellaco y gallofero eres. Busca, busca un amo a quien sirvas.»
> «¿Y adónde se hallará ése —decía yo entre mí— si Dios agora de nuevo, como crió el mundo, no le criase?» (Tratado 2)

> Así, como he contado, me dejó mi pobre tercero amo, do acabé de conocer mi ruin dicha, pues, señalándose todo lo que podría contra mí, hacía mis negocios tan al revés, que los amos, que suelen ser dejados de los mozos, en mí no fuese ansí, mas que mi amo me dejase y huyese de mí. (Tratado 3)

These meditations, pronounced as he leaves (or is left by) each of his first three masters, emphasize the tribulations of his marginalized class position. Even though Lazarillo does not join up with gangs of pícaros, like Guzmán and Pablos, his tale nonetheless presents the mistreatment he endures as typical and endemic. It is his clever response to an unjust society, rather than the miserable circumstance, that is presented as unique.

Far more than Lazarillo, Guzmán uses direct address as he seeks to convince the reader that his crimes are the result of unfavorable social conditions rather than an inherently defective or base nature. In his depiction of the initial fall into criminal activity, Guzmán provides a lengthy justification,

¿Qué fuera entonces de mi? ¿No *consideras* qué turbado, qué afligido estaría y qué triste, quitado el oficio, sin saber de qué valerme ni rincón adonde abrigarme? Con cuanto gané, jugué y hurté, ni compré juro, censo, casa ni capa o cosa con que me cobijar. Habíase todo ido, entrada por salida, comido por servido, jugado por ganado y frutos por pensión.

Del mal el menos: con todas estas desdichas mi caudal estaba en pie, la vergüenza perdida, *que al pobre no le es de provecho tenerla*, y cuanta menos poseyere le dolerán menos los yerros que hiciere.

Ya me sabía la tierra y había dineros para esportón; mas antes de resolverme a volverlo al hombro, visitaba las noches y a mediodía los amigos y conocidos de mi amo, si alguno por ventura quisiera recebirme: porque ya sabía un poquillo y holgara saber algo más, para con ello ganar de comer. Algunos me ayudaban, entreteniéndome con un pedazo de pan. Debieron de oír tales cosas de mí, que a poco tiempo me despedían sin querer acogerme. *Donde la fuerza oprime, la ley se quiebra.* (1.I.viii; emphasis added)

Like Lazarillo, Guzmán depicts an unjust urban environment in which criminal deception is the only option for those who seek to rise above primate levels of subsistence. Lazarillo and Guzmán guide readers to form a ToM that "absolves" the pícaro; in a society where every level of master and religious servant is corrupt, how can we expect virtue and honesty from a pauper? The recent investigations of poverty-relief policy provide an ideological framework that strongly favors sympathetic evaluation of the deceptions practiced by the urban poor. Of course, this group of studies is not the first to see the pícaro as a sympathetic character and to emphasize social satire. As many studies have noted, Lazarillo depicts a society marked by widespread greed and abuse as well as dishonesty; the negative portrayals of the first three masters are reinforced by the episodes with fraudulent indulgences and the adulterous Archpriest (Maiorino 138; Ife 100; F. Sánchez, *Bourgeois* 80; Cruz xiii; Johnson, *Inside* 51–54). In addition, the analyses by Sánchez and Ruan of the picaresque as a form of conduct manual for class mobility provide further evidence for an early modern discourse of tolerance. In these studies, the ToM formed for the protagonist is not based solely upon an individualist response to a single character's self-presentation, but rather on using statements from the text to place the pícaro in a larger social category and to form a broader Theory-Theory-based ToM for which Lazarillo, Guzmán, and their literary descendants serve as exemplars. In this context, the fraudulent activities propagated by the impoverished can be viewed as a necessary form of Social Intelligence, and justified as an "art of survival" in the face of discriminatory legal practices rather than as a moral failure. This model of Social Intelligence provides support for critical approaches that challenge the period's binaristic and essentialist discourses concerning birth and merit and which question earlier generations of literary study that accepted those judgments at face value.

Apart from these ideological studies of the picaresque, one other primary current employs narratology to foreground the aesthetic strategies these novels employ. Here, the implicit ToM involves an assumption that our admiration for the characters' skills as an author form the basis for a favorable impression, despite the various ethical and moral lapses, misjudgments, and possible insincerities. Zunshine's model of literary ToM emphasizes the relations between reader and narrator. She highlights "source tagging," as a primary cognitive act by which readers evaluate characters and narrators and label them—as victims or villains, reliable narrators or frauds (*Why* 51). Zunshine's study focuses upon the complex source-tagging acts provided by nineteenth- and twentieth-century novels; however, the metacognitive paradigm can also provide useful insights concerning early modern Spanish picaresque fictions. Like the works of Austen, Richardson, and Nabokov that Zunshine analyzes, picaresque novels highlight "numerous interacting minds" as a key thematic component and also foreground readers' evaluation of a potentially unreliable narrator (*Why* 10). Zunshine asserts that reconsiderations of source tags is central to metarepresentational (or metacognitive) fiction, where the climax occurs precisely at the moment where the reader "reweighs" the reliability of the narrator (*Why* 61). Reweighing is ubiquitous in picaresque literature, both within picaresque escapades as well as in the relationship developed between protagonist narrators and their reading public. All three of the picaresque narratives are metacognitive in the first sense; as seen in previous sections, they foreground source-tagging activity among the characters who swindle each other. However, the type of contradictory self-presentation that invokes metacognition on the part of readers plays only a small and perfunctory role in Quevedo's socially conservative novel, which seeks to reinforce rather than challenge social norms (Davis 129; Cruz 117; H. Reed 19). The more-complex first-person narrators, Lazarillo and Guzmán, offer paradoxical self-portrayals that elicit significant metacognitive reflection on the part of their readers—and academic critics.

Barry Ife's important book *Reading and Fiction in Golden Age Spain* reminds contemporary readers that, in the early modern age, theological doctrine and moral discourses played a central role in shaping the source tagging of all fictional texts and authors. Each reader who sat down with a new novel was deeply aware that a primary social institution of his or her culture had deemed all such works to be, at best, frivolous (15–24). Thus, in order for readers to move beyond the idea of leisure reading as a guilty pleasure, in order to posit any sort of significance or intellectual merit to a novel, required a reweighing of this cultural source tag. The assumption of an initial negative evaluation and a desire to provoke an immediate reweighing can be seen in the prologues to many early modern narratives, from *Libro de buen amor* to *Lazarillo* to *Don Quixote*, all of which acknowledge fiction's problematic social status (Ife 93; H. Reed 38). The picaresque novel provides an even greater challenge in this regard, due to the unique nature of the avowed rogue as protagonist and narrator.

Narratological studies characterize the picaresque novel as a sort of proto Kunstbildungsroman, or an autobiographical self-begetting novel, portraying the circuitous path by which a deviant becomes an accomplished writer. The ToM that I infer from such studies is, like that of the ideological studies, one that exonerates the criminal mind due to mitigating circumstances. Here, however, the redemptive variant of ToM is that which academic readers will form in response to an innovative crafter of a new artistic form. Such indulgence has been prevalent since the Romantic era, when the mythologized ToM of the mad or misunderstood artistic genius first arose. We belong to a generation that, influenced by the counterculture era's revival of Romanticism, was trained to prize the creative explosions of alcoholics, addicts, manic depressives, and other assorted misfits. Having learned to accord a reverent ToM to such figures, we will have no trouble with the comparatively tame exploits of early modern pícaro narrators, especially in light of the durability of the narrative model they were purported to create.

Ulrich Wicks offers a reading of *Lazarillo* that is typical of this variant of narratological study. He posits that the ideal reader will adapt the same cognitive stance as Lazarillo himself, employing "narrative distance" in order to avoid being duped (58–59). Wicks characterizes Lazarillo as a "trickster of narration" and yet also an "admirable figure"; for a scholar with a fondness for narrative complexity, the formation of a ToM will focus on the protagonist as inventive author rather than as compromised cuckold (237–38). In a similar vein, Ife notes that the narrative structure guides the reader in an emotional shift from empathy for the young victim Lazarillo to "complicity" with the cynical adult Lázaro (115–17). The compliant reader will have no choice but to pardon the narrator and hence to project a complacent rather than condemnatory ToM. Employing Bakhtin's model of dialogism, Helen Reed praises the "double voiced" quality of the picaresque narrative structure, which "demands a high degree of reader participation" and which also enables authors to present a sympathetic view of the pícaro without fear of retribution or censorship (Bakhtin 325–28; H. Reed 26–38). And, even though she characterizes the class discourse as bifurcated, Reed indicates that her own ToM focuses upon the "necessity" of fraudulent acts (21). David Castillo asserts, "with his life story, Lázaro manufactures an anamorphic web that could be said to entrap, not just the implied reader 'Vuestra Merced,' but also contemporary readers who may see their own presuppositions, biases, and indeed desires reflected in the text" (34). This same approach can be found in recent studies of *Guzmán*. Nina Davis concedes that the protagonist may be feigning his conversion, but asserts that this is actually a positive phenomenon because readers derive great pleasure from teasing out the truth in a complex text (72). The linguistic virtuosity that Guzmán displays in "concealment by disclosure" appeals to deceived characters and extradiegetic scholar alike, and both forgive the lesser transgressions out of appreciation for artistic merit (Davis 77). These readings conflate or equate picaresque manipulations and the art of narration, and grant the same—favorable—ToM to both character and authorial voice. The polyphonic nature of the picaresque texts requires readers to devote significant attention to the source tags they place upon protagonists and narrators; postmodern critical paradigms currently in vogue reward such metacognitive tactics. This overview of the metacognitive aspects of the pseudoautobiographical picaresque narrator, although brief, nonetheless demonstrates the rich potential of this new branch of literary study for early modern Spanish literature.

Although the early modern age did not possess the technology or the disciplinary knowledge necessary to investigate complex human cognitive activity, the picaresque novel and courtier manual nonetheless display a keen awareness of the important role played by ToM and MI within social interactions. Cognitive theory and terminology add an important new dimension to the exploration of ideological approaches to the deceptions represented in picaresque and courtier literature. The homologies outlined here, concerning the ways that pícaros and cortesanos alike use ToM and MI, further highlight the ubiquity of mechanisms of deception for purposes of advancement between and within all social classes in early modern Spain. By representing MI as a necessary component of survival and prosperity practiced at all social levels, the texts disrupt hierarchical discourses of ethics and honesty. Cognitive theories of social interaction help us to understand the mechanisms that these literary forms use to undermine social binaries concerning birth rank, character, and mental competence.

Contextualism, Skepticism, and Honor

Contextualism can be seen as the polar opposite of the mechanistic models of cognitive activity such as Artificial Intelligence and Skinnerian behaviorism discussed in Chapter 1 (Mancing, "Embodied" 26–27). Diane Gillespie's *The Mind's We: Contextualism in Cognitive Psychology* (1992), rejects quantitative and cause-and-effect emphases in favor of an orientation toward interactive, dynamic, experiential, situational, and context-dependent modalities (Mancing, "Embodied" 29). Gillespie also emphasizes the integration of present and past and the importance of "narrative epistemology"—the validation of storytelling as a cognitive process. Contextualist cognition overlaps in important ways with both the model of the embodied mind and with Carol Gilligan's feminist psychology, in which "data" concerning moral reasoning is obtained by listening to the stories subjects tell about moments of moral decision-making in their lives. Gilligan's *In a Different Voice* offers this contextualist research in place of the traditional and more mechanistic process of posing abstract reasoning tasks that incorporate dualistic presuppositions of correct (mature) and incorrect (immature) moral reasoning processes. Contextualist models of cognition can play an important role in literary analysis, in particular regarding texts that foreground epistemological norms, as well as in narratives with frame tales or other devices that emphasize narrated experience as a cognitive force. This chapter will explore the ways that the contextualist paradigm opens up new perspectives on the epistemological processes that are used to determine female virtue in early modern Spain, as seen in canonical honor drama and in María de Zayas's feminist challenges to the honor code.

The contextualist model of cognitive functionality is dependent upon new models of the brain itself. In recent decades, new paths of research on brain-injured patients and new insights gained from ever-improving technologies such as positron emission (PET) scans of the brain and magnetic resonance imaging (MRI) have drastically reshaped scientific knowledge of brain structures and functions, highlighting the engagement of numerous areas of the brain in mental activity (Damasio 14; Sacks 62–63). One early mode of the contextualist brain, offered by Jerry Fodor in 1983, proposed that thinking is "modular" rather than linear in nature; that is to say, that at any given time, separate compartments of the brain work simultaneously but independently—at a nonconscious level—to process different types of information (37–46). The nonconscious level is viewed as automatic, like the brain level that controls breathing, and is not in any way related to the Freudian unconscious mind. Like Fodor's modular model, Ray Jackendoff's *Consciousness and the Computational Mind* (1987) posits consciousness as disunified, because of varying modalities of experience at the computational, or nonconscious level (Varela et al. 50–55).

Subsequent research in several different fields has shown Fodor's model to be incomplete; however, the new explanations expand upon rather than rejecting the modular theory concerning the multiplicity of brain function. Patricia Churchland delineates a model of parallel processing in *Neurophilosophy* (461–62). In *Beyond Modularity* (1992), developmental psychologist Annette Karmiloff-Smith seeks to move beyond both Piaget and Fodor with her model of representational redescription, a cognitive model that emphasizes the link between inter- and intra-domain relations as the process by which knowledge in a specific domain is continually refined and modified through communication with other domains (Karmiloff-Smith 15–21; Mancing, *Voices*). In an even more radical departure from mechanistic cognitive models, Esther Thelen and Linda Smith use the metaphor of the cognitive process as an organic system with "a multiple, parallel, and continuously dynamic interplay" (xix; cited by Mancing, *Voices*). Similarly, Joaquín Fuster explains that neurological research has contributed to the development of a networked model, in which Fodor's individual modules are now viewed as the starting point for more complex networks that link noncontiguous areas (4–15; Mancing, *Voices*). Combining developmental theory and neuroscience, Gerald Edelman proposes "Neural Darwinism" as the key to early brain development. In this "use it or lose it" model, axons, dendrites, and synapses are strengthened to create the most powerful neuronal networks or "maps" in areas of the brain that are used extensively, while those that are underutilized whither away. These neuronal networks are not simply extended modules, because they interact with other networks (32–47; Mancing, *Voices*). All of the theories that have enriched and developed Fodor's modularity reinforce the tenet that consciousness derives from simultaneous or parallel and multifaceted nonconscious processes that provide the conscious mind with varied and even conflicting knowledges. Ellen Spolsky was among the first to use this cognitive model for literary analysis; her study *Gaps in Nature: Literary Interpretation and the Modular Mind* establishes a paradigm for applying Fodor, Jackendoff, and Edelman's insights to a wide variety of texts across genres and time periods. This model of multifaceted cognitive processes is particularly appropriate for exploration of the dense and complex representations of human thought processes found in early modern texts.

Contextualism and Early Modern Skepticism

The contextualist approach to cognitive functionality offers exciting new opportunities for analysis of philosophical skepticism as presented in early modern literature and culture. Spolsky uses the paradigm of modularity to explain the basis of skepticism as a philosophical system; she notes that this school is based upon the premise that sensory information is unreliable and often contradictory (*Gaps* 20–41). Spolsky attributes the conflicting information streams that skepticism highlights to the varying data provided to the conscious mind by different modules. She writes that for many early modern characters, quandaries about judgment and knowledge arise from "the multiplicity of knowledge itself" (*Satisfying* 80). For early modern tragic protagonists, embodied knowledge based upon personal interactions often diverges from data obtained by the senses, especially sight, "this state of brain affairs is the description of the skeptic's dilemma" (*Satisfying* 80). Tragic figures are often marked by an obsessive desire for perfect or complete knowledge, and early modern skeptical texts emphasize the lack of any such fully consistent epistemic ground.

For Spolsky, the modular brain provides an embodied explanation for a human cognitive plight and the related philosophical system that has re-arisen, phoenixlike, across more than two millennia (she identifies postmodernism as a current incarnation). Although such a model was not available to early modern skeptical philosophers, they were able nonetheless to create systems and narratives based on the human and social *manifestations* of a contextualist brain. The analysis of skepticism in this chapter seeks to break new ground on two fronts: in the consideration of epistemological processes as represented in early modern Spanish honor literature, and in demonstrating the relevance of the cognitive model of contextualism for studies of philosophical skepticism.

The re-emergence of philosophical skepticism in the sixteenth century is associated with Latin translations of the Pyrrhonian skeptic, Sextus Empiricus, published as early as 1520. His classic text, *Outlines of Pyrrhonism,* was available throughout Europe by the 1560s, and was widely read. Renaissance skepticism is an important turning point in human history, part of the general movement to seek out scientific explanations for "supernatural" phenomena as well as to feel comfortable with the discoveries of Copernicus and Galileo. José Raimundo Maia Neto cites one important factor in European acceptance of a pagan philosophy: French thinkers such as Foucher, Bayle, and Pascal all asserted that skepticism is the form of ancient philosophy that is most compatible with Christian beliefs (6–8). Richard Popkin explains that the basic tenet of Pyrrhonian skepticism, the most influential form of skepticism in the sixteenth century, is the rejection of Academic skepticism's belief that nothing at all can be known for certain because of the unreliability of sensory perception, and the resultant impossibility of establishing reliable criteria for judgment. Pyrrhonists emphasize the cultivation of an *attitude*, rather than the development of an epistemological statement. This attitude consists of an ability for "opposing evidence, both pro and con, on any question about what was non-evident, so that one would suspend judgment" on questions of truth and knowledge. The Pyrrhonic skeptical attitude entails reservations concerning the establishment of criteria for judgment, rather than an outright denial of any valid criterion (Popkin xv). This "attitude," based on awareness of contradictory sensory data, has affinities with the multiple information streams posited by the contemporary contextualist paradigm.

Cornelius Agrippa's "On Certainty, " published in Antwerp in 1530, was the first skeptical treatise written in the early modern period. Agrippa bases his rejection of the possibility of certain knowledge in his elaboration of the many scientific and religious issues on which qualified experts hold conflicting opinions (Chaudhuri 6). Sukanta Chaudhuri refers to the episode in Rabelais's *Tiers Livre* where Panurge hears totally antithetical opinions concerning his prospective marriage from authorities in different fields: theology, medicine, law, and philosophy, as a relevant example of the way that this skeptical tenet is adapted and circulated (15). Thus, Agrippa attributes contradictory knowledge to different sources, while contextualism credits this phenomenon to multifaceted neuronal networks.

Erasmus conveys a conventional skeptical attitude in his writings about the debates arising out of the Reformation. He expresses doubt concerning Luther's belief in human capacity to ascertain the one true meaning of the Bible (Popkin 6). Another skeptic, Francisco Sánches (a Portuguese *converso* who studied medicine in Toulouse and Rome) wrote the treatise "That Nothing Can Be Known" (1581), in which he abandons the Aristotelian "demonstrative" model of scientific inquiry in favor of development of a more precise methodology employing experimentation and empirical observation (D. Thompson 25; Popkin 41). Although Spain, as the home of the Counter Reformation, did not produce as much skeptical writing as other Western European nations, Erasmus's writings exercised substantial influence (Ihrie 26). Maureen Ihrie and Anthony Cascardi have identified a strong skeptical current in the writings of J. L. Vives and Pedro de Valencia, the court historian for Philip III (Ihrie 20–23; Cascardi, *Limits* 5–12). Although he was born in Portugal, Francisco Sánches is viewed as an important contributor to the history of Iberian skepticism (D. Thompson 28). However, even if Spain had produced no skeptical philosophers of its own, the widespread circulation of Continental and Latin skeptical texts during this period would have assured at least some familiarity with this movement. For example, Otis Green notes that Quevedo quotes Montaigne in the *Buscón* (II: 71). Maureen Ihrie, Anthony Cascardi, Barbara Mujica, and Henry Sullivan have published important books and essays concerning skepticism in the writings of Cervantes, Calderón, and Tirso (my own previous essays on this topic address Lope's and

Tirso's dramas). This study seeks to further their lines of inquiry in its analysis of the central role of the skeptical paradigm within early modern representations of honor conflicts and self-reflexive drama.

Although research in several different cognitive fields has shown Fodor's initial model of a modular mind to be incomplete, the new explanations expand upon rather than rejecting the modular theory's central proposition concerning the multiplicity of brain function. For this reason, Spolsky's argument about the modular mind and skepticism requires further development but need not be jettisoned. All of the later models share an underlying assumption that modules—or something like them—provide the building blocks for even more dynamic and interactive communication networks than Fodor originally proposed. However, none of these models contest the central assertion that cognitive processes are fluid, participatory, and complex. Thus, although Spolsky's citation of Fodor's modularity as the model of neurological processes has been superseded, subsequent developments in the field have confirmed the underlying premises that connect philosophical skepticism to contemporary cognitive theory. Thus, as the rest of this section will demonstrate, contemporary cognitive sciences that enrich our understanding of human mental processes can be used to explore and illuminate the functions of skepticism in early modern texts.

Skepticism and Female Honor

Spolsky emphasizes concerns about absolute knowledge of the female mind and its potential for true virtue as a key epistemological fault line where early modern literary characters apply skeptical modes of inquiry. She cites various written and visual reinscriptions of the Roman myth of the rape and subsequent suicide of Lucretia in the sixteenth century, as well as the plot line of a spouse who errs in believing his wife has been unfaithful as presented in *Othello* and Shakespeare's late tragicomedies, to illustrate this thesis ("Women's Work" 76; *Satisfying* 68). The protagonist of *Othello* experiences the typical "skeptical quandary" concerning whether or not his wife has betrayed him, because different modalities provide conflicting knowledges, and "multiple versions of reality, once produced, demand judgment and choices" (*Satisfying* 67).

Lies, misleading appearances, and a tortured imagination conflict with Othello's "experiential and bodily knowledge" of his wife's love and fidelity (*Satisfying* 78).

This very same scenario of scrutinized spousal fidelity is at the forefront of early modern Spanish honor literature; I will propose that, like Shakespeare, Calderón also presented conflicting modalities of cognition as the basis for his critique of the early modern obsession with honor and *fama* in *El médico de su honra*. María de Zayas's wife-murder novellas, such as "La más infame venganza" ("Infame"), highlight these same problematic cognitive paradigms but reinscribe them from a "pro woman" or proto-feminist perspective; she identifies epistemologic flaws in the honor code as a key factor in women's oppression (Soufas, "Feminist Approach" 127; Vollendorf, *Recovering* 10). The conflicting emotional and cognitive norms associated with male homosocial bonding and heterosexual marriage play an additional significant role in many honor texts (Sedgwick 1–6). I will use this perspective as a point of departure in order to explore the "El curioso impertinente" episode of *Don Quixote* and Zayas's "El verdugo de su esposa." Spolsky asserts that many honor dramas point to "the impossibility of knowing the things one most needs to know by seeing alone—by judging outward appearances" and suggests that in the late romances, Shakespeare chose tragicomedy as the genre that allows for an embodied knowledge that is "sufficiently satisfying so as to avoid the death of innocent women" ("Women's Work" 78). In early modern Spain, "tragicomic" resolutions to the skeptic's dilemma can be found in many honor plays, as well as in a few of the novellas in *Desengaños amorosos*. This chapter will explore Lope de Vega's *El animal de Hungría* and Zayas's "La inocencia castigada" and "La perseguida triunfante" as representative examples of the tragicomic solution. A comparative analysis of these tragic and tragicomic texts, which foreground the problem of how to evaluate complex and conflicting data about gender and honor, will enable a fuller appreciation of the homologies between early modern skepticisms and the current model of knowledge as derived from embodied, contextualist, and networked cognitive processes.

Hispanists have traced the outlines of the central quandaries in representations of the search for truth about wives and fidelity. Georgina Dopico Black notes that the virtue of *married* women emerges as a particularly thorny cognitive problem in Counter

Reformation Spain, because the experience of conjugal intimacy robs a woman both of her maidenhead and of the impression of virtue (19–25). Thus, at the same time that purity of blood lines is seen as crucial to aristocratic hegemony, there is no concrete marker to prove fidelity and hence the legitimacy and *limpieza* of offspring. Dopico Black hints at the epistemological issues that underlie honor drama, but because her book focuses on the obsession with chastity as a displacement for larger concerns with racial and religious purity, she does not develop this line of thought (20, 27, 112). Likewise, Ruth El Saffar points toward questions of knowledge, "the linguistic precision, the use of syllogistic reasoning, and the constant play with dualities, conceived as opposites, suggests ... an on-going longing for that elusive ever-absent cohesion" ("Anxiety" 118, cited in Blue, "*Médico*" 413). However, she asserts that the ground for truth will be found outside of the philosophical realm; in her psychoanalytic reading, it is "embodied in the figure of the father and the king. It is a cohesion, finally, that the child is required to invent out of his desire for it" ("Anxiety" 118, cited in Blue, "*Médico*" 413). Matthew Stroud's analysis of the neo-Stoic aspects of the epistemology in honor tragedies provides important background on early modern conceptualizations of obtaining and testing knowledge (*Fatal* 116–40). Cory Reed uses chaos theory to characterize early modern marriage as a "chaotic system" and uses this model to explore specific flaws in Gutierre's purportedly scientific investigation (29–31). Teresa Soufas's exploration of humoral theory in Calderonian honor tragedy also devotes attention to melancholia as a cause for distorted processing of evidence (*Melancholy* 197–201). The insights provided by cognitive theory supplement these findings and enable a more complete analysis of the cognitive processes depicted in honor literature.

Within the history of Hispanic literary criticism, the ideological content of honor drama has been among the most hotly debated topics. As Melveena McKendrick notes, "the traditional Hispanic mode of reading these plays, and those like them by other dramatists, saw the endings in the context of the plots as a whole as prescriptive exercises in male triumphalism" (217). In addition, feminist literary scholarship has emphasized the oppositional nature of honor drama's critique of the cultural obsession with women's chastity and the public honor with which it is associated (Vollendorf, *Reclaiming* 10; Yarbro-Bejarano 75).

Georgina Dopico Black notes that honor plays, due to their "migrating signs. … are plagued by semiotic instability that troubles the very notion of legibility or, indeed of epistemologic certainty" (20). Steven Wagschal's recent study *The Literature of Jealousy in the Age of Cervantes* provides an important introduction to the links between epistemology, jealousy, and honor (20–49). Analysis of honor drama's presentation of normative epistemological operations furthers the feminist project, highlighting the consistent undermining of the grounds for certainty about an area of human existence that is shown to be subject to pervasive misunderstandings. The cognitive model of the networked brain, through its illumination of the processes that give rise to skepticism as a philosophical model, provides additional support for the stance that many of the texts addressing the honor code do so from a distinctly critical perspective.

In her study of *Othello* and "The Rape of Lucrece," Spolsky notes that early modern literature often features suspicious husbands who doubt their wives and agonize over the "the universal skeptical dilemma of knowing whether available information is reliable" ("Women's Work" 78). Husbands typically limit the type of information concerning fidelity that is deemed worthy of consideration to that which can be perceived via visual or rational faculties; Spolsky asserts that one primary source of tragic outcomes is "Too great a faith that outward signs mirror inner truths"—that is to say, over-emphasizing the "rational" faculties of judgment and ignoring important alternate modes of emotional and embodied epistemology ("Women's Work" 78). Naomi Rokotnitz asserts a similar cognitive weakness on the part of Leontes in *A Winter's Tale*, who draws tragedy down upon himself because he loses "the ability to weigh the evidence presented by different modalities, inventing hypotheses that deepen his mistrust" (126). Calderón's *El médico de su honra* presents a similar cognitive world, in which a jealous male is ever-vigilant concerning female transgression and employs a similarly limited repertoire of tactics and modalities in his evaluation of evidence (López-Peláez Casellas 94–96).

Gutierre's Skeptical Dilemma: *El médico de su honra*

As Calderón's *El médico de su honra* opens, we see that the epistemology of honor has so distorted society that the female protagonist Mencía actually welcomes a potentially compromising situation—the reappearance of her former suitor, Prince Enrique. Yvonne Yarbro-Bejarano notes this same phenomenon in her analysis of gender conventions within Lope's honor plays about innocent wives (75–77). Because Mencía has complete faith in her own capacity to remain loyal, this test appears auspicious in the sense that it arises in circumstances where she feels competent to handle and defuse the threat. Further, she implies that in passing this particular test, she has a chance to definitively prove her virtue so that it will not be subject to future scrutiny

> y solamente me huelgo
> de tener hoy que sentir,
> por tener en mis deseos
> que vencer; pues no hay virtud
> sin experiencia. Perfeto
> está el oro en el crisol,
> el imán en el acero,
> el diamante en el diamante,
> los metales en el fuego;
> y así mi honor en sí mismo
> se acrisola, cuando llego
> a vencerme, pues no fuera
> sin experiencias perfecto. (I.140–52)

Mencía has internalized the value systems and cognitive norms of her society so completely that she takes no offense at the belief that women's honor is highly suspect and thus ever-subject to surveillance and interpretation (Carrión, "Burden" 450). What makes her situation particularly complex is that she seeks to prove herself before two different men; in addition to demonstrating her loyalty to her new husband, Gutierre, she also wishes to find a way to make Enrique understand that she abandoned him for valid and honorable reasons rather than because of typical female *mudanza*.

Even as she enters into the process of proving her virtue, Mencía is acutely aware of the inherent dangers. After listening to Enrique's remonstrance concerning her infidelity, her response is marked primarily by concern over how this accusation could be interpreted,

> Quien oyere a vuestra alteza
> quejas, agravios, desprecios,

> podrá formar de mi honor
> presunciones y concetos
> indignos de él; y yo agora,
> por si acaso llevó el viento
> cabal alguna razón,
> sin que en partidos acentos
> la troncase, responder
> a tantos agravios quiero,
> porque donde fueron quejas,
> vayan con el mismo aliento
> desengaños. (I.278–90)

As a woman intent on proving her innocence within a proscribed cognitive system, Mencía seeks to identify the words and actions that will provide the appropriate masculine enlightenment. The near impossibility of this goal is made manifest at the end of this speech, when she asks Enrique not to leave her house. Although she makes this request seeking to avoid the gossip that would ensue if the public witnessed a hasty departure on the part of her former lover, this utterance can—and will—be interpreted by a vigilant husband as proof of illicit desire. Mencía confronts a situation in which there is no available action that will enable her to soothe the suspicions of three separate audiences: Enrique, Gutierre, and the general public. This triple bind situation highlights the insufficiency of the normative evaluation techniques practiced in her social milieu.

The conventional practices for judging women's honor can easily be characterized as negligent. When the King interrogates Gutierre concerning the reason why he broke off his engagement to his former fiancée, Leonor, Gutierre explains that he saw a man leaving her house under cover of darkness and tried to follow him, but never found out who he was. Gutierre then describes the next—and final—step in his investigation,

> Y aunque escuché
> satisfacciones, y nunca
> di a mi agravio *entera fe*,
> fue bastante esta aprensión
> a no casarme. (I.922–26; emphasis added)

Gutierre characterizes the explanation he received as "satisfacciones" rather than using a pejorative term like excuses, lies, or falsehoods, and admits that he was not *entirely* certain of her guilt. Nonetheless, he believes that his decision-making process was valid—so much that he is willing to defend himself at sword point when Arias attacks him. When Gutierre finds himself alone at the end of this scene, about to be jailed for dueling before the King, the only regret he voices is that he will not return home to his wife that night. Within the context of this exploration of cognitive practices and literary critiques of the honor code, the King's judgment can be interpreted as a condemnation of Gutierre's perfunctory reasoning process.

The way that the King acts when presented with Leonor's story of an unjust abandonment supports the idea that he found Gutierre's investigation inadequate. Rather than taking her testimony at face value, he presents a model of careful judicial process as he seeks out Gutierre's perspective,

> Oigamos a la otra parte
> disculpas suyas; que es bien
> guardar el segundo oído
> para quien llega después (I.685–88)

In addition, the King also allows Arias to present additional pertinent information. By hearing from all relevant parties, this sovereign presents himself here as a model of careful and thorough adjudication, a role that he will reprise when investigating Mencía's death in the third act.

The second act opens with two scenes that reinforce women's powerlessness in the face of a masculine culture that is always ready to judge hastily and harshly. First, Enrique reminds Mencía that she dare not make a public protest against this renewed pursuit, because such occurrences always redound against the woman, "A ti misma te infamas" (II.1143–44). Then, when Gutierre arrives unexpectedly, Mencía behaves like the guilty protagonist of an infidelity comedy out of fear that she will be misjudged; she hides Enrique in her room and then uses the subterfuge of a supposed intruder to help him escape. Mencía defends this deception to her maid Jacinta,

> si yo no se lo dijera
> y Gutierre lo sintiera,
> la presunción era clara,

pues no se desengañara
de que yo cómplice era. (II.1350–54)

Further, she asserts that her desperate plight justifies the standard comic tactic of "engañar con la verdad"; in this situation Enrique can indeed be described as a thief, for he seeks to steal the *fama* that is a married woman's most valuable possession (II. 1358). The juxtaposition of a conventional device of comic emplotment within this drama of innocent virtue and potential tragedy underscores the fragility of women's reputations and lives in a culture where men are free to act against women upon the slightest of doubts, and where even women's attempts to defend themselves from pursuit are interpreted as markers of guilt. It is appropriate that this scene has been used to credit Calderón with sympathies that align with contemporary feminist discourse; however, it is likely that this pro-woman viewpoint is the by—product of the larger scrutiny of honor code norms, rather than an end in itself (Williamsen, "Fatal" 35).

Many scholars have noted that Gutierre does make a sustained effort to uncover the truth about Mencía's relationship with Enrique (Benabu; García Gómez; Honig; Johnston; O'Connor, "Interplay"; Ruiz Ramón; Stroud, *Fatal Union*; Soufas, "Calderón" and *Melancholy*; Wardropper. Feminist responses include Williamsen, "Fatal"; and McKendrick). Gutierre undertakes a step-by-step analysis of the evidence; the anaphoric use of "en cuanto a" to introduce each new piece of data contributes to the atmosphere of careful deliberation (II.1627–40). In a much-cited speech, Gutierre condemns the rigors of the honor code as an "injusta ley" (II.1661). He decides to test Mencía by entering his home secretly the next evening, to spy on her, in an effort to gather additional facts. Gutierre transforms Mencía's garden into both a stage and a laboratory, where she must perform and prove her fidelity without even being aware that she is being observed and tested. Unfortunately, the words that Mencía utters to discourage the man she believes to be the Infante are easy to misinterpret as evidence of infidelity. This scene demonstrates that because the honor code is so rigid, normal virtuous behavior is insufficiently convincing and elaborate demonstrations are necessary when doubts arise. Later, when the King asks Gutierre to hide behind a curtain so that both can gain insight concerning his brother's behavior, Gutierre misinterprets

Enrique's declaration of his own passion as further evidence of his wife's guilt.

As Gutierre began his judicial process, he consistently admitted exculpatory evidence, with each condemnatory "en cuanto" balanced by a mitigating "pero." Stroud questions the good faith of this effort, alleging that murderous husbands like Gutierre merely "wish to appear to be acting from reason rather than passion" (*Fatal Union* 137). However, as the second act concludes and the final curtain rises, Gutierre's rational process deteriorates and he ceases to look at both sides; he describes himself as overcome by rage: " Todo soy rabia, y todo fuego" (II.1950). Cory Reed astutely observes that,

> Gutierre may be a scientist, but he is not a very good one. In many ways, he is presented as a figure of the emerging Western scientist, an intellectual who relies on reason in his attempt to discern orderly and predictable behavior in the world around him. But Calderón shows that such unquestioned reliance on determinism and logic can result in an incorrect or incomplete analysis, particularly when the imagination is detached from reality. Gutierre is thus both part of the emergent empiricism of his times and a parody of it. (34)

Spolsky and Rokotnitz also highlight this tendency to prioritize the wrong kinds of data in their studies of husbands in Shakespearean drama. In early modern European dramatic texts, husbands consistently emphasize the types of evidence that validate suspicions of spousal transgression and ignore the embodied evidence of their own marital experience (Spolsky, *Satisfying* 83; Rokotnitz 124). Gutierre even concedes that his suspicions are partly a result of his own obsessive nature; when the King asks at the beginning of Act II exactly what his subject has seen that would provoke suspicion, the jealous husband describes his cognitive process as defective:

> Nada; que hombres como yo
> no ven. Basta que imaginen,
> que sospechen, que prevengan,
> que recelen, que adivinen,
> que ... no sé como lo diga;
> que no hay voz que signifique

una cosa, que no sea
un átomo indivisible. (III.2927–34)

Blue notes that, as Gutierre's obsession deepens, he compromises his own integrity,

> Whereas in Act I, Mencía was duplicitous and Gutierre straightforward, from Act II on, Mencía insists on and believes in the innocence of her words and acts, while Gutierre believes her to be duplicitous and guilty. Whereas Mencía spoke duplicitously in Act I, Gutierre spoke literally. From Act II on, Mencía believes she speaks literally while Gutierre becomes more and more adept at double-talk. ("*Médico*" 412)

Calderón further complicates the matter by providing a rival whom the faithful wife may indeed love; although she commits no immoral physical act, in an honor-grounded society even "lust in the heart" is transgressive.

The multiple significances of the final scene of this tragedy have received sustained and thoughtful critical attention. One topic of dissent has been how to interpret the King's mandate that Gutierre must marry Leonor (Fox 72; Benabu 20–23). Soufas depicts the monarch as an unreliable arbiter, because he like Gutierre suffers from melancholia ("Calderón" 195). Cory Reed sees Pedro's problematic decision as an "emblem of the unstable order in the play" (34). King Pedro's declaration, "es tiempo que satisfaga / vuestro valor lo que debe," can be seen as an indication that Gutierre owes reparation to Leonor. This coerced union has been viewed as a form of "punishment" (Stroud, *Fatal Union* 61; McKendrick 227). If the marriage to Leonor is indeed a punishment, as the denial of Gutierre's request for a period of mourning would imply, his crime lies at least partially in the cognitive realm. The final lines of the play remind the audience of the earlier scene in which Pedro determined Leonor's innocence through a very thorough investigation involving multiple witnesses. As Gutierre presents the King with a series of potentially incriminating events that he might face in the future, Pedro counters each with advice that implies a multifaceted and careful approach, beginning with "no dar crédito a sospechas," and being cautious with informers who might have a bias, such as servants that may be bribed, as well as seeking support from authorities (III.2904–20). Most importantly, the king urges faith in a spouse who shows herself to be "una constante muralla," thus granting credence to embodied knowledge (III.2923).

In this context, I believe that excess attention has been focused on the very last observation the King makes, which appears to accept uxoricide as a remedy, at the expense of the contradictory position described here (III.2931). The lengthy exchange, in which Gutierre suggests a series of scenarios that mirror all of the misleading incriminations against Leonor and Mencía, highlights the need for care and prudence rather than condoning a hasty application of vengeful violence. King Pedro's advice for suspicious husbands combines rational thought, understanding of social interactions, and emotional intelligence; this approach is consistent with early modern skeptical practice as well as the networked thought processes of contextualist and embodied cognition. However, although the King's observations are correct, he did not act in any meaningful way to prevent Mencía's death and Gutierre's punishment is negligible compared to the cold comforts of the grave. Amy Williamsen ("Fatal") and Melveena McKendrick have offered sustained feminist readings of the deficiencies in male application of the honor code in this play; the insights of cognitive contextualism provide an additional perspective concerning patriarchal modes of judgment.

Cognition and Curiosity in Cervantes

The Cervantine reinscription of literary codes of honor and masculine friendship in the interpolated novella "El curioso impertinente," has been studied exhaustively; analysis of epistemological issues has also flourished in recent years. Explorations of male friendship begin, of course, with Girard's model of mimetic desire; important studies of "El curioso" include those of Ayala, Jehenson, Kaplan, and Gil-Oslé. Epistemological approaches to this episode include Avalle-Arce and recent essays by Michael Gerli and David Arbesú Fernández. (See also Wagschal's study of jealousy in early modern texts.) My goal in this section is not to offer a comprehensive new reading, but to relate existing scholarship to the contextualist paradigm. In this short tale, Cervantes explores the relations between knowledge and the honor code through a multigeneric extravaganza. The text begins with a ludicrous pseudo-scientific proposal and presents the initial heroic loyalty of friend and spouse, develops the plot into a cloak-and-dagger comedy of betrayal and deception, descends into bitter farce as Camila stages a Lucretia-like scene of heroic resistance to convince her husband of her continued fidelity, and concludes with the deaths of all three protagonists. Howard Mancing uses Jerome Bruner's binary model of logical and narrative cognition to assert that Cervantes gives priority to the "narrative logic" that Camila provides in the second half of the novella. Mancing posits that her narrative logic overwhelms the conventional formal logical processes that the male protagonist deploys in devising the test of his wife's virtue ("Camila" 9–11). His demystification of the myth of storytelling as a degraded, feminine form of knowledge akin to gossip is an important insight for evaluating the cultural gendering of cognitive modes. Alison Krueger also depicts the novella as a comparison of differing cognitive modalities, "authority, reason and experience"—but concludes that the novella does not in fact support any of the three. Rather, Krueger explains, Cervantes presents detailed depictions of each modality in order to highlight the respective limitations (164). Viewing this episode through the lens of contextualist cognition, both the narrative logic that Mancing proposes and the empirical mode that Krueger describes are antecedents or complements to the embodied knowledge paradigm of cognitive theory. And, although Mancing is correct that Camila's narrative logic is presented as superior to conventional rationalist processes, Krueger is also persuasive in her observation that no single cognitive force proves adequate to bringing about a positive outcome. Camila's narrative logic does enable her to take the upper hand in the situation that has been forced upon her, but does not enable her to fashion a happy ending for herself. Nonetheless, I do not agree that this conclusion constitutes the nihilism that Krueger purports; rather, the novella highlights the importance of employing all available modes of epistemological inquiry because no single method is sufficient unto itself. Rather than pointing toward a pessimistic nihilism, this representation of all models of knowledge as partial and provisionary corresponds to the skeptical paradigm of early modernity that Maureen Ihrie has proposed as a central component of Cervantes's philosophical framework. This novella scrutinizes honor literature from multiple perspectives, calling into question conventions of gender, genre, and epistemology. The series of shifts in tone and genre arise in conjunction with the proliferation of conflicting forms of evidence provided by the different modalities within a complex neural network. This depiction of knowledge as multiple and fragmented, as rational and embodied, is consonant with the contextualist cognitive paradigm.

Cognitive Malpractice and Wife Murder in Zayas's Novellas

María de Zayas also focuses upon cognition in her tragic tales of marriage and honor. *Desengaños amorosos* presents ten novellas within a frame tale that depicts a literary *sarao* as part of the festivities before a wedding. Important early analyses of feminist reinscription and the representation of female characters in the novella collection can be found in the introductions to Patsy Boyer's translation and Alicia Yllera's critical edition and in early studies by Ordóñez, Foa, and Maroto Camino. The anthology *María de Zayas: The Dynamics of Discourse*, edited by Amy Williamsen and Judith Whitenack, also contributed significant feminist studies of the novellas. More recent books by Lisa Vollendorf, Yolanda Gamboa Tusquets, Marina Brownlee, and Margaret Greer have provided extended and complex interdisciplinary and historicized analyses of gender dynamics in the novellas. The study of embodied and gendered cognition offered here complements these approaches. Zayas's portrait of the way that a typical husband evaluates his wife's virtue does coincide with Calderón's depiction of Gutierre; not in his lengthy deliberation of the evidence against Mencía, but rather in his swift and careless condemnation of Leonor in the absence of solid evidence. Her feminist analysis of the shortcomings in the honor code emphasizes lack of male interest in determining the truth about their wives' chastity.

In "La más infame venganza," Zayas condemns not only rash and hasty judgments, but also the masculine obsession with public opinion, which leads them to value appearances over truth. In this novella, Juan pursues and then rapes Camila, because he seeks to avenge himself of an *agravio* that Camila's husband, Carlos, has committed against Juan's sister. A Milanese official who is also her husband's own father investigates the case and proclaims Camila's complete innocence, "no había sido su agravio"; he also accepts that Camila's silence about Juan's pursuit is due to her "recato y retiro" as well as fear of harming Carlos's reputation (194).

Nonetheless, Carlos is determined to be rid of her because Juan has publicized the rape as the culmination of his revenge; Camila suffers a horrible and lingering death because her husband botches his effort at poisoning her (195). In presenting the spousal judgment process, Zayas does not present even a single moment where Carlos engages in deliberation about how to react to the unfortunate scandal. This type of thoughtless attack against an innocent woman will be repeated several times in other novellas.

In many of the *desengaños*, Zayas devotes intense scrutiny to the cognitive processes associated with evaluation of honor cases. Within the tale itself, the narrator discusses the public reaction to the rape; she notes that the verdict was mixed, with some pardoning Camila, some blaming her because she failed to inform her husband that Juan had pursued her before resorting to rape when she rejected him, while others asserted that even in a case of unprovoked rape "no quedaba Carlos con honor si no la mataba" (194). Throughout the entire book, the frame tale foregrounds the discussions about marriage and honor among the participants of the *sarao*. In reacting to this novella, opinion is divided among the "real life" guests, just as it was among the Milanese public; Isabel argues that Camila bears "alguna culpa" because telling Carlos about Juan's advances might have prevented the rape (Brownlee 138). However, Lisis vehemently denounces the suggestion that telling Carlos would have been appropriate,

> no sé qué mujer hubiera en el mundo tan necia que se atreva a decirle a su marido que ningún galán la pretende, pues se pueden seguir de muchos riesgos, y el mayor es si está un hombre seguro de celos, despertarle para que los tenga y no viva seguro de su mujer. (196)

Lisis, the bride-to-be and sponsor of the festivities, notes that a predisposition to jealousy is an important cognitive attribute, in the sense that this emotion obliterates other modes of knowledge and thus limits masculine ability to evaluate evidence correctly. Lisis weighs the relative merits of both cases, pointing to additional factors such as Camila's repeated rejections of Juan and the fact that Carlos had previously abandoned Juan's sister, Octavia—an indication that Carlos is fickle and for this reason might be happy to have an excuse to get rid of Camila. Lisis thus takes into account the embodied knowledge that derives from deep knowledge of a person's character as he or she behaves over an extended period of time. After performing a carefully constructed deliberation, she determines that the death sentence was unjust. Lisis is given the last word in the narrative frame as an implicit affirmation of her cognitive process; Ruth El Saffar has posited that this protagonist serves as alter ego for Zayas herself ("Ana/Lysis" 192–95). Where Calderón contrasts the decision-making procedures of a rational monarch and a thoughtful although excessively suspicious husband, Zayas presents a husband who cares about *fama* rather than truth, juxtaposed with the more careful and complete judgment process of the female protagonist of the frame tale.

In "Mal presagio casar lejos" and "Estragos que causa el vicio," Zayas focuses upon wife murders committed in the heat of unfounded jealous rages. In the first tale, two sisters are killed by their husbands at the very moment that a potentially compromising situation first arises. These two uxoricides do not even involve the heroine, Blanca; they are merely the "backdrop" for the far more brutal murder she later endures. In the tale that closes the collection, "Estragos," Dionís also kills his wife the moment that he sees a male servant leave her bedroom. He begins to deliver sword thrusts without uttering a single word, and this silence prevents Magdalena from offering any sort of defense: "le tendió en el suelo, sin poder decir más que '¡Jesús sea conmigo!'" (496). Throughout the ten *desengaños*, husbands routinely attempt to kill their wives upon the slightest hint of scandal or in the heat of reactive rage; cool-headed investigation is not deemed necessary because every accusation of infidelity merely confirms the many forms of cultural discourse that predict rampant female wantonness. Zayas further undermines the validity of such discourses by presenting several unfaithful men; in addition to Carlos's fickleness as cited above, Dionís is himself guilty of adultery and has just left his lover's bed at the moment he kills his wife.

Zayas's "El verdugo de su esposa," like Cervantes's "El curioso impertinente," begins with a description of the bond between "dos amigos" that is disturbed when one of them marries (200–02). Zayas depicts Don Pedro as suffering the same regrets that Anselmo had lamented, once he realizes that his best friend can no longer be his inseparable companion due to fear of gossip about his wife Rosaleta's virtue. But, where Anselmo provided the spark for the love triangle by asking his friend to test his wife's virtue,

Pedro merely provides the matches and kindling of opportunity by insisting that Juan dine with him and his new bride on a regular basis. As in Cervantes's tale, it is the male friend who is first to cede to passion; like Lotario, Juan ignores all the laws of male bonding to pursue the forbidden female. However, Zayas goes even further than Cervantes in rejecting the truth value of conventions of ideal male friendship, for Juan does not attempt in any way to resist the passion that he feels for Rosaleta out of respect for his bond with Pedro. Rather, pursuit follows immediately upon the awakening of desire. In addition, Juan laughs off Rosaleta's threat to inform Pedro, because giving voice to such an accusation is a form of social suicide; even when a woman is innocent, any intimation of impropriety nonetheless tarnishes her honor. More importantly, Zayas depicts Rosaleta as a far more perfect wife than Camila. Where Cervantes critiques the ideas that women are likely to initiate illicit relations if they are alone with a man, and that they will succumb easily to any suitor that presents himself, he falls short of presenting Camila as a true Penelope or Lucretia figure. Zayas does take that extra step; Rosaleta is adamant in her complete fidelity and even places herself in jeopardy by telling her husband of his friend's untoward actions. In these circumstances, Pedro faces a unique dilemma. Most honor plays involve a husband who must ponder conflicting evidence concerning his wife's chastity; Pedro instead is presented with incontrovertible proof that his dearest friend has committed an unpardonable transgression against his honor.

In this tale, Zayas emphasizes the ways that gender influences modalities of knowledge. As demonstrated above, she regularly presents male characters who react with immediate and unthinking violence in the face of possible marital infidelity. But when Pedro faces betrayal by a beloved male, his rage cools quickly, "Ya la cólera no le daba lugar a aguardar tiempo para su venganza, y ya el amor que a don Juan tenía le atajaba tomarla" (212). Thus, although Pedro does formulate and attempt to carry out a plan to kill Juan, he does not appear terribly disappointed when he learns of his friend's miraculous rescue at the hands of the Virgin. Instead, when Juan reappears, Pedro allows him to apologize and retreat to a monastery rather than make another attempt to avenge himself. In relations among men, emotional intelligence serves as a mitigating force, allowing tempers to cool and pity or empathy to replace furor. This aspect of contextualist cognition is either absent or easily subordinated in canonical literary representations of marriage and honor.

The discrepancy in masculine evaluations of accusations about male and female disloyalty is readily apparent in "El verdugo." The narrator of this tale interrupts herself after Juan completes his explanation of his own guilt and Rosaleta's perfect loyalty to observe, "Bien pensaréis, señores, que estos prodigios sucesos serían causa para que don Pedro estimase y quisiese más a su esposa" (219). However, when Angeliana, a woman that Juan had courted previously, tells Pedro that Rosaleta did indeed have an affair with Juan, Pedro readily believes her lies. He does not take any action to investigate the details of this accusation: that the letter to Rosaleta from Juan complaining of the disdain that Rosaleta had shown him came from the earliest moments of Juan's pursuit; that his wife had resisted only briefly before giving in; that she told Pedro as a form of vengeance when Juan abandoned her to court Angeliana. The narrator attributes Pedro's cognitive error to two possible factors; either the impact of the honor code, because the story has become public and hence caused Pedro to turn against Rosaleta, or masculine inconstancy, which leads men to want to believe the worst of their wives so that they have justification for killing them and moving on to the next pretty face. These are the same forms of evidence that Lisis had pointed to during her examination of Carlos's motivations in the frame tale discussion following "Infame." The repeated assertions of masculine *mudanza* offers a definition of essential male character that is the polar opposite of patriarchal norms, turning on its head the honor code dictum that it is the degraded *feminine* nature that must be under constant surveillance because of an innate tendency to seek novelty (see Chapter 2 for an exploration of cognitive theories of male infidelity and neophilia).

In "El verdugo" Zayas presents a portrait of masculine reasoning and mental processing that completely contradicts the canonical honor dramas. Where Gutierre devoted several soliloquies to pondering evidence about Mencía, Pedro hesitates only when his male friend is implicated. The manner in which he kills his wife, by untying the bandage after Rosaleta has been bled due to an illness, distinctly evokes Mencía's unjust fate. But, where Calderón had attacked the honor code by evoking sympathy for the suffering that both husband and wife endure, Zayas emphasizes the complete lack of humanity on Pedro's part. She devotes two full paragraphs to laying bare the hypocrisy of the public face of sorrow that Pedro displays, mocking his "lágrimas falsas" and "extremos" (221). Zayas also emphasizes the public evaluation of Pedro's veracity; although his feigned grief initially convinces, "en muchos acreditaba sentimientos," his subsequent behavior speaks louder than any performance (221). As the months pass and Pedro courts and then marries Angeliana, a public consensus emerges that he did indeed kill his wife, but there is no investigation, because "no se podía averigüar" (222). Zayas's final indictment of the epistemological system underlying the honor code is that too little effort is dedicated to finding out the truth in cases of uxoricide. There is gossip but no judicial consequences, "paró solo en murmurarlo" (222). When honor is questioned, women are damned by the power of rumor and the indifference to embodied truth on the part of spouses, the judicial system, and the general public.

As she had done in "Infame," Zayas dedicates significant attention in "El verdugo" to debates concerning gender and honor, both within the narrative itself as well as in the frame tale. These discussions highlight vast disparities in how honor cases are judged. Here, the narrator Nise reports on the public reaction to the story of Rosaleta and Pedro in their hometown of Palermo. One controversy addresses whether or not Pedro's *attempt* to kill Juan was sufficient or if actual bloodshed is necessary to truly cleanse his honor. Another topic is "la honestidad de Rosaleta, diciendo si había sido o no; y juzgando si le movió diferentes accidentes que la honestidad a avisar a su marido de las pretensiones de Juan" (219). This discussion demonstrates the "double bind" married women face; the general public and the typical husband alike question their motivations both when they report an affront and when they keep silent. When every possible course of action is interpreted as evidence of guilt, then an accused wife is left with no means to demonstrate her innocence. This is a clear indication of a serious flaw in the cultural conventions of evaluation and judgment. In addition, fragmented public opinion can also be attributed to contradictory forms of knowledge—the discrepancy between Pedro's embodied narrative of ideal wifely virtue and normative social discourses of female vice.

Within "El verdugo," the narrator Nise gives no indication of a connection between the gender of the Palermo residents in the tale and their evaluations. However, the notion of gender-based and biased forms of cognition does arise in the frame tale segment that follows the conclusion of Nise's story. The omniscient narrator who conveys the discussions that take place at the *sarao* explicitly points out that the assignment of blame concerning Roseleta's death is divided along gender lines, "Los caballeros le disculparon [a Pedro], alegando que un marido ... no está obligado a averigüar nada" (223). On the contrary, "las damas decían lo contrario" and chastised Pedro for his complete lack of critical acumen. The female listeners assert that Pedro should have realized that statements concerning his wife, when uttered by a woman who was pursuing him and wanted to marry him, would be completely unreliable (Zayas, *Desengaños amorosos* 223; Williamsen, "Challenging" 145). These women hold high expectations concerning the cognitive obligations of husbands, expecting men to employ embodied knowledge of how people behave in common social situations. Across all ten novellas in *Desengaños amorosos*, Zayas lays bare the inconsistency in a society where masculine power and female marginalization are grounded in assertions of superior male intellect, but where men set a very low standard for the cognitive responsibilities of their peers in honor cases.

Satisfied Skepticism: Lope's *El animal de Hungría*

Shakespeare's tragicomic late romances offer a new angle from which to scrutinize the relationship between knowledge and public honor. In those late plays, the husband's murderous impulse is not actually carried through, so that reconciliation may occur at a later date. In her analysis of *Cymbeline*, Spolsky asserts that "by retelling the story of the wife suspected of adultery as a tragicomedy, Shakespeare was able to employ a set of conventions by means of which the audience could be satisfied that it can know what it needs to know" ("Women's Work" 78). In these situations, spouse and audience alike abandon the pursuit of absolute certainty in favor of an attitude that Rokotnitz characterizes as "prudent skepticism" (127). Rokotnitz traces a similar cognitive shift in *The Winter's Tale,* as characters move away from over-emphasis on reason and visual perception as the ground for knowledge and toward a valorization of the embodied modalities of "emotional intelligence" (127). Rokotnitz astutely notes that it is the female characters Paulina and Camila who provide the role models for a more balanced cognitive process (127). Lope de Vega's little-studied honor drama *El animal de Hungría* also presents a similar pattern of failed murder and eventual tragicomic reconciliation (Yarbro-Bejarano 17–20).

Unlike Shakespearean and Calderonian honor drama, *El animal de Hungría* does not stage the crucial scenes where a husband scrutinizes and wrongly condemns his wife for an imagined affair. The English plays regularly devote several scenes to the husband's growing doubts about his wife's fidelity and final decision to avenge his honor. Instead, Lope's play opens with a scene in which the already exiled Queen of Hungary, Teodosia, recounts the tale of unjust suspicion and narrow escape from a death sentence in order to explain her existence as a "monstruo" (12). Lope dedicates less than a page to a narration of how the Queen's sister had fallen in love with her husband and subsequently fabricated a fictitious rival and false evidence in order to deceive the King and induce him to eliminate his wife. Lope dispenses of the entire epistemological enterprise with a recitation that lasts just a few lines, "Creyólo el rey, que era fácil / y porque vio contrahechas / algunas cartas, o acaso / porque ya adoraba en ella" (12). Here, Lope depicts a man, both husband and monarch, who shows little interest in determining the truth. The first act does not devote any sustained attention to cognitive acts, describing instead the way that Teodosia sustains herself in the forest through her enactment of a strange wild creature in order to maintain the belief that she has perished and hence avoid further attacks. The second act scrutinizes the process by which Rosaura, who is raised in the wild by Teodosia, learns the rules of civilization. In the scenes of adolescent education, the emphasis is on the formation of moral reasoning rather than on epistemology.

In Shakespearean tragicomedy, the misguided husbands occasionally lament their lost wives and thus prepare the grounds for their return and final reconciliation. However, as the third act of Lope's play opens, the King continues to stand by the hurried pronouncement he made over a decade earlier. When Teodosia, disguised as a laborer, informs him that there has been "murmuración" because of his hasty remarriage, he dismisses out of hand the opinion of "el vulgo ciego" and insists, that "tengo satisfacción de la justicia que tuve" (96–97). He shows no inclination at all to reconsider his earlier decision-making procedures. In addition, when presented with the case of Felipe, a disguised nobleman who killed a peasant in order defend the "monster's child," the King continues to rely on standard judicial practice, "Dios quiso que hubiese muerte / para castigar la culpa. Yo firmo lo que es razón" (104). The young monster, in actuality Rosaura, the daughter whom Teodosia had kidnapped and raised in the wild, offers instead a contextualized analysis. She rejects unthinking adherence to the law as "injusta inclinación" and proclaims that in "siguiendo mi natural" the correct verdict would be to punish the peasant who had initiated all the troubles, rather than her protector (and lover) (104). After the King witnesses Rosaura's profound abjection in the face of the death sentence, he concedes that the situation "me entristece" but this emotional response does not alter his verdict (105). Rosaura's critique is especially noteworthy because, throughout the second act, as she reaches adolescence and comes into contact with other humans for the first time, she has been represented as the incarnation of natural innocence, purity, and instinctive wisdom. The scenes between mother and daughter dramatize both her innate virtue and her intellect as she studies and questions the norms of court society; the drama thus characterizes embodied cognition as a positive force, intimately connected with essential and uncorrupted human nature.

In the final scenes of the play, when the machinations of Teodosia's sister Faustina are uncovered, Lope provides a detailed—although belated—account of the procedures a husband should undertake when examining an allegation of betrayal. First, the very tardy arrival of Teodosia's father (the King of England), and her supposed suitor, the Prince of Scotland, sheds new light upon the alleged adultery. The King accepts as decisive evidence the testimony of the Prince that there was no amorous activity, and the declaration by Teodosia's father that his elder daughter had always been considered "santa." He gives voice to a sentimentalized *anagnorisis* and remorse "ya estoy / llorando lágrimas tiernas" (122). Upon receiving a letter about his wife's scheme to poison him and marry the court official who had helped her to frame Teodosia, in order to keep the throne, the Hungarian King does not react with unthinking rage. Instead he arranges for a test; thus, when he informs the English King of his younger daughter's perfidy, he is able to substantiate his claim with evidence, "Hice al veneno la prueba / y hallé ser todo verdad" (121). Even after two decisive demonstrations of Faustina's guilt, her husband does not give in to furor and order an immediate execution as he had done previously with Teodosia. This new prudence makes possible a tragicomic ending in which none of the major characters dies.

Yet even in the final scene, discretion is still somewhat lacking. When Teodosia, still disguised as a peasant, reveals that there is a legitimate heir to the throne, because the "animal" is actually the King's long lost daughter, the two kings do not immediately believe "him." However, their doubt is related not to his evidence but to his subject position; villanos, like wives, are assumed to have ulterior motives that nullify the possibility of truth-telling. For this reason, the monarchs do not follow the cognitive process for confirming the identity of a lost child that is standard for comic *anagnorisis* and reconciliation; they do not ask about birth tokens or examine her face for family resemblance. This failure stands in direct contrast to a scene earlier in this very same act, where the true identity of Felipe, the heir to the Spanish throne, was validated by using these two pieces of data. Instead, the peasant is denounced as "ambicioso" and it is agreed that the only way to test his honesty is via *torture*. Further, the kings declare that only a miracle, such as validation by a resuscitated Teodosia, could convince them. Comparing this reaction with the ready acceptance of the Scottish prince's words highlights the class-based discrepancy. It is deeply ironic that Teodosia, whose testimony of her own innocence was completely ignored in the first scene, is declared the only arbiter of truth in the final one. Only after she has become a quasi-martryr and saint do the monarchs grant cognitive force to a woman's words.

In the denouement, Teodosia offers one final corrective to the norms of tragic honor drama: even though her sister has been proven guilty of deceit, infidelity, and attempted murder, she will not reconcile with her husband unless Faustina is allowed to retreat to a convent. Here, Lope rejects the cultural norms that punish women with death for infractions of the honor code. If the King can be pardoned for his negligent judgments and the unjust death sentence he had placed upon his innocent wife, then Faustina also merits a chance at redemption. In this case, embodied knowledge produces mercy for all; contextualized cognition is thus superior not only in purely epistemological terms but also from a Christian perspective.

In tragic honor dramas, Shakespeare and Calderón devote intense scrutiny to the careful but nonetheless flawed process by which a man arrives at the erroneous conclusion that his wife is an adulteress. In her tragic novellas, Zayas grounds her feminist critique of the honor code in the assertion that men do not engage in any such cognitive effort but instead rush to form ill-founded conclusions. I believe that both approaches serve to question the legitimacy of the honor code by placing in doubt the validity of the available mechanisms for determining female fidelity. Although Lope's depiction of the King's reasoning process is reduced to the rather generic observation "era fácil," this initial condemnation does not lead to a sustained exploration of how men do—or should—judge their wives. Instead, Lope presents a sprawling, adventure-filled drama in which Teodosia performs a series of valorous (*varonil*) acts that, although unrelated to physical chastity, nonetheless mark her as a virtuous person. Lope thus introduces a third possible approach to questioning the validity of honor killings, by presenting a number of highly visible and measurable signs that a husband could use when attempting to determine his wife's loyalty in the face of accusations, rumor, or an ambiguous piece of evidence such as a letter or conversation. The process this play presents, which involves taking into account the entirety of a person's actions and character over time, is homologous to the paradigm of embodied contextualist knowledge. The emphasis upon the need for careful processes of knowledge gathering and evaluation, a prominent feature in the final scenes, provides the necessary rational complement. The concluding act stages a combination of emotional and logical intelligences that enables the characters in *El animal de Hungría* to avoid the consequences of tragic misunderstandings and to reach Spolsky's "satisfying" level of knowledge.

Too Good to Be True: Zayas Deconstructs Happy Endings

In the novellas "La inocencia castigada" and "La perseguida triunfante," María de Zayas also uses the model of mixed genres and multiple cognitive modalities in order to create a narrative in which a falsely accused wife narrowly (and implausibly) escapes from unjust punishment. However, where the male dramatist envisions a tragicomic world in which the wronged wives reconcile with their would-be murderers, the *autora* creates instead a form of hagiography in which the wife enters a convent and leads an exemplary, even saintly, monastic life (Greer, *Baroque* 144; Grieve 86–88). I will show that these modifications of the tragicomic model serve two functions: they highlight the aristocratic masculine cognitive process as inherently flawed and also provide a plot arc that allows a more certain knowledge of women's virtue.

"La inocencia castigada" features an honor narrative that is similar to the Lucretia motif, in that Inés, the chaste wife, engages in adulterous but nonetheless blameless sexual activity. She is courted by the *galán* Don Diego, who refuses to give up in the face of consistent rejection. Instead, he consults a Moorish wizard for magical assistance, and receives a voodoo doll and an enchanted candle that enable him to summon Inés to his bedside. Zayas takes care to highlight that sexual acts performed under these circumstances do not constitute infidelity. The woman does not actually engage in sexual activity but behaves like a robotic sleepwalker:

> Inés estaba fuera de su sentido con el mal encanto, y que no teniá facultad para hablar, teniendo aquellos, aunque favores, por muertos, conociendo claro que si la dama estuviera en su juicio, no se los hiciera, que era verdad, que antes pasara por muerte. (277–78)

Zayas further reinforces her innocence and noncooperation in noting that Diego does not enjoy his ill-gotten favors as much as he had hoped because Inés is so passive, and he is left feeling "algo pesaroso" (277). Vollendorf very aptly characterizes Diego's coercive behavior as a form of rape, thus underlining the connection to the Lucretia tale; Whitenack's use of the term *necrophilia* is another valid analogy for this involuntary sexual act (Volendorf, *Reclaiming* 152; Whitenack 175). Inés further reinforces her virtue in her reaction to these events, which she interprets as nightmares; she is wracked by guilt and seeks guidance from her confessor over what seem to be merely mental acts. Taking into account the wisdom derived from embodied knowledge, both narrator and seducer are in agreement with contemporary feminist scholarship; despite her activity in another man's bed, Inés is not guilty of willful and active infidelity.

The next segment of the novella widens the cognitive framework by establishing Inés's innocence within the rational discourses of patriarchal law. The magistrate who investigates the case performs the rite with candle and waxen image repeatedly in order to be sure that this is the true cause of her acts and ultimately declares that her innocence is "averiguado" (281). Inés herself continues to uphold her image as a model wife, asking for death because "aunque sin su voluntad, había manchado su honor" (281). Publicly, her brother Francisco upholds rational thought, rejecting any such vengeance and assuring her that "no erais parte para no hacerle" (281). However, all of the males in Inés's orbit, family and husband alike, care more about the shame associated with public knowledge of the affair than with the truth or her victimhood. Their reactions are described as counter-rational: "loco de pena" and "en lo interior estaba vertiendo pozoña y crueldad" (281). Despite the official judgment of the magistrate, her husband and brother ignore all legal and embodied evidence and fall back on the misogynist cultural truisms concerning flawed female nature in order to determine that Inés must have been feigning the enchantment "por quedar libre de su culpa" and thus deserves punishment (282). The men's desire to alleviate the humiliating gossip influences their cognitive processes more strongly than the relative validity of the multiple forms of evaluation available. The narrator, Laura, emphasizes that male authors bear significant responsibility for propagating this erroneous view of women, "escriben libros y componen comedias, alcanzándolo todo en seguir la opinión del vulgacho, que en común da la culpa de todos los malos sucesos a las mujeres" (290). In such circumstances, the search for truth among contradictory modalities is not governed by a desire for the clearest and best knowledge. Rather, Inés's family members favor the discourse and modality that will enable them to cover up an inconvenient truth. As seen above, Spolsky characterizes dramatized wife murders as the result of an inappropriate obsession with absolute knowledge. This analysis is appropriate to the cognitive deliberations of the Shakespearean play, in which Othello makes a good faith, if ultimately flawed, attempt to know the facts about Desdemona. Zayas, however, presents an alternative model of masculine thought, in which sincerity is abandoned and the skeptical mentality is deliberately misused for the sake of expedience.

This novella emphasizes (or exaggerates) the total lack of reason in masculine response to public dishonor. The act of incarcerating Inés in a tiny closet where she spends six years, standing upright in her own bodily wastes, goes beyond any sort of rational adjudication and approaches torture or martyrdom (Williamsen, "Challenging" 142; Vollendorf, *Reclaiming* 154). Ironically, it is this inhumane and "grotesque" sentence, whose purpose is described as a desire to prolong her punishment "por que no muriese tan presto," that enables a nontragic denouement (Vollendorf, *Reclaiming* 155; Zayas 383).

Just as in Shakespeare's romances, and in *El animal de Hungría*, there is a demonstrable lack of verisimilitude in the happy ending, both in the wife's survival of a harrowing ordeal and in the quasi-apotheistic rescue. However, Zayas's projection of what occurs after a wronged wife regains her freedom is far more plausible than the Bard's or Lope's. The possibility of reconciliation is not even raised; rather, the guilty family members are executed for their heinous crime. The novella emphasizes Inés's innate goodness in the closing pages; her first act upon being rescued is to ask for holy communion, and the narrator assures the salon audience that she lives on to their very day in a convent, "haciendo vida de una santa" (288). Inés's eventual triumph over her persecutors, as facilitated by a kindly neighbor acting as dea-ex-machina, provides a secularized version of the miracle tale or hagiographic *vida* in place of Shakespeare's (re)marriage plot (Greer, "M(Other)" 90–100). This conclusion foregrounds the innocent woman, her virtue on display as if in a spotlight, leaving the audience with no doubt at all concerning her absolute chastity. Where even the most sympathetic male-authored honor drama, such as *El médico*, depicts women's mental fidelity as questionable or unknowable, Inés's exemplary life leaves no room for doubt. One of the male members of the salon audience is sufficiently enlightened by this story to declare that unthinking circulation of cultural discourses of female vice is itself "un vicio" (290). The first part of this novella critiques conventional honor literature by proving that there are viable methods for a husband to obtain secure knowledge about his wife's virtue if he truly seeks it. In addition, the embodied wisdom of "true" female experience that Zayas presents in this novella and many of the others opens a new path of skeptical inquiry. The tales treat the issue of male anxiety as mostly baseless and hence irrational and refocus readers' attention upon what Zayas depicts as a far graver cognitive problem: how can women gain secure knowledge concerning the way their future husbands will treat them? Throughout the ten novellas that make up *Desengaños*,

Zayas scrutinizes the entire domain of gender, honor, and knowledge as she depicts an endless parade of husbands who doubt and abuse their faithful wives, before offering a novel solution, to be explored below.

The ninth novella, "La perseguida triunfante," reinscribes both "El curiososo" and *El animal de Hungría* and juxtaposes these with Marianist elements from Berceo's *Milagros de nuestra señora*. Once again, Zayas combines tragic honor drama with hagiography in order to continue the reinscription of honor and gender norms. In addition, this tale revisits motifs presented previously in "Inocencia" and "El verdugo" and offers a new twist on the husband who is betrayed by a trusted male companion (Greer, *Baroque* 144). Through this combined reinscription of male-authored and her own narratives, Zayas continues to demystify the male reasoning process. Like Cervantes's Camila, and Rosaleta in "El verdugo," the protagonist Beatriz is pursued by the male who is dearest to her husband's heart—in this case, King Ladislao's rival is his very own brother, Federico. This is one of the most significant reinscriptions of *El animal*, where the heroine's sister rather than her brother-in-law had presented the false accusations. Here, Zayas inverts the standard motif of women who compete with and betray one another and presents the masculine as the traitorous gender.

As indicated above, early modern women feared revealing such plights because of the dictum that men never pursue women unless enticed; thus, when a woman launches an accusation, her evidence will always be weighed against a prominent truth of patriarchal literary and moral culture. The narrator, Estefanía, highlights the way in which the sibling bond further complicates Beatriz's credibility in her husband's mind: "pues era dificultoso de creer contra su mismo hermano podía haber intentado tal traición" (418–19). Worse yet, unlike Rosaleta, Beatriz cannot present the evidence of the letter from Federico, because in her anger over his temerity she has torn it to bits. Ironically, the very act that every unwilling and offended *dama* is expected to perform in order to prove her virtue to an unwanted suitor later prevents her from providing supporting evidence of Federico's advances to her husband.

Because of this confluence of enforced silence and misplaced trust, the King assigns joint custody of his kingdom to his brother and wife when he goes off to war. During his extended absence, Beatriz is forced to imprison Federico to protect herself from continual harassment; this desperate act is intended to prove her fidelity upon her husband's return. However, Federico uses the time to prepare his own evidence; he ceases eating and personal grooming so that when his brother returns, he presents an emaciated and pathetic figure. Although she acknowledges the portrait of victimhood that Federico enacts so well, narrator Estefanía nonetheless condemns the inadequacy of Ladislao's reasoning process. She complains that even though his brother's appearance is terrible and his tears appear sincere, the King "creyó como fácil. Gran falta es en un rey, que si ha de guardar justicia, si da un oído a la acusación, ha de dar otro a la defensa de ella" (428). As a monarch who has been formally trained in adjudication, Estefanía implies, Ladislao has a special responsibility to practice cognitive responsibility. Instead, his reasoning process is compromised, because he judges as a husband and brother, and because the accuser is male and the plaintiff female (428). The narrator characterizes the King as "ciego de ira" at the moment when he greets Beatriz, delivers a blow to her check, and pronounces a death sentence, "sin más aguardar ni oírla" (429). In contrast to Othello and Gutierre, who do make an effort, if flawed, to contemplate evidence, Ladislao does not conduct any sort of inquiry and rushes to his criminal judgment. Where the former two erred in searching for perfect truth, Ladislao commits a more egregious cognitive crime in failing to search at all. Zayas condemns this cognitive flaw repeatedly throughout the rest of the novella; when Federico announces the death sentence he is to carry out on the King's behalf, Beatriz declares that her only real regret in the whole affair is that her husband "haya dado crédito a [las] traiciones, sin averiguar la verdad" (430). Similarly, the narrator lambastes Ladislao for turning over the reins of his kingdom to his brother "sin haber más averiguación de la verdad" (435).

In this novella, Zayas explores at unusual length the cognitive deliberations of two groups that evaluate Beatriz's situation. Immediately after Federico presents his case to the returning king, the narrator describes the reactions of the courtiers who accompanied him. As they perform the cognitive task of weighing multiple factors, these noblemen present a mixed reaction concerning the truth value of Federico's accusation. The very first piece of evidence they take into account is the embodied knowledge of their experience of the Queen's performance in ruling the court during her husband's absence, "su virtud y honestidad la acreditaba" (428).

However, when they weigh experience against a logical consideration such as the great risk Federico would be taking if he were to be caught in a lie in this circumstance, as well as the complication of denouncing the crown prince and sole inheritor before the king has produced an heir, the initial favorable evidence does not prove decisive. A similar consensus emerges when Beatriz's family and home court in Britain hear the news. Her parents doubt the story because of their faith in their embodied knowledge of "la virtud que de su hija habían conocido" (439). However, even among her own courtiers, many believe the tale immediately simply because of her gender, "juzgándola mujer, de quien por nuestra desdicha se cree más presto lo malo que lo bueno" (439). The ambassadors who investigate the allegations return to England convinced of her guilt.

In Zayas's revisioning of how patriarchy evaluates women's chastity, she emphasizes an over-reliance on the embodied experience of homosocial bonding and on a reasoning process that privileges cultural discourses of masculine honesty. She also indicts the ways that these two forces work against women. Like Shakespeare's kings, Ladislao and the two groups of aristocrats give little credence to the emotional intelligence and embodied knowledge that could be derived from taking into cognitive account their personal relations with Beatriz. Even though the courtiers do consider that form of evidence, they give it only secondary importance. The immediate credulity of king and courtier alike concerning Federico's tirade against Beatriz certainly owes much to misogynist cultural narratives, which Zayas consistently lays bare as unreliable data sources.

Once the King's rage has cooled—well after Beatriz has already been taken to the forest to be blinded and left for dead—Ladislao finally becomes aware of his embodied knowledge, "acordándose con la honestidad y el amor que la reina le había salido a recibir" upon his return (435). Now that he is "sosegado," his rational processes also begin to function, and a piece of overlooked evidence takes on significance: it is unlikely that a guilty wife would have greeted him in public so gladly and lovingly. At this point he finally begins to conduct a proper investigation, summoning the Queen's ladies-in-waiting to present their case. The information that they provide makes clear that the death sentence was unmerited. Here, Zayas provides a model of the ideal husband, who combines embodied and rational knowledges in order to consider all relevant data, and who includes the wife's female companions as reliable witnesses. Clearly, the British diplomats who had been sent to investigate did not deign to collect testimony from women, or they would have reached a different conclusion. However, this paradigm of rational consideration provides little basis for optimism. The entire novella collection makes clear that if such a model investigation occurs at all, it is only after the damage has been done. In one tale after another, the narratives condemn the honor code because it allows for killing in the heat of passion, before reasoned inquiry and contextualist data can be used to identify the truth (O'Brien 225).

Zayas emphasizes the unlikelihood that a serious investigation will ever occur or that it will impact reality; she displaces the entire development into the world of the supernatural by introducing a magical ring that erases the king's memory (Armon 102). Similarly, it is only through the repeated miraculous interventions of the Virgin that Beatriz is able to recover her sight after the King's men blind her, and to survive her long years of exile (Matos-Nin 140–45). The narrator Estefanía interrupts her tale to hammer home the point that even the most perfect wife is subject to unreasonable suspicion and hasty murder, or

> para defenderse de la lasciva crueldad de un hombre, no le bastase su santidad, su honestidad, con todas las demás virtudes que se cuentan de que era dotada ... Nada bastaba contra la soberbia e ira de este hombre, sino que era menester todo el favor y amparo de la Madre de Dios. (458)

As in "Inocencia," the generic dimensions of the miracle tale play an important role in the "happy ending" that Beatriz ultimately achieves. Unlike the Shakespearean wives who finally reunite with their husbands, or Lope's Teodosia, Beatriz instead opts for retreat to a convent and the "esposo celestial" that so many of Zayas's heroines ultimately prefer to flesh and blood mates (466). Beatriz rejects utterly the possibility that a woman could forgive so grave an offense and "volver a ocasionarse más desdichas y padecidas" (466). Ladislao himself unwittingly confirms the sanity of this decision, for even as he begs Beatriz's pardon for having failed to employ embodied wisdom, he excuses himself with the pathetic query, "¿Mas cómo no me había de engañar si mi propio hermano te descreditaba con tan aparentes maldades?" (465). He treats this case as an aberration rather than as the norm, and thus does not recognize the need for a drastic reconsideration of his and his culture's cognitive priorities. Beatriz seeks refuge in a convent precisely because her husband's failure to acknowledge the systemic problem opens the possibility for future misunderstandings and danger (Romero Díaz, "Revisiting" 174; Greer, *Baroque* 354). When women live within an epistemological system that places so little value on the contextualist data that provides the strongest evidence of female fidelity, a prudent, embodied female skepticism dictates avoidance of men and marriage.

In her novella collection, Zayas presents a gender-grounded cognitive paradox. When men seek truth about the women in their lives, they favor theological and literary discourses that present data of women as flawed and prone to infidelity. In many honor plays, such data directly contradicts the husband's embodied experience, for wives are generally faithful—or at worst, not the initiators of the adulterous acts they commit. Women encounter a complementary but opposite paradox: although literature and theology provide data of the male as a rational, faithful protector, the embodied experience of marriage as presented by Zayas reveals men to be raging homicidal maniacs. In both cases, the consequences of the contradiction between embodied experience and rational discourse are to the detriment of women. When Lisis ultimately closes the frame tale with her decision to renounce marriage in favor of the veil, it is because she has deduced from the tales that no matter what wives do, they cannot prevent men from pursuing them—nor can they prove themselves innocent of adultery—because of the inadequate cognitive procedures available to them. Lisis lists the misfortunes of each heroine by name in order to emphasize the lesson to be found in these tales: none of the sensible precautions or virtuous behaviors of the female protagonists, as prescribed in masculine literature, enabled them to form acceptable marriages nor to protect their honor against calumny. She explains that the tales by her friends have left her completely "desengañada; que aunque no lo estoy por experiencia, lo estoy por ciencia" (508). Lisis describes her form of disillusionment as one that is grounded in a gender-based skepticism: she has learned that male-authored depictions of courtship and marriage are biased and do not provide reliable information for or about women.

In listening to the stories of women's lived experiences, and their redefinitions of masculine behavior, she has gained new knowledge about gender relations. In this context, life in a convent is not the last resort for a woman no man desires; the narrative voice that closes the book explains to a male reader that, "no es trágico fin, sino el más felice que se pudo dar, pues codiciosa y deseada de muchos, no se sujetó a ninguno" (Zayas, *Desengaños amorosos* 510–11; Vollendorf, *Reclaiming* 215; Greer, *Baroque* 355). In Zayas's reformulation, retreat to a convent, whether for social or devotional purposes, is presented as the one avenue that brings security to women. Lisis rejects marriage because she has been unable to identify a cognitive process that would enable women to make a good decision about selecting a spouse. This epistemological frame constitutes an extreme version of skepticism, both the opposite of but also a parallel to the cognitive process that led Othello and other doubting spouses to murder.

It can be argued that Lisis's research method is not completely valid because she herself "skewed" the data (Armon xii; Brownlee xiv–xv). By requesting that her guests recount only *des*engaños, she predetermined the results of her study. Further, by asking for only true stories, she placed complete reliance on embodied experience, ignoring other forms of discourse and alternate modes of knowing that are crucial to a fully realized contextualist cognitive paradigm. Lisis influenced the outcome of her investigation by presupposing that marriage will make women unhappy, just as male-authored marriage manuals do in taking as their point of departure that woman is a flawed creature in need of education and surveillance in order to be a good wife. However, I do not see this as evidence of a faulty intellect on Lisis's part. Rather, I would like to propose that Lisis's model is a deliberately produced mirror image of standard masculine epistemological practice, presented for the explicit purpose of laying bare the radical incompleteness of patriarchal cognitive norms.

Early modern texts that critique the honor code often highlight its defective epistemological ground. Calderón, Cervantes, and Lope de Vega represent a serious flaw in the honor code through their critique of husbands who display an obsession with seeking absolute certainty about an immeasurable entity, the mental and physical chastity of a woman who is no longer a virgin. María de Zayas goes even further in her attack on the way that the honor code distorts masculine approaches to knowledge and decision-making. The contextualist cognitive paradigm provides new insights into the sources of the discrepant forms of sensory data and divergent mental processes with which men struggle and which they fail to process adequately. The conventional early modern cognitive model is shown to be partial and inadequate for judging human behavior, because it ignores embodied and emotional intelligence and relies on biased forms of textual data concerning both men and women, which are mislabeled as rational and truthful. Calderón and Cervantes depict their male protagonists as aberrant cases of cognitive malpractice; this aspect is also relevant for Lope's King although not a central issue. These men are seen as symptomatic of a larger malfunction in the epistemological order, but the flaws in the general paradigm are attributed to neutral philosophical forces rather than deliberately articulated power structures. In contrast, Zayas's novella collection presents numerous examples of the damage done to women's lives and their public reputation—as individuals and as a social group—by the cumulative cognitive failures of the honor code as an essential component of the patriarchal system. The texts of Calderón, Cervantes, Lope, and Zayas presented here take different paths to lead to a similar conclusion; all four present marriage as a locus for potential tragedy because of inadequacies in the cultural models for acquiring and assessing knowledge of honor, gender, and human nature. In addition, albeit from different angles, all four authors suggest alternative cognitive paradigms, which bear homologies both to early modern skepticism and to the current model of the contextualist mind. Zayas's fervent emphasis upon the dangers inherent in neglect of embodied cognition may be seen as both incorporating and going beyond the claims of contextualism.

Chapter Six

Contextualism and Performance in Lope's *Lo fingido verdadero*

Contextualist models of the brain depict perception as a complex cognitive activity that requires conscious and nonconscious processing of multiple streams of information about the reality that surrounds us (Chapter 5). Contextualist cognition can be seen as analogous to the "baroque" preoccupation with the indeterminacy of reality itself (Warnke 69). One of the most striking cultural manifestations of this baroque epistemology is literary reflexivity or meta-art, works that foreground the quandary, how can art hope to imitate a perceived reality when the artist—and his audience—share doubts about the reliability of perception? One of the defining features of baroque (or early modern) literature of all genres is its emphasis on the work of art as a set of arbitrary conventions, rather than as a direct or natural imitation of reality. J.R. Mulryne examines the self-reflexivity of the Dover Cliffs scene in *King Lear*, which lays bare stage conventions concerning exotic locales, as an illustration of the way that early modern meta-art explores epistemology, presenting the relationship between illusion and truth as a "necessary and mutually sustaining co-presence" rather than as polar opposites (60). William Egginton goes even further, asserting that the metatheatrical "innovation in the practices in spectacle is an integral element in a complex process of change that is not merely linked to an aesthetic or mentality, but is rather constitutive of it" (*World* 77). Egginton's valuable study links this new mode of spectacle to the postmodern notions of subjectivity related to performance, the gaze, and surveillance (*World* 13–20). In this chapter, I, too, seek to relate early modern theatrical aesthetics to contemporary cultural theory, but with a cognitive focus. Although the importance of meta-art in early modern Spanish dramaturgy has been definitively established over the past three decades, far less critical attention has been devoted

177

to the emergence of philosophical skepticism in the seventeenth century, and even less to the synergetic relationship between metatheater and skepticism as an emergent philosophical mode of inquiry (Egginton, *World* 80–84, 99–104; Simerka, "Early Modern Skepticism" 39–45). This chapter will examine Lope de Vega's *Lo fingido verdadero* (ca. 1608–10), a martyr play in which the relationship between self-referential dramaturgy, philosophical skepticism, and contextualist cognition is particularly noteworthy and mutually sustaining because the characters ponder not only the liminal spaces between real life and the stage, but also between material existence and the divine.

The contextualist model of cognitive functionality has emerged from new discoveries concerning brain structures and interactions, captured via ever-improving imaging technologies (Damasio 14; Sacks 62–63). Back in 1983, early imaging data had led Jerry Fodor to suggest that brain functioning is modular rather than linear in nature, so that the separate modes can process different information streams, or different aspects of the same information stream, simultaneously (37–46). More advanced imaging technologies revealed thought processes to be even more complex than supposed with the modular model; current models indicate parallel processing, interconnectivity, and dynamic interfacing as the key activities in a completely networked brain (Churchland; Karmiloff-Smith; Fuster; Edelman; see Chapter 5 for an extended description of contextualism).

Ellen Spolsky was the first literary scholar to recognize the potential of the modular model for studies of early modern literature and philosophy. In her studies of epistemology in *Othello* and Shakespearean tragicomedy, Spolsky develops connections between contextualism and the search for true knowledge in early modern British texts (*Satisfying* 80). Spolsky demonstrates that the competing and contradictory information streams encountered and processed by a modular (or networked) brain offer an embodied explanation for the central quandary of skepticism as a philosophical system: the difficulty in determining how to be certain of knowledge in a world of deceptive appearances. Although such a model was not available to early modern skeptical philosophers, they were able nonetheless to create systems and narratives based on the human and social manifestations of a contextualist brain (see Chapter 5 for an expanded introduction to skepticism and contextualism). Historians of philosophy have linked the rise of early modern skepticism to the proliferation of religious discourses: mystic Catholicism, various strands of Protestantism, as well as the new awareness of non-Christian theologies in the east and in the Americas (Kors viii). This competition among theologies could certainly contribute to the conflicting data streams that contextualist models of cognition address.

Moriscos and the Performance of Christian Identity

In Lope's *Lo fingido verdadero*, skepticism concerning certain knowledge of embodied experience is even more complex because the play dramatizes the act of religious conversion. Scholarship dates this play to the very same years during which Spain undertook the expulsion of its *morisco* population, which had come to be seen as a group of "false converts" and "internal enemies" (Perry, *Handless* 1). The cognitive premise underlying such an expulsion was the profound conviction that a sizable portion of the populace that had been coerced to convert in the previous half-century continued to engage in Islamic practices, and that determining which converts were sincere Christians was a difficult challenge. In addition, a subject position of loyalty to a particular *religion* was seen as inseparable from *nationalist* identity; only true Christians could be counted upon for loyalty to the Spanish crown in the event of Turkish attacks (Perry, *Handless* 1–2). Thus, as Mary Elizabeth Perry and Barbara Fuchs have shown, Moorish conversion to Christianity was viewed by many as a highly suspect *performance* of faith and allegiance, a public display that obscured private heresy and treason (Perry, *Handless* 3–4; Fuchs 4–10). The tenets of skepticism as a philosophical system and contextualist models of thought are extremely relevant to the search for certain knowledge concerning religious converts. The debate concerning *conversos* can be viewed as the ultimate moment of skeptical exploration; skilled performances of Catholic faith provided one stream of information, while the various *morisco* rebellions of the sixteenth century provided material evidence of potentially treasonous allegiances, and social discourses about secret subversive religious practices also abounded. Ultimately, because Counter Reformation culture could not determine satisfactory criteria for evaluating the validity of each conversion, expulsion was deemed the only recourse that would completely purge Spain of internal religious enemies.

The connection between early modern conversions from Islam and Roman conversions from paganism has not been discussed in the literature on this play, perhaps because the aspects of hagiography and martyrdom overshadowed more contemporary homologies. Interestingly, this same aporia exists in scholarship on Rotrou's version of the legend *Le véritable St. Genest*, which tends to focus on the moral issues of the day (Ekstein 3–7). Despite the fact that France engaged in fifteen years of civil war to prevent the accession of a Huguenot to the throne at the end of the sixteenth century, and even though Henri of Navarre was assassinated in 1610 because of concern about the authenticity of his conversion to Catholicism, the issue of pragmatic or politically motivated performances of conversion among the playwrights' own contemporaries does not arise as a topic of interest in French studies of martyred pagan converts. Scholarship concerning Spanish and French dramas about pagan conversion offer uncanny parallels in that both overlook the connections to forced conversions of the early modern age. This chapter thus breaks new ground not only in linking contextualism and skepticism but also in connecting *pagan* conversion drama with the frenzied politics of religious identity that swept across early modern Europe. From this perspective, Lope's conversion drama has important analogies to Cervantine plays such as *Los tratos de Argel*, as well as to hagiographic literature (Fuchs 10).

Metatheater and Skepticism

The form of contextualist skepticism to be explored in relation to Lope's martyr play arises from the epistemology of metatheater. Lionel Abel's groundbreaking *Metatheater: A New View of Dramatic Form* (1963) provided important early insights concerning theatrical reflexivity. In particular, his construct of the metatheatrical character as a self-aware playwright, scripting his or her own role in the world, is highly relevant for the analysis of the conversion and martyrdom of Saint Genesius (San Ginés) (Witt 22–30). Abel's insights have been used to illuminate a wide variety of early modern Spanish texts, although many Hispanists argue that his theories must be modified to be applicable to Golden Age texts.

(Hispanists who foreground the sacred dimension of Spanish metatheater include O'Connor, Casa, Case, Sito Alba, and Stoll. Other studies of metadrama in Golden Age Spain, often applying Abel's character-as-dramatist approach, include three essays by Fischer; de Armas, "Lope"; Paredes; Ponce; Hall; Gómez; E. Sánchez; Kirby; Moore; Smith; and Larson, "Metatheater.")

This book will expand critical attention beyond the relationship between the characters and their roles to include as well the dynamic of audience reception. This re-direction will facilitate the examination of socio-historical aspects of early modern self-referential drama not directly related to Abel's character-oriented approach, in particular social anxiety about the difficulty in distinguishing sincere conversion from the mere public performance of Catholic religious identity. In self-reflexive drama, discrepant information streams are not the result only of the gap between material and intellectual experience of social norms. Rather, the cognitive conflict arises from encounters with various forms of reality: "real life," theatrical illusion, and the miraculous are staged as three supposedly distinct yet uncannily overlapping forms of embodied experience.

Richard Hornby asserts that, when the dominant theological discourse characterizes the material world as illusory or false, then the dramatic device of the play-within-the-play becomes a metaphor for life itself. The fact that the inner play is an obvious illusion (since we see other characters watching it), reminds us that the play we are watching is also an illusion, despite its vividness and excitement; by extension, the reality of the world in which we live, which also seems to be so vivid, is implicated as well. In Lope's play, the representation of actors who metamorphose into the characters they play, and of the confusion this transformation causes for the on-stage spectators, is a graphic reminder that the "all the world's a stage" *topos* is not merely an aesthetic device, but is associated with highly complex cognitive circumstances. Audiences encounter a multifaceted vision of ontology and acting, witness the possibility of performed conversion as a positive phenomenon, and are asked to consider the enactment of conversion as a pathway to authentic Christian belief. These self-reflexive musings could then interact with cultural codes concerning which social groups are cognitively and morally capable of true conversion. The contextualist cognitive model illuminates these conflicting perceptions of real and dramatized religious identity as the result of multiple information streams within the networked brain.

In *Partial Magic*, Robert Alter defines a related aesthetic approach, which he calls "self-conscious" writing. Although his definition is used to describe developments in the history of the novel as a genre, it is also applicable to dramatic art. Alter describes the self-conscious work of art as one that "flaunts" its status as artifact in order to examine the relationship between "real-seeming artifice and reality" (x). In these works, the fictional world is "set up as an authorial construct against a background of literary tradition and convention" (xi). This interplay is at the heart of contextualist skepticism's emotional and intellectual power. Lope's dramatization of religious conversion exemplifies the type of exploration that Alter advocates.

Timothy Reiss identifies an increasing self-consciousness as a dominant feature of early modern drama. He writes that, while "at first this new direction was apparent only in occasional references by playwrights, they soon undertook a complete re-examination of the nature of the theater" (55). Reiss points to characters using theatrical terminology to describe the unconvincing actions of other characters as role-playing more appropriate to the stage; this staging of the uncertain line between acting and being is central to the contextualist aspect of metatheater (56). Through this type of diction, the theatrical experience is fragmented into differing "levels of action": the audience is made aware of the production of the play as separate from both reality and the story that is enacted (Reiss 133). The representation of a play-within-the-play provides dramatists with an excellent opportunity to examine the difficulties in discerning between the theater and the "real world" and among various types of performances, both on and off the stage. In this age of heightened anxiety about purity of blood, the performance of religious identity, as well as class conformity as studied in earlier chapters, was necessary for participation in many forms of social life—not only for converts.

Reiss points out that one primary technique for blurring the boundary between stage and audience is to present the actors of the company appearing as themselves; that is, when the script calls for the actors to be called by their real names as they rehearse a play or talk about a play they are involved with, and also to talk of their "real" lives (129). Of course, this still takes place on a stage, it has been scripted in advance, the names are likely to be stage names; thus it is a representation that immediately undermines its own premise of showing the "reality " of theatrical life. An important factor to consider in evaluating the audience reaction to such scenes is the typical composition of acting troupes of the time, in which stock characters such as the jealous husband, the ingénue, and the braggart captain are always played by the same actor, so that, "for the audiences of the time, the real personalities of these actors are confused with their stage personalities" (Reiss 129). In Lope's *Lo fingido verdadero*, the fame that the actor has achieved for his skillful portrayal of Christian martyr Saint Genesius is central to the cognitive doubts arising in the play-within-the-play about the moment of sincere conversion. Genesius may be viewed as a symbol for the *morisco* population as a whole; incarnating a continuum from those who merely enacted the conversion forced upon them in the late sixteenth century, to those whose beliefs became sincere over time, to long-standing voluntary converts from the earliest centuries of the Reconquest. The cognitive quandary in which the actor's colleagues find themselves sheds light on seventeenth-century Spanish citizens: if a person's closest peers are confused by conflicting streams of information about a friends' conversion, how can members of one entire social group hope to judge the sincerity of a marginalized group with whom there is limited social interaction?

Reiss emphasizes that metatheatrical scenes go far beyond providing a forum for theatrical apologies. They also reveal the complex nature of human identity through the layers that are peeled back to reveal: character, actor as character, actor as "celebrity" (the public perception of the actor), and a "real person." Reiss writes that this type of confusion produces "a sense of fluctuating psychical distance" for the spectator (130). He attributes this distance to the "deliberately precarious" nature of the "illusion" created in the drama of the period, and asserts that it is this fluctuating distance that forces the spectator to confront the problem of illusion and reality, in part by blocking identification with any of the characters (108, 137). In the context of the ubiquitous dictum of the period—that we are all mere actors—this "deconstruction" of the actor would be seen as relevant to all human beings, thus linking existential and epistemological concerns; this fluctuation and deconstruction is similar to the epistemological vertigo posited by the contextualist model of cognition. Although Reiss is writing about baroque French drama, his theories of reflexive theater are equally relevant to the Spanish drama of this same era—in particular because of the strong influence of the *comedia* on the theater north of the Pyrenees. Further, this model reveals all components of human social identity to be a compendium of various degrees of authentic and enacted social modalities, which are processed by different networks within the contextualist mind.

Hornby and Reiss produce readings of metadrama that recall Brechtian theories of alienation, underscoring the value of dramatic technique that fosters distance and critical thought. This approach to theatrical reflexivity leads to analyses that vary significantly from most early analyses of meta-art. As noted previously, Golden Age Spanish scholars often evaluate works within Abel's framework of character study, or seek to reconcile Abel and the Counter Reformation; both approaches take for granted that metadrama serves ideological hegemony. Likewise, in his exploration of the evolution of studies of Shakespearean metadrama, Richard Fly notes approvingly that a few scholars, including Lionel Abel, believe that reflexivity ultimately serves to reinforce harmony, closure, and the restoration of order; however, recent studies have emphasized the transgressive possibilities (127–30). William Egginton's *How the World Became a Stage* opens a space for more nuanced readings of Lope's play and offers an important exception to the conservative tendency among Hispanists. Catherine Larson's recent survey of the potential for new uses of metatheatrical analysis of Golden Age drama also develops this line of thought ("Metatheater" 216). Jonathan Thacker's *Role-Play and the World as Stage* links self-reflexive drama and gender ideology; he identifies female protagonists in comic drama who use role play to challenge and evade gender codes. Similarly, R. A. Martin rejects readings of Shakespearean metatheater that emphasize harmony and reintegration. He writes that, although scholars generally view the Prince Hal who emerges at the end of *Henry IV, Part 1* as a coherent and mature figure who synthesizes the best characteristics of Hotspur and Falstaff, he instead views the character as displaying "a discontinuous, heterogeneous, and metatheatrical sense of selfhood which guarantees that a man's name and the role that name implies can never coincide—even for a man who is also a king" (263). This discontinuity is also evident in early modern portrayals of Saint Genesius, a figure whose iconic martyrdom is inextricable from his vocation as actor. This heterogeneous and reflexive self can be seen as the embodiment both of the contested figure of the early modern *morisco* and of contextualist modes of skeptical cognition.

The Real Genesius: Role Playing and Reality

According to Frank Warnke, in baroque drama the staging of the relationship between theater and life goes beyond simple resemblance, "not a similarity but an identity" (69). One of the most obvious issues is the multiple layers of the actor's role. In Lope's play about Saint Genesius, the confusion of roles occurs at a deeper level, involving the actors as well as the spectators, as the events the protagonists enact come to influence their real lives. The theme of *theatrum mundi* is expressed by many of the characters; the Emperor Carinus's (Carino's) companion Celius (Celio) informs him that there is little difference between his life and that of actors who represent kings:

> La diferencia sabida,
> es que les dura hora y media
> su comedia, y tu comedia
> te dura toda la vida
> Tú representas también,
> mas estás de rey vestido
> hasta la muerte. (Act I p. 206)

Carinus dismisses these words, asserting his innate superiority:

> ni puede humano suceso
> contra el divino poder.
> Somes los emperadores,
> como sabéis, casi iguales
> a los dioses celestiales :
> somos del mundo señores,
> como ellos lo son del cielo. (I.207)

However, these words are almost immediately shown to be rash, for Carinus is killed at the end of the scene. With his dying words, he acknowledges the truth of Celius's earlier assertion of equality:

> Poned aquestos vestidos
> de un representante rey,
> pues es tan común la ley
> a cuantos fueran nacidos,
> a donde mi sucesor
> los vuelva luego a tomar,
> porque ha de representar. (I.214)

Susan Fischer characterizes the Emperor's *desengaño* as an example of meta-art's power to help viewers analyze "role-playing as an artistic, psychological and metaphysical phenomenon" ("Lope" 160). Awareness and valorization of the polyphonic nature of role-playing is key to the skeptical and contextualist view of Genesius's conversion that will be posited in this essay. Fischer points to this moment of enlightenment as a preparation for Genesius's own conversion, implying a more conventional interpretation ("Lope" 160). Yet, the imperial subplot also supports a skeptical interpretation; the series of crownings and murders points to epistemological confusion in Roman culture, as seen in its inability to determine adequate criteria for knowing who will be a good ruler. Contextualist skepticism is relevant not only to theatrical role-playing but also to conceptualizing politics as an interdependent or symbiotic fusion of governance and spectacle.

This early examination of multiple levels of confusion about role-playing and life (and death) is further developed in the play through the actor Genesius's dual portrayals of a jealous lover and a Christian martyr (Egginton, *World* 113–20). As Rufinus, Genesius enacts a suffering lover; he loves Fabia, a character played by the actress whom Genesius loves; but, she loves one of the other actors in the company. The resemblance between the real and the enacted situations causes Genesius to abandon his role and to call his leading lady by her real name, Marcella (Marcela). When Marcella/Marcela asks if he is breaking character, Genesius/Ginés responds that he is enacting his real pain for the one who caused it (II.242). Here, Genesius conflates two different meanings of the word *act*, eliminating the distinction between the theatrical and the everyday uses of the word. This conflation is similar to the model of self-fashioning posited in Goffman's *The Presentation of Self in Everyday Life* and deployed by aspiring courtiers (see Chapter 4). In early modern Spain, concerns about religion and subjectivity overlap with preoccupations about other troubling forms of social mobility and manipulated identity.

The similarities among the suffering lovers cause Genesius to confuse his role and his life and to create a liminal space at the edge of the fourth wall. This form of boundary straddling proves to be contagious; next, Marcella also breaks out of character. As in real life, Octavius (Octavio) is Rufinus's rival, and as in real life, the woman's father prefers Rufinus. When Octavius asks Fabia to run away with him, Marcella exclaims, "¡Ay cielo, si verdad fuera / la comedia! ... quisiera que a Ginés / le hiciéramos este tiro" (II.248). Because Marcella does not appear on cue for her next scene, even after Genesius repeats the cue line, the actor who is Marcella's father appears on-stage in order to apologize to the Emperor for whom the play is being performed. He announces that his daughter Marcella has run away with her true love, just like the character Fabia that she portrayed. After the audience has dispersed, Genesius again conflates stage and life, repeating the very same lines his character had said when Fabia ran off. Genesius is quite conscious of this conflation, for he points out, "Quiero volver a decir, /pues que mi tormento es cierto" (II.255). The second act emphasizes the difficulties in distinguishing between fantasy and reality: if those who earn their living by pretending cannot consistently draw a line between self and character, how can the audience be expected to do so? This question points to the basic tenet of contextualist skepticism, that epistemological certainty is an elusive goal in all areas of social living because of the ubiquity of performances of identity.

Elizabeth Sánchez and Susan Fischer relate this particular form of reflexivity to the issue of authorial control of characters, and to the popular device of characters who escape from their creator to take on a life of their own (E. Sánchez 36–37; Fischer, "Lope" 163). Sánchez also notes that, by exposing the composition process, authors reveal the ways in which artistic experience mediates and shapes our perceptions of reality (39). Alan Trueblood points out the complexity of this scene, which "appears to proclaim an identity of role and actuality. In fact, it does just the opposite through a subtle play of irony" (314). This scene also involves scrutiny of a debate during the period concerning the preparation for a role, and whether or not an actor must feel an emotion in order to portray it effectively (Fischer, "Lope" 161). In fact, the confused reactions of all three actors involved highlight the idea that excessive similarity between true and enacted feelings actually causes problems—and eventually disrupts the play as the actors decide to use scripted behaviors to solve real-life problems. As true emotions emerge from and overtake scripted selves, these three actors corroborate Cicero's dictum that one should use his/her imagination rather than life experiences to understand characters and situations—but also reveal the difficulty inherent in this task. This debate is also relevant to social norms for judging the relative ease or difficulty of feigning conversion and of detecting such pretenses.

It is in the role in which Genesius is said to most excel, that of a Christian martyr, that the conflation of actor and role becomes irreversible. As Genesius muses about how to enact this role for the Emperor, he asks himself,

> ¿Como haré yo que parezca
> que soy el mismo cristiano
> cuando al tormento me ... ofrezco?
> ¿Con que acción, que rostra y mano
> en que alabariza merezca?
> (III.265; accent marks silently corrected)

The enactment here of an actor's struggle to choose the most convincing ways to express emotions that are totally foreign to him is a particularly effective tool for breaking the audience's identification with actor or character, and for stimulating reflection upon the "role" that deliberate presentations of the self play on- and off-stage. This could also stimulate audience reflection on the tactics of feigned conversion in its own era. As Genesius continues, describing various scenarios in which the martyr shows his courage, the stage directions call for a painting of a Christian scene to be revealed and spotlighted, and an "off-stage voice" to address the actor in the following manner, "No le imitarás en vano, / Ginés, que te has de salvar" (III.266). At this point, Genesius begins to think that the Christian God has spoken to him, and to speculate about Christian beliefs, when he notices that another actor is present and has been trying to get his attention. Thus, Genesius decides that it must be Fabius's voice he heard, and apologizes,

Perdona, que divertido
en imitar al cristiano,
fuera me vi de sentido,
pensando que el soberano
ángel me hablaba al oído. (III.268–69)

However, this explanation will not satisfy the off-stage audience, who has seen the painting that Genesius did not see, and the "miracle" of its appearance and disappearance. For the "real" audience, Christian and stage miracle are conflated, for even the devout spectator who believes that God did indeed intervene in the actor's life is still aware that the apparently miraculous revelation of the picture is actually a result of stage machinery. This may very well be one of the most subversive moments of Lope's play, for it demonstrates the ease with which miracles may be contrived. Although the play does appear to support belief in Christian ideology, through the representation of Genesius's heroic acceptance of martyrdom and his firm belief in a glorious afterlife, it simultaneously draws attention to the possibilities for deception. Not only everyday life, but also extraordinary occurrences, are shown to be opaque rather than obvious, and subject to interpretation. The contextualist model of cognition emphasizes the embodied cerebral activity that underlies such moments of epistemological vertigo. This scene encourages the audience to reflect upon the nature of faith in its internal and external manifestations; if the miraculous is so easy to stage convincingly, a public façade of conformity to the state-sponsored doctrine would pose no challenge at all.

An Actor Performs Authentic Conversion

In the play-within-the-play, the audience becomes aware that the encounter between Genesius and the "angel" is not a part of the script only because the other actors break character to comment that he is improvising once again. Because there have been previous indications that Genesius's brilliance consists, in part, of this very improvisational ability, neither the audience represented onstage nor the real audience suspects that the encounter is "real." This becomes apparent when the other actors attempt to prompt their star player, so that he will return to the script. Genesius rejects their cues, explaining,

Pues no ves
que el cielo me apunta ya ...
desde que a un ángel oí
detrás de su azul cortina ...
pero después que apuntó
el ángel del vestuario
del cielo, y lo necesario
para acertar me enseñó ...
Oyeron de mi buen celo
la comedia, y era justo,
y en verdad que di gran gusto,
pues que llevan al cielo:
De Dios soy de aquí adelante,
que siéndolo de su fe,
dice el cielo que seré
el mejor representante. (III.276)

Even in this moment of religious ecstasy, the famed actor sees his conversion as yet another role to play—but this does not mean that his conversion lacks sincerity. Rather, it is a restatement of the Emperor Carinus's dying words in Act I, of the baroque *topos* that all of life and human identity is as illusory as an actor's costume. This speech could also be seen as indicative of the fluid nature of all conversions, which must always use an embodied display to convey a disembodied spiritual practice. This conflation of faith as role and reality inspires the most profound of skeptical meditations concerning the elusive and contradictory nature of truth.

When Fabius, the boy actor who plays the role of the angel, comes out on-stage to begin that scene, the two different audiences suddenly realize that the encounter with the angel was a "true" miracle. Upon hearing that the scene is over, the boy protests that he has not entered the stage nor spoken yet. The on-stage audience becomes angered at this indication that the actors don't know the play thoroughly. The question of who actually "played" the angel is never resolved, so this is an element of uncertainty that the "real" audience members must resolve in accordance with their own belief systems. This moment also lays bare the theatrical convention of disguised identities: for example, it is a commonplace of early modern drama that female characters who dress as males are accepted as men by the other characters and the audience. Taking this convention a step further, the two levels of audience must accept that to the acting company, the "real" angel was indistinguishable from the actor who played that role in order to decide that a real angel did indeed appear to Genesius. Staging practices would also be crucial to the interpretation of this scene, as the manager would have to choose whether or not to use the same actor and costume for the two angels.

However, the protagonist diverts attention from the matter when he addresses the Emperors directly concerning his conversion:

> Césares, yo soy cristiano:
> ya tengo el santo bautismo:
> esto represento yo,
> porque es *mi* autor Jesucristo;
> en la segunda jornada
> está vuestro enojo escrito;
> que en llegando la tercera
> representaré el martirio. (III.278)

Genesius highlights the theme of the shadowy line between acting and essence (which Michael McGaha also emphasizes with his translation of Lope's title, *Acting Is Believing*) in a soliloquy addressed to his new God:

> Mi Dios, cuando por burlas fui cristiano
> y me llamastes a tan altas veras,
> representaba burlas verdaderas
> en el teatro de mi intento vano.
> Mas como el auditorio soberano
> en las gradas de altísimas esferas,
> y Vos por las celestes vidrieras
> vistes de mi comedia el acto humano,
> he pensado que lástima tuvistes
> que estuviese en tan mala compañía
> y que para la vuestra me quisistes. (III.282)

Thus, it is not only the two levels of the audience that are affected by this dramatic *tour de force*; Heaven itself was so moved by the performance that it decided to make the act a reality. Apparently, there are no limits to what can be accomplished by a truly skillful actor, no audience that cannot be influenced. In this case the outcome is positive, from the Christian point of view, at least.

This scene, of course, raises the possibility of divine intervention in order to make real the coerced *morisco* conversions. However, in baroque literature, as in early modern Spanish life, the ability to play a role convincingly is seldom viewed as the unequivocally beneficial talent that is represented here.

Diocletian's (Diocleciano's) reaction also foregrounds the possibilities of audience confusion at the collapse of the border between acting and existing. He focuses at first on the role he is supposed to play within the improvisations. When Marcella's father announces that she has run off with Octavius, the Emperor wonders,

> ¿Es esto representar
> y a la invención convenible,
> o quieres mostrar, Ginés,
> que con burlas semejantes
> nos haces representantes? (II.254)

When he is informed that the elopement is real, Diocletian is still uncertain, declaring,

> ¡Por Jupiter, que sospecho,
> y no se si lo rehuse,
> que quieres que represente!
> ¿Hablas de veras o no? (II.254)

At this point, the actor Pinabellus (Pinabelo) enters to inform everyone that Marcella and Octavius have returned. Diocletian's rage subsides, as he decides,

> De la burla estoy contento,
> y pues he representado
> mi figura en vuestra historia,
> no es razón que el tesorero
> os pague. (II.254)

After the on-stage audience leaves, Pinabellus reveals that the Emperor is still confused about the truth, although he doesn't know it, because Pinabellus lied about the actors' return. Here, the off-stage spectators can be confident about their own knowledge of the truth, but skepticism is nonetheless reinforced as they see how easily truth can be manipulated. In courtier societies, whether Roman or early modern, catering to the whims of an absolute ruler adds an additional stream of contextualist data, for some truths cannot be told safely and plausible fictions must be invented for self-preservation.

Diocletian finally realizes that Genesius is sincere when the actor involves the Emperor in his drama, saying,

> en la segunda jornada está
> vuestro enojo escrito;
> que en llegando la tercera
> representaré el martirio. (III.278)

Diocletian then begins to frame his own actions within theatrical norms, prefacing the death sentence with "Pues ya quiero hacer mi dicho" and concluding it with "acabaré mi papel" (III.278). Michel Darbord notes that in *Don Quixote*, when the protagonist ruptures the fourth wall to intervene in Maese Pedro's puppet show, Cervantes provides a typical and negative example of the naïve spectator (25). In the Saint Genesius plays, however, the actors themselves invite or even force the audience of the play-within-the-play to take on dramatic roles, as they deliberately rupture that wall. The permeability of the border between make believe and truth is emphasized throughout this scene, as Genesius's initial transgression paves the way for other characters and "real people"—Marcella and Octavius as well as the Emperor—to speak and act as if inhabiting two planes of existence. *Morisco* conversions were envisioned as similarly dualistic, combining clandestine Islamic rituals with public conformity to Christian norms of clothing, diet, and worship.

Many scholars interpret the final scene in a way that minimizes the role of metadrama, skepticism, or both. Hall compares this ending to *La vida es sueño*, and Genesius's acting to Segismundo's dreams, in order to assert that these forms of illusion ultimately lead to certain knowledge, an assertion also made or implied by Fischer and Trueblood. Jean-Claude Vuillemin views the closing of Rotrou's play as a homage to the pleasures of theatrical illusion, within a context in which theatricality and the staging of identity are connected to Louis XIV's penchant for the staging of power as a political tool (314). Margaret Greer and Stephen Orgel have made related claims concerning the court spectacles of the reigns of Philip IV in Spain and James I in England. However, while this paradigm may help to illuminate the presentation of the Emperor, that model cannot be applied mechanically to the character Saint Genesius, because the reflexive scenes in which this character participates are more strongly connected to issues of cognition and religion than to political power. Thus, it is more problematic to assert here that reflexivity is used primarily to celebrate illusion. Rather, the many layers of reflexivity present in these plays stimulate critical reflection concerning doubt and knowledge in response to the self-conscious staging of religious themes. The atmosphere of skepticism concerning where performance ends and true existence begins is prominent in the final lines.

Theatrical metaphors are pervasive in the dying words of this illustrious martyr, who refers to earthly life as "la humana comedia" and "la segunda parte" (which McGaha cleverly translates as "sequel"). The linkage of the most important event of Christian dogma with theatricality—and hence pretense—serves to undermine the orthodox theological message. The ubiquity of self-conscious questioning of the perception, reality, and illusion throughout this drama paves the way for a heterodox interpretation of the concluding lines. The precarious relationship between illusion and knowledge is of special importance in the closing scenes of martyrdom; for, as Harry Berger notes, the staging of death is the most metatheatrical of dramatic moments because the audience is always aware that "the corpse will return for a curtain call" (98). Richard Sanderson's observations on the reflexive aspects of one particular form of staged death, suicide, are particularly relevant to Genesius's martyrdom, for both are voluntary, deliberately chosen forms of death that involve elements of staging and self-conscious (even if sincere) role-playing. Sanderson characterizes the staging of death as a special form of the "play-within-the-play," and asserts that the perpetrators of voluntary death envision themselves in a dual role, as the one who dies and as a spectator who will remain to observe the desired responses to that death, whether as vengeance for a suicide or eternal life in heaven for the martyr (206, 201). Lope's protagonist envisions a wonderful outcome, although even here, metadrama intrudes as he declares, "en Vos acabe la comedia mía" (III.282). The boundary between life and death is crossed several times, as the actor first portrays the death of a previous martyr, then breaks out of this role to declare his real conversion as Genesius, and later endures his own "real" death, only to return once more as the actor who played both Genesius and the other martyr in the curtain call. Awareness of the networked and contextualist nature of the human brain facilitates our understanding of how audiences engage cognitively with such complex representations of reality and competing levels of illusion.

In addition, both suicide and martyrdom are communicative, in the sense that they seek to transmit a message to and create a lasting image for those left behind (Sanderson 201). The impaled Genesius opens his final speech, "Pueblo romano, escuchadme" (III.285) and assures them,

> Voy al cielo a que me paguen,
> Que de *mi* fe y esperanza
> Y *mi* caridad. (III.286)

Sanderson stipulates that those who commit suicide urge their supporters to avenge them; here the martyr's drastic affirmation of heroic adherence to his faith is meant to encourage other Romans to accept the new faith and profess it despite the consequences, because of the value of the ultimate reward. This scene could be interpreted as a conversion call to the small number of crypto Moors and Jews who remained in Spain after the expulsions.

H. Gaston Hall notes that even if an author sincerely believes in the power of theater to bring about miracles and redemption, and epistemological certainty concerning life, death, and the afterworld, the conclusion could still appear illusory because of the social changes from Roman to early modern times, when miracles play a much smaller role (43). The rampant repetition of the *theatrum mundi* motif is all the more significant in that the play dramatizes the central story of Christian mythography: the martyrdom of the persecuted believer. The staging of martyrdom evokes the death of the first and most revered Christian martyr, but also distances the spectator and ruptures identity with Genesius and Christ through the reflexive nature of the actor's conversion and death. Ironically, the mixed messages that this self-reflexive and hagiographic play sends serve to undermine faith in the human capacity to attain meaningful knowledge of the relationship between material reality and divine revelation. In the context of this narrative of the ultimate gesture of faith, the meta-artistry in this play can be seen as a radical affirmation of skeptical thought. This questioning of human ability to perceive the difference between theatrical illusion and material reality offers an unexpected analogy for interpretations of true and feigned conversion. As Barbara Fuchs has noted, the phenomenon of performed conversions or "passing" posed a radical challenge to "the very notion of a transparent, easily classified identity on which the state can rely for exclusionary purposes" (7). Thus, on one level this play's metatheatrical dimension—in particular its staging of sincere and feigned conversions as indistinguishable—calls into question the validity of the cognitive underpinnings of a highly significant and even traumatic political event, the expulsion of the entire *morisco* community. Contextualist models of cognition offer new ways to explore the epistemological quandaries that self-reflexive and hagiographic dramas stage.

Chapter Seven

Cognition and Reading
in *Don Quixote*

The field of cognitive studies includes a wide variety of approaches that explore many aspects of the human mind/brain and embodied cognition. In this chapter, I will present an overview of several approaches that appear to me to provide the most valuable insights concerning Cervantes's master work, addressing characters, aesthetics, and ideology. Some topics, such as social intelligence and modularity, have been covered in previous chapters in relation to other genres. But, because of the uniquely "modern" (or even postmodern) nature of this novel, there are several aspects of cognitive study, particularly in the areas of reading and perception, that are not as readily applicable to other early modern Spanish texts. *Don Quixote* is a text that both illustrates the utility of current cognitive theories of reading and also offers one of the earliest known examples of a narrative that self-consciously represents norms and aberrations in the reading process as an object of scrutiny.

In *Cognition and Reality,* Ulric Neisser analyzes the nature of human perception. He writes that normal human beings are acutely aware of the difference between imagination and perception, because the former depends upon internal stimulus, such as the recall of previously seen objects and events or anticipation of future events, while the latter entails a mental process in which new information is continually acquired from external stimuli and processed (129). One aspect of Don Quixote's mental aberration is that he reacts to new and external stimuli, which normally evoke perception, via his imagination. And, where normal humans navigate the external world though cognitive schemata that are based upon prior lived experiences, Don Quixote's orientation is instead shaped by imaginative experience (135). Further, humans normally create and modify templates of human experience, known among cognitivists as schemata—to reflect and incorporate new experiences that contradict expectations (Turner 52–55). In Don Quixote's case, those modifications are very slow to come. He holds on to his chivalric schema despite very concrete physical evidence that it is unreliable. Neisser notes that "selective perception" is an essential aspect of human cognition, because advanced human society presents so many types and sources of stimuli (85). Normal mental screening activity entails focusing attention upon the stimuli that are most relevant to the tasks and goals at hand. However, Don Quixote ignores the clues that Sancho and others find most pertinent, focusing instead upon any detail, however minute, that corresponds to the chivalric schema. It is this aberrant perception that leads him to notice only that Maritornes is a female figure who comes near him with stealthy step in darkness, and to disregard the scents and textures that reveal her to be a peasant and prostitute rather than the fair princess of his schema.

The Paradox of Fiction

In the study of reading from a cognitive perspective; researchers have analyzed both the practices of fictional characters and also the experiences of actual readers. One key area of research concerns the "paradox of fiction," which is defined as the fact that psychologically stable readers experience emotional responses to fictional characters and events (Levinson 20; Zunshine, *Why* 195). Blakey Vermeule recently dedicated an entire book-length study to the question, *Why Do We Care about Literary Characters?* Her answer foregrounds the cognitive stimulation provided by active engagement with the mental activities of literary characters, which is both enjoyable and a way to develop real-life socio-cognitive skills (12–16). Jerrold Levinson writes that both psychologists and literary scholars have attempted to resolve this paradox by explaining it away; for example, by asserting the well-known "willing suspension of disbelief," or by claiming that the emotions felt toward characters are not the same as those felt for real people, or that fictional events trigger emotional responses to similar events readers remember from their own real lives (23). Levinson finds all of these explanations unconvincing as they do not take into account the full range of textual responses. Kendall Walton seeks to dismantle the paradox from a different angle, by showing that normal humans have emotional responses to many types of nonpresent events; he asserts that mental processing of memories, nostalgia, and anxiety about future events is cognitively similar to reading about fictional events. Walton writes that emotions like regret and remorse are also akin to emotional responses to reading; all consist of producing mental "simulations" that are perceived and responded to as if real and present (46). These insights concerning *emotional* reactions to fictional characters are also relevant to analyzing reader's *intellectual* responses, such as the formation of a Theory of Mind for protagonists or narrators (Chapter 1).

George Butte was among the first to study the thought processes of literary characters, with a decade of study and critical essays culminating in *I Know That You Know That I Know* (2004). He does not cite any of the major cognitive theorists, but instead bases his work upon the phenomenological philosophers, especially Merleau-Ponty, who also inspired many cognitivists. (The complete absence of reference to cognitivists is somewhat startling given that his title is so clearly connected to Dennett's model of intentionality.) Butte uses the term *intersubjectivity* rather than ToM or MR to describe his object of study, "the way that stories portray consciousness of consciousness" (vii). Butte's subtitle indicates that his object of study is novel and film subjectivity from Defoe to Hitchcock; he asserts that literary representations of intersubjectivity appear in a nascent state with *Moll Flanders* and achieve full flowering in the novels of Jane Austen. Howard Mancing has pointed out that this construct, based on Ian Watt's premise that the modern novel begins in eighteenth-century England, completely ignores the existence of earlier non-British novelistic narratives, such as *Don Quixote* and the Spanish picaresque tradition, which presented numerous examples of intersubjectivity or ToM ("Sancho" 128). Despite this significant flaw, Butte's readings of Austen and others are of interest for those scholars who seek to address character subjectivity and consciousness through a non-psychoanalytic frame.

Alan Palmer further develops the groundwork for analysis of the mental processes of literary characters. The introduction and first section of *Fictional Minds* (2004) reveal the inadequacies of conventional narratology and speech act theory for analysis of character. He links the reading of characters' mental states to reader response theory, claiming that one of the primary gap-filling activities is the use of textual clues to construct a coherent mindset for each character (3). He also links this model of active reading to the possible worlds theoretical model (32–36, 196–98). Where other theorists—such as Jerome Bruner, Marie-Laure Ryan, Thomas Pavel, and Lubromír Doležel—emphasize the mental construct of a story *world,* Palmer explores the construction of "continuing consciousness" for fictional *entities.* He points out that, even in real life, people have very partial and incomplete access to the consciousnesses of those around them, so that "our real-life cognitive frame" prepares us for the gaps in our knowledge of textual minds as well as textual worlds (199). Thus, although there is a clear ontological difference between people and characters, encounters with both require us to "make inferences and construct hypotheses based on limited information" (200). Within literary texts, where characters discuss each other as people, they repeatedly lament this self-same paucity of information—or worse, make faulty judgments based on lack of awareness of that lack. Palmer's book clearly demonstrates both the validity of using cognitive theories designed for observation of real people to discuss literary characters, as well as the benefits of studying "fictional minds." Like Butte, Palmer emphasizes the nineteenth-century social novel, but also addresses the early modern writing of Aphra Behn (Palmer further develops this line of thought in *Social Minds in the Novel,* which appeared after this book was completed).

Long before cognitive theory gave us the concrete concept of a ToM, awareness of this ability produced "metarepresentation," which Zunshine defines as the aesthetic technique of foregrounding mind reading activity within fictional texts (*Why* 50–60). Zunshine coined the neologism metarepresentational to designate a select group of texts in which ToM is a central thematic concern (5). However, this term may be confusing to scholars who associate representation with other literary theoretical paradigms; therefore, I prefer the phrase "intense mind reading novel" that Blakey Vermeule offers for similar texts—or my own neologism of metacognitive (Vermeule 70–71). Zunshine delineates source monitoring and source tagging as key components of such texts; these are the processes by which both characters and readers use their ToM to keep track of which characters do or do not possess particular information and also to gauge the reliability of narrators and characters as they are presented over the course of a novel (*Why* 50–60). This cognitive process is different from "semantic memory," which is used to obtain and store stable, objective facts for which the source is of no import. Source tagging enables us to distinguish universal facts from contingent or provisional information whose validity may be reconsidered at any time (Zunshine, *Why* 52). Source tagging is a central activity for character development, which often hinges upon the moments when a character forms and then later "reweighs" beliefs or feelings, and adapts or modifies behaviors based on an initial or revised understanding of a source (Zunshine, *Why* 61). The concept of reweighing in some ways resembles Aristoteles' paradigm of tragic *anagnorisis*, as well as the modern notion of the epiphany as the psychological turning point. However, the reweighing model requires that the new level of awareness derive from a very specific form of reconsideration—concerning how characters use their own ToM to evaluate the reliability of other characters and information. Source monitoring is also an essential tool for readers of metacognitive texts whose aesthetic interest derives from the unraveling of the complexity of character action, interaction, and motivation—or from discerning the narrator(s) as reliable or not (Zunshine, *Why* 76). As they lay bare the processes by which characters form and modify their perceptions of events and other characters, metacognitive narratives provide readers with a new way to conceptualize the sourcing strategies that all authors use, "turning formerly trusting readers into 'detectives' querying the author's motives" (64). In addition, metacognition can induce readers to scrutinize real-life social interactions from a new perspective, with more awareness of everyday source tagging and monitoring activity. Zunshine asserts that readers get pleasure from virtual mind reading tasks because they are a form of play or rehearsal that confirms our success at real-life MR; certainly, one aspect of our enjoyment of the *comedia* derives from our ability to follow and untangle the complex and multilayered levels of MR and intentionality (18).

The one flaw in Zunshine's ground-breaking study is the lack of any attempt to historicize literary deployment of ToM and metacognition. Although Zunshine acknowledges *Tristram Shandy* as an early example of this tactic, she does not seek to address the social contexts that might foster or support its manifestation at particular moments across three centuries. And, like Butte (and Palmer to a lesser extent) she mostly ignores the early modern period—apart from a brief analysis of Don Quixote as the exemplar of a reader with defective source monitoring. However, Zunshine's most recent anthology, *Cognitive Cultural Study*, contains essays that fill both of those gaps. In addition, Vermeule's study provides an excellent role model of historicized cognitive analysis. She carefully traces the connections between the rise of the "intense mind reading novel" and a newly monetarized nineteenth-century economic culture in which the ability to form an accurate ToM is crucial for decisions regarding credit-worthiness (7–9). Paula Leverage, Howard Mancing, Richard Schweickert, and Jennifer William's anthology *Theory of Mind and Literature* also offers several essays that situate mind-reading activities within specific social frameworks. This chapter, like the rest of the book, builds upon these foundations by situating the reading practices on display in *Don Quixote* within the specific context of how early modern culture responded to the invention of the printing press and the rise of entertainment fiction (Ong 31).

In many studies of the paradox of fiction, Don Quixote is alluded to as an example of a reader who devotes excessive emotional energy to his literary experiences. Keith Oatley and Mitra Gholomain address a related form of response, where readers identify with a literary character as if he or she were real. They describe identification as leaving behind one's own world to experience the fictional life or world vicariously (269). Identification can take several guises, ranging from admiration to idealization to eroticization (276). Of particular note is the form of unhealthy identification where a reader seeks "to mirror a fictional character so different from him- or herself that all possibility of attaining the character's status is dismissed" (Oatley and Gholomain 276). Of course, the gravity of Don Quixote's problematic mirroring stems precisely from his identification with medieval chivalric characters; putting aside all of the fantastical and magical powers that no real knight could ever have possessed, even those details of daily life that did reflect actual medieval knight errantry are too far removed from the realities of 1605 to be accessible to the protagonist. This distance is highlighted when the obsessed reader seeks to make use of the armor his ancestors had actually used in earlier times, "Y lo primero que hizo fue limpiar unas armas que habían sido de sus bisabuelos, que, tomadas de orín y llenas de moho, luengos siglos había que estaban puestas y olvidadas en un rincón" (I.1.75). The rust and mildew provide graphic physical evidence of a doomed pursuit of identification. Temporal distance separates this reader irrevocably from the characters he seeks to mirror. This combination of impossible identification and a total disregard for the paradox of fiction lies at the heart of Don Quixote's anomalous reading habits.

Overactive Reading: Immersion and Participatory Response

Cognitive theorists have moved beyond theoretical speculation to explore what readers actually do—how their reading practices respond to the paradox of fiction (László 96; Miall 11–22). In particular, there is interest in the nature of leisure reading and of immersion. Oatley and Gholomain cite Janice Radway's landmark study of actual romance novel readers, which separated genre fiction fans into two groups: those who use identification with romance heroines as an occasional and harmless "retreat" and those who are "compulsive" in their habitual escape from the problems of adult life (Oatley and Gholomain 287; Radway 84). Clearly, Don Quixote's form of identification is at the far end of the compulsive continuum, where identification is not merely frequent but constant for weeks on end. Oatley and Gholomain assert that one main feature separating trivial genre fiction from artistic or literary texts is the difference between works that deliberately invite identification and obsession vs. those that use aesthetic and other tactics to stimulate thought and reflection (274–75). This distinction is similar to that made by the priest and the barber as they survey Don Quixote's library, praising epic poetry and condemning chivalric and pastoral fiction in terms similar to those Radway uses for romantic fiction. Thus, when the curate praises *Tirante el blanco* as the rare example of a good chivalric novel, his analysis indicates that this book is an exception because it does *not* invite inappropriate identification, "por su estilo, es éste el mejor libro del mundo: aquí comen los caballeros, y duermen, y mueren en sus camas, y hacen testamento antes de su muerte, con estas cosas de que todos los demás libros deste género carecen" (I.6.117). The realistic and even moralistic qualities that the curate praises mark this novel as less likely to incite compulsive and escapist consumption. The psychological implications of leisure reading, which Cervantes interrogates in relation to pastoral, Moorish, and exemplary fiction as well as chivalric tales, is a central concern for cognitive studies of the reading process and reader response (Alcalá Galán 41–56).

Victor Nell's *Lost in a Book* seeks to analyze ludic reading and readers, from a theoretical and experimental perspective, in order to reconceptualize this activity and to destigmatize some forms of leisure reading. Nell links concerns about entertainment fiction to moments of religious reform: both during the Reformation era in Germany and the Puritan movement in England, the scrutiny of popular fiction was linked to social discourses that praised industry and disparaged leisure activity as a form of idleness that could foster sinful activity (26–27). Nell's study does not include consideration of post-Tridentine Spain; however, Counter Reformation Spain was equally suspicious of worldly pleasures. And, of course, the topic of "idleness" is ubiquitous in the Cervantine novel, where it is depicted as provoking a socioeconomic crisis as well as a spiritual decline. The importance of unproductive leisure arises at key moments, beginning with the very first sentence of the prologue, which simultaneously apostrophizes and reprimands its "desocupado lector." Don Quixote himself, as well as the pseudoshepherds who follow Marcela into the woods, and the Duke and Duchess, are denigrated with the adjective *ocioso*. The forms of unhealthy reading in which these characters engage is intimately linked to the idleness of their social groups.

Howard Mancing points to Richard Gerrig's book *Experiencing Narrative Worlds* as an extremely valuable contribution to the study of narrative and thus as a potent potential tool for analysis of *Don Quixote* (*Reference* 133). Gerrig proposes the metaphor of immersive consumption as the sense of being transported to a narrative world (13). However, he cautions that this voyage is purely intellectual; the normal reader or viewer knows that it is not possible to interact with the narrative world. Given that caveat, Gerrig delineates a continuum of normal participatory responses (p-responses) ranging from expressing hopes and fear about the outcome to gap-filling mental activities, such as imagining physical details or motivations that the author does not specify (66–68). In the very first chapter, as Cervantes establishes his protagonist's eccentricities, he describes the gap-filling aspects in a way that introduces the reader to the hidalgo's hopeless entanglement in the paradox of fiction. Immersion manifests itself here in discussions that treat the characters and narrative world as if they were real; first he confuses fictional and historical figures, and then compounds this error in his musings about his favorite heroes, "No estaba muy bien con las heridas que don Belianís daba y recebía, porque se imaginaba que, por grandes maestros que le hubiesen curado, no dejaría de tener el rostro y todo el cuerpo lleno de cicatrices y señales" (I.1.72). It is a clear sign of anomalous immersion that he questions the verisimilitude of engaging in battle without incurring scars, but accepts at face value common fantastic elements such as enchanters. In the second volume, Cervantes continues to explore Don Quixote's gap-filling as he shares with the priest and barber the mental images he has formed of various chivalric heroes:

> —De Reinaldos —respondió don Quijote— me atrevo a decir que era ancho de rostro, de color bermejo, los ojos bailadores y algo saltados, puntoso y colérico en demasía ... De Roldán, o Rotolando, o Orlando, que con todos estos nombres le nombran las historias, soy de parecer y me afirmo que fue de mediana estatura, ancho de espaldas, algo estevado, moreno de rostro y barbitaheño, velloso en el cuerpo y de vista amenazadora, corto de razones, pero muy comedido y bien criado.
> —Si no fue Roldán más gentilhombre que vuestra merced ha dicho —replicó el cura, no fue maravilla que la señora Angélica la Bella le desdeñase. ... (II.1.51)

Cervantes once again signals the idiosyncratic nature of these imaginative practices; Don Quixote is unconventional even in such an ordinary aspect of reading as filling in gaps concerning details about physical appearance. As his friends indicate, his projections do not correspond at all to the idealizations normally associated with chivalric texts. This scene may be construed both as an additional piece of evidence for his defective reading practices, as well as a parody on Cervantes's part concerning the convention that all knights-errant must be handsome, just as all of their damsels must be beautiful.

Nell describes a continuum of intensive reading responses, ranging from entrancement to addictive immersion (1–2, 212). His qualitative research points to two different types of immersive response related to positions on this continuum. The beneficial and intellectually respectable form of entrancement is classified as "looking for heightened excitement" (9). Entranced reading also requires an active and engaged mental process (77). By contrast, the activity that he stigmatizes is characterized as escapist or addictive and denigrated by the metaphor of gluttony, in which a text is consumed so greedily that its flavors are not even noticed, much less savored (239). This reading process is characterized as passive rather than active in the sense that there is a lack of critical engagement with the text. Nell links the negative forms of immersion to consumption of mass-marketed genre fiction, such as the western, romance novel, or science fiction, which is depicted as highly repetitive and predictable, so that intellectual nutrition is scarce at best. Nell's book posits Don Quixote as a prime example of the stigmatized gluttonous reader. A *superficial* initial scrutiny of the protagonist would agree with that assessment, in particular because Cervantes explicitly critiques the repetitive and escapist natures of the genre narratives—especially *novelas de caballería* and pastoral literature—that he and other characters devour. However, it can likewise be argued that the characters' ludic consumption of texts falls into both categories, for their active engagement with the story worlds also represents the characters' attempts to effect change and self-actualization in their lives.

This escapist but active form of reading may be linked to Gerrig's studies of reading arousal (177–90). Reading enjoyment derives in part from the alternate cognitive state that immersion produces; however, in normal readers the return to normal cognition is also enjoyable. When Don Quixote stays up all night reading and then becomes a knight, when Marcela's admirers follow her into the pastures and woods, and even when the Duke and Duchess re-create a chivalric world for their deluded guest, each is seeking to achieve and then prolong a state of alternative cognition in the hope of bringing about some change in their external circumstances or their internal perspectives. Yet Cervantes is quite harsh in his treatment of this aspect of arousal, for the pseudo-shepherds and the ducal couple are depicted as self-indulgent.

One primary sign of abnormal p-response or addiction is to continue to think intensively about the plot and characters after putting down the book, and to neglect real life obligations because of immersion. Don Quixote clearly falls into this category; not only does he sell off his only patrimony to buy books, but he neglects the few responsibilities of an hidalgo in order to dedicate himself wholly to reading, "En resolución, él se enfrascó tanto en su lectura, que se le pasaban las noches leyendo de claro en claro, y los días de turbio en turbio " (I.1.73). Two decades before Cervantes sought to demystify and hence deliver a death blow to the chivalric novel, Teresa de Ávila in her *Libro de su vida* also blamed excessive engagement with chivalric novels for character defects: both her mother's lax parenting and her own deviations from childhood virtue were attributed to this pastime. Saint Teresa writes of her mother's reading habits as escapist, "lo hacía para no pensar en grandes trabajos que tenía, y ocupar sus hijos, que no anduviesen en otras cosas perdidos" (119). She characterizes her own reading as addictive, "era tan en extremo lo que en esto me embebía, que si no tenía libro nuevo, no estaba contenta" (119). At its most extreme, immersion may manifest itself in "replotting"—the term Gerrig uses to describe mental activities and conversations in which readers or viewers "mentally simulate alternative plot events or endings" (67–96). Saint Teresa explains that once engaged with chivalric literature, she and her brother abandoned their previous favorite form of active replotting—re-enactments of biblical tales—in favor of knightly adventures. In the case of children and teenagers, such a playtime pursuit is relatively harmless (although Teresa herself judges this "fall" rather harshly).

The early chapters of *Don Quixote* delineate the process by which an aging adult moves from entrancement to obsessive p-responses—at first, merely thinking about and discussing his favorite chivalric characters, to the neglect of his estate. Later, his eccentric p-response culminates in a highly anomalous form of replotting, in which the template of chivalric adventures serves as the point of departure for new tales in which he serves as the protagonist. The fact that Don Quixote lives out these adventures in public, rather than imagining, discussing, acting out at home, or even writing them down, as in fan fiction, is clearly a pathological form of live action replotting, which places him at the extreme edge of the p-response continuum. Cervantes repeatedly emphasizes the unique and bizarre nature of such immersion; each time that a new group of people encounters and comes to understand his excessive p-response, the reaction is described as "admirado(s)." A search of an English-language on-line translation reveals no fewer than thirty-one instances where characters are "amazed" or "astonished" by their first encounter with Don Quixote's immersive activities and his rupture of the paradox of fiction.

Don Quixote's uniqueness as a reader derives from the near-total identification with his idols and his long-term devotion to replotting. However, across the two volumes, Cervantes demonstrates that although this p-response is extreme and based on a complete erasure of the paradox of fiction, this reader is in fact not completely unique but merely occupies the far end of a replotting continuum. For example, the first *novela intercalada* features a group of wealthy peasants who live out the conventions of pastoral literature. While Marcela and most of her swains remain grounded in reality, it is arguable that a Grisóstomo, who either commits suicide or dies of a broken heart, mirrors Don Quixote's obsessive p-response. In addition, the priest and barber have no trouble luring the occupants of the inn to enact chivalric roles, ostensibly in order to convince their friend to return home. However, because live action replotting requires a solid familiarity with literary codes and genre norms as well as an emotional investment, the text implies a certain level of entrancement on the part of all these readers (László 143). In the second volume, Sansón Carrasco's absorption goes one step further, for his determination to avenge his initial defeat constitutes an identification with the values of chivalric literature approaching that of the protagonist himself, for individual revenge is part of a chivalric code prohibited both by Catholic dogma and early modern law.

It is especially noteworthy that by the mid-point of the second volume, it is more often Don Quixote who is astonished by strange events, rather than his actions astonishing others. In fact, the scenarios the ducal couple and the nobility of Barcelona created are also examples of live action replotting. Although these characters are more firmly rooted in the reality of their era, and do not confuse history and fiction, they nonetheless constitute a related category of anomalous reader, like the faux shepherds of the first volume. The effort and imagination that the Duke and Duchess devote to creating elaborate adventures reveals that even apparently sane readers from the highest social levels are prone to excessive forms of immersion. Cervantes emphasizes their intensive efforts to bring their former guests back to the palace for one final hoax,

> tanto era lo que gustaba de las cosas de Sancho y de don Qui-
> jote; y haciendo tomar los caminos cerca y lejos del castillo, por
> todas las partes que imaginó que podría volver don Quijote,

> con muchos criados suyos de a pie y de a caballo, para que por
> fuerza o de grado le trujesen al castillo. (II.70.564)

Thus, although these two characters have not forgotten their true identities, their obsession with replotting borders on the obsessive and pathological. Indeed, this quest for one final adventure leads Cide Hamete to question their mental stability, "que tiene para sí ser tan locos los burladores como los burlados y que no estaban los duques dos dedos de parecer tontos, pues tanto ahínco ponían en burlarse de dos tontos" (II.70.564–65). It is deeply ironic that readers who enjoyed the first volume, which warned continually against the dangers of immersion through Don Quixote's negative example, nonetheless find themselves sufficiently entranced by *his* world that they go to great lengths to take an active role in the adventures of their favorite protagonist. It is equally paradoxical that Cervantes posits such a reaction to his *own* fiction, for in the first volume there are several indications that a reformulated chivalric novel, presenting adventure and valor rather than magical nonsense, would elicit beneficial entrancement rather than addiction,

> sin duda podrían salir algunos con la perfección que vuestra
> merced ha dicho, enriqueciendo nuestra lengua del agradable
> y precioso tesoro de la elocuencia, dando ocasión que los libros
> viejos se escureciesen a la luz de los nuevos que saliesen, para
> honesto pasatiempo, no solamente de los ociosos, sino de los
> más ocupados. (I.48.572)

If even Cide Hamete's (Cervantes's) own best recuperative efforts nonetheless result in obsessive consumption, then perhaps the human mind is inherently susceptible to consuming all entertainment fictions in an unproductive manner. Nell notes that throughout the history of book publication, the "elitist fallacy" has posited that poorer, less-educated readers would be most likely to want an escape from reality and thus would be most prone to pathological immersion (4). However, in Cervantes's case we see that readers from all social levels succumb to this temptation; indeed, in this earlier age when poor people were mostly illiterate, it is among the prosperous and leisured classes that reading addiction is most prominent.

The end of Don Quixote's reading arousal and replotting coincides with the end of his life. One of the most popular and enduring explanations of his death is that he succumbs to extreme melancholy; life is not worth living once he can no longer engage in his preferred from of replotting (Soufas, *Melancholy*; Friedman, "Executing"; Lo Ré). The narrator suggests "ya fuese de la melancolía que le causaba el verse vencido, o ya por la disposición del cielo, que así lo ordenaba" and his friends concur, " creyendo que la pesadumbre de verse vencido y de no ver cumplido su deseo en la libertad y desencanto de Dulcinea le tenía de aquella suerte, por todas las vías posibles procuraban alegrarle" (II.74.586). This interpretation is indicative of a long-standing Western paradigm concerning the deranged psychological state of readers who engage in the most intensive forms of immersion, such as replotting. Thus, just as a Grisóstomo infected by courtly love norms could not withstand Marcela's rejection, Don Quixote cannot live without adventures. The final indictment of formulaic literary genres that incite excessive immersion—and of those readers that fall into addiction—is that for the most severely afflicted, life in the real world becomes unbearable. Cognitive studies provide a new vocabulary that enriches our understanding of the reading process and reader responses to various types of fiction, enabling a deeper scrutiny of Don Quixote's engagement with fiction as well as that of other characters. In particular, the tracing of a continuum of reading immersion permits a fuller contextualization of the protagonist both within this novel and in comparison to other literary characters. Mercedes Alcalá Galán asserts that the Cervantine novel moved beyond moral condemnation to play a key role in *normalizing* novelistic fiction (56–57). Thus, as is so often the case with Cervantes, we find an awareness of human cognitive processes that appears to "anticipate" the paradigms of twenty-first-century research.

ToM and Machiavellian Intelligence in *Don Quixote*

As discussed in Chapter 1, Theory of Mind or ToM entails the study of how people—and primates—conceptualize the thoughts and rationales behind the actions of others (Whiten 150; Zunshine, *Why* 4). Possession of a ToM concerning one's cohorts enables the development of Machiavellian or Social Intelligence, through which primates and humans pursue social goals by misleading others concerning what they are thinking (Byrne and

Whiten, "Manipulation" 211). As Howard Mancing has demonstrated, Sancho Panza is capable of forming a highly detailed and sophisticated ToM concerning Don Quixote, which enabled him to use MI to deceive his master about Dulcinea's enchantment ("Sancho" 125–28). In this episode, Cervantes does not depict the use of social intelligence solely as a conventional sign of inherent dishonesty among laborers, in order to reinforce the deserved marginality of peasants as a class. On the one hand, Cervantes emphasizes Sancho's gleeful and even smug reaction to the successful deception, "Harto tenía que hacer el socarrón de Sancho en disimular la risa, oyendo las sandeces de su amo, tan delicadamente engañado" (II.10.113). The adjective *socarrón* in particular reinforces binary discourses of class hierarchy. However, Sancho had earlier justified his plan to himself in a way that presented him in a more favorable light, "Quizá con esta porfía acabaré con él que no me envíe otra vez a semejantes mensajerías" (II.10.107). The incident of manipulation is thus depicted both as malicious and also as a defense mechanism, a necessary evil in the face of a master who demands the impossible—the very type of SI so prevalent and so vehemently justified in picaresque narrative.

This same combination of malice and righteousness is present in Sancho's other elaborate deception of his master, concerning the whippings he is to inflict upon himself to achieve Dulcinea's disenchantment. By the time Sancho strips off his shirt in chapter 71, Cervantes had already established such physical punishment as a symptom of class-based cruelty. When Sancho had been commanded to submit to pain in order to help resuscitate Altisidora, his refusal explicitly rejects such hierarchical injustices,

> —¡Voto a tal, así me deje yo sellar el rostro ni manosearme la cara como volverme moro! ¡Cuerpo de mí! ¿Qué tiene que ver manosearme el rostro con la resurreción desta doncella? Regostóse la vieja a los bledos ... ¡Encantan a Dulcinea, y azótanme para que se desencante; muérese Altisidora de males que Dios quiso darle, y hanla de resucitar hacerme a mí veinte y cuatro mamonas y acribarme el cuerpo a alfilerazos y acardenalarme los brazos a pellizcos! (II.69.560)

Even though Cervantes repeats the epithet "socarrón" in describing the ruse whereby Sancho lashes tree bark rather than his own back, it is once again in a context of critiquing the infliction of physical harm,

> Hasta seis o ocho se habría dado Sancho, cuando le pareció ser
> pesada la burla y muy barato el precio della, y, deteniéndose
> un poco, dijo a su amo que se llamaba a engaño, porque me-
> recía cada azote de aquellos ser pagado a medio real, no que a
> cuartillo.
>
> —Prosigue, Sancho amigo, y no desmayes —le dijo don
> Quijote—, que yo doblo la parada del precio.
>
> —Dese modo —dijo Sancho—, ¡a la mano de Dios, y llue-
> van azotes!
>
> Pero el socarrón dejó de dárselos en las espaldas y daba en
> los árboles, con unos suspiros de cuando en cuando, que parecía
> que con cada uno dellos se le arrancaba el alma. Tierna la de
> don Quijote, temeroso de que no se le acabase la vida y no con-
> siguiese su deseo por la imprudencia de Sancho. ... (II.72.572)

The beginning of this passage reveals that enduring such pain is
not worth the initial substantial amount that Sancho was prom-
ised, while the final words indicate that Don Quixote's tenderness
is evenly divided between genuine concern for his servant and
self-centered worry that excessive lashing might cause the squire to
kill himself before fulfilling the ultimate goal. These two episodes
in particular emphasize that MI is one of the few weapons available to the lower classes in their quest to defend themselves from
the abuses of a hierarchical society, that it is a lack of social power
rather than genetic inferiority that "breeds" dishonesty. Although
he does not discuss ideological implications, it is surely not coincidental that the two other early modern characters whom Mancing identifies as using MI are Lazarillo and Celestina ("Sancho"
128–29).

Sancho's capabilities with ToM are also crucial to his successful encounters with the inhabitants of Barataria whom he had to
judge; for example, enabling him to create the appropriate scenario to test the alleged rape victim. These variable uses of MI complicate readers' evaluations of his mind and character. One mark
of the total folly of the scenarios created by the Duke and Duchess
and their retainers is Sancho's inability to use his ToM in those
circumstances. No rational peasant, taught that the nobles are his
intellectual and moral superiors, would posit such contemptuous
motivations to explain the mysterious adventures that befall him.
For this reason, despite his ingenuity in many other situations, he
fails to comprehend the courtiers who ostensibly serve him and
hence cannot use his ToM or MI to resolve the problem of inade-

quate food supply or armed attack. In most instances, Sancho's successful use of ToM and MI is not employed to denigrate him as a deceitful and thus despicable character; but rather, to reveal the social constructions of knowledge and power that are designed to create and maintain hierarchies. Cognitive readings can enhance materialist scholarship by enlarging the field of investigation, providing additional tools for the exploration of mental activity. Ideological criticism has tended to foreground characters' behavior and social circumstances, scrutinized via binary constructs such as oppression and resistance or marginalization and claiming a voice; cognitive study provides an important complement.

The use of ToM is not limited to Sancho; clearly, it is their awareness of Don Quixote's unique cognitive processes that animate the Duke and Duchess. In this case, the term MI does merit all of the pejorative connotations associated with the notorious Italian author, for the couple abuses their wealth and power to arrange the series of humiliating and damaging adventures for no purpose beyond their own decadent amusement. As their own resident priest informs them on the very first night of Don Quixote's sojourn, such behavior is harmful both to him and to their own souls,

> —Vuestra Excelencia, señor mío, tiene que dar cuenta a Nuestro Señor de lo que hace este buen hombre. Este don Quijote, o don Tonto, o como se llama, imagino yo que no debe de ser tan mentecato como Vuestra Excelencia quiere que sea dándole ocasiones a la mano para que lleve adelante sus sandeces y vaciedades. (II.31.281–82)

The ducal couple is repeatedly captured in moments of gloating over their successful pranks; the narrator also emphasizes that they never regret the physical harm that sometimes befalls their hapless guests as a result of their machinations. This noble pair's "cavalier" misuse of ToM serves as a foil and counter point to Sancho's more defensible actions, contributing to the novel's scrutiny of social hierarchies by linking gratuitous dishonesty to the aristocrat rather than the *labrador*.

ToM also lies at the heart of the many efforts to use the norms of Don Quixote's own chivalric world in order to induce him to give up his adventures and return home. In this circumstance, which involves a more beneficent form of deception, cognitivists substitute the term Social Intelligence for MI (Strum 74). However, while the end goal of protecting their neighbor from future harm is worthy, the elaborate scenario that the priest and barber create with Dorotea's assistance is not univocally positive. Although they do succeed in bringing him home, the old man is humiliated in the process. Because of the fictitious enchantment, Don Quixote is forced to endure a week-long ride through the countryside in a cage, the object of amusement to passersby such as the literary critic canon. He is even reduced to soiling himself because enchanted men ostensibly do not have physical needs. And, where the peasant neighbor who had found Don Quixote lying on the ground in chapter 5 waited until nightfall so that the village would not witness his first ignominious return, his so-called friends show no such discretion,

> llegaron a la aldea de don Quijote, adonde entraron en la mitad del día, que acertó a ser domingo, y la gente estaba toda en la plaza, por mitad de la cual atravesó el carro de don Quijote. Acudieron todos a ver lo que en el carro venía y, cuando conocieron a su compatrioto, quedaron maravillados. (I.52.602)

The mock duels that Sansón Carrasco arranges to lure Don Quixote home in the second volume present this same combination of beneficial deception and cruelty; his return at the end of the second volume provides another unflattering spectacle. Although their understanding of Don Quixote's ToM does enable his friends to put an end to his risky escapades, a reader cannot help but use his or her own ToM to suspect that they derive some bit of fun for themselves at his expense. Mancing correctly asserts that ToM is pervasive in *Don Quixote*,

> If one doesn't read *Don Quixote* as a constantly evolving, ever more intricate, series of scenes involving thoughtful fictional minds interacting with each other in the widest possible variety of ways, both theorizing about how other minds work and simulating the feelings of other minds, the novel simply cannot be understood. ("James Parr" 140)

The contradictory manner in which characters use SI to impact each other also stimulates—and frustrates—the readers' ToM, for few novels of any era present such a wide variety of character motivations. The ethical ambiguity readers attribute to these characters derives in part from our inability to establish a stable ToM for any of the main characters—or the primary narrators.

Source Monitoring and Metacognition

As indicated above, Lisa Zunshine identifies *Don Quixote* as the initiator of metarepresentational technique and deems all such subsequent texts, from *Clarissa* to *Pale Fire*, as Cervantes's "progeny" (*Why* 75). Zunshine provides a rather cursory analysis of Don Quixote's source monitoring and source tagging abilities, and does not address any other characters in that novel, because her purpose is to establish the foundation for a detailed analysis of later, purportedly more audacious texts. She notes that the protagonist

> suffers from a selective failure of source monitoring. He takes in representations that "normal" people store with a restrictive agent-specifying source tag such as "as told by the author of a romance" as lacking any such tag. He thus lets the information contained in romances circulate among his mental databases as architectural truth, contaminating his knowledge about the world that we assume has hitherto been relatively accurate. (*Why* 75)

Damaged source monitoring is the root cause for Don Quixote's inability to negotiate the paradox of fiction, to distinguish between historical and fictional figures and events.

The conversation with the priest and barber at the beginning of the second volume is just one of many in which Don Quixote violates the norms of source tagging; he refers, in the same breath and sentence, to real although inflated historical figures, such as Roland or the Cid, in conjunction with Amadís and his fictitious progeny. This discussion is especially noteworthy because of the way in which the hidalgo defends the existence of his heroes and the giants they defeated. Here, he assimilates the miraculous and the fantastic of Christian and chivalric myth:

> —En esto de gigantes —respondió don Quijote— hay diferentes opiniones, si los ha habido o no en el mundo; pero la Santa Escritura, que no puede faltar un átomo en la verdad, nos muestra que los hubo, contándonos la historia de aquel filisteazo de Golías, que tenía siete codos y medio de altura, que es una desmesurada grandeza. (II.1.48)

As Cervantes contrasts three completely different forms of source tag: the historical, fictional, and biblical, readers are made aware that, despite the vastly different status attributed to each, there is in fact considerable overlap concerning outsized or exaggerated deeds and beings among the three ostensibly distinct modes of narrative. This overlap undermines confidence concerning source tagging and even blurs the clear distinctions between historical fact and the modes of non-truth that F.G. Bailey has identified, from fiction and fabulation to a continuum of actual lies—from polite and harmless to decisively malicious (14–21). Thus, although Don Quixote is unique in his drastically flawed source monitoring and also delusional concerning the goals that this error leads him to pursue, Cervantes also makes clear that even for a reasonable human being, the unstable nature of cultural narratives presents an obstacle to accurate source tagging.

Source monitoring problems and metacognitional episodes are not limited to the protagonist; they are also central to Sancho's development as a character. Spain's cultural code granted significant source authority to the gentry, so it is not surprising that this peasant would give initial credence to his master's promises of significant reward. However, as Sancho begins to develop an awareness of the problems with Don Quixote's source tagging, the logical response would be to "reweigh" his ToM concerning his master and the reliability and pertinence of chivalric codes. In fact, this is precisely what happens on numerous occasions. After the ungrateful galley slaves attack their liberators, Sancho urges a retreat into the Sierra Nevada to escape legal repercussions, because "le hago saber que con la Santa Hermandad no hay usar de caballerías, que no se le da a ella por cuantos caballeros andantes hay dos maravedís" (I.23.277). Sancho is willing to continue on with the chivalric adventures and to take the risk that the promise of great wealth may never come to pass. But, when his safety is at stake, the squire rejects the chivalric source tag, and instead insists on prudence in order to avoid the jail sentence associated with violating real world source tags. This pattern is repeated on numerous occasions; where Don Quixote's chivalric source deems all hesitation in the face of danger as cowardice, Sancho repeatedly asserts an alternate code of pragmatism in order to protect himself from harm. This caution, he deems "buen gobierno" (I.23.277).

Sancho's source monitoring is even more complex than Don Quixote's, for he is willing to accept the chivalric codes in those situations that benefit him, for example by accepting the right to "spoils of war" in the encounters that are characterized as battles. However, this process is extremely unstable, for all Sancho's acts of reweighing are temporary and provisional. And, Cervantes's careful plotting assures that each time this reweighing seems about to lead Sancho to a genuine epiphany, some material reward emerges to lure him back to acceptance of chivalric source codes. For example, when the pair escapes to the Sierra Morena after a series of highly unpleasant and unproductive adventures, they immediately discover Cardenio's valise, with the gold coins that are worth several months of a peasant's earnings. Chivalric codes enable him to keep the gold, when other source tags would have required that the treasure be restored to its original owner. Similarly, the pair encounters the Duke and Duchess and enter a world of luxury precisely at the moment in the second volume when a series of disasters had caused Sancho to lose all faith in the chivalric source tags and to decide to return home. Thus, Sancho's journey provides just enough economic benefit that the chivalric source appears plausible, yet also presents innumerable instances where Don Quixote's source monitoring is not merely delusional but impacts both of them with directly negative and often painful repercussions. The unreliable nature of the code Sancho has learned to employ is an important component of his own paradoxical state as both *simple* and *agudo*. It is not *entirely* irrational for Sancho to accept Don Quixote's source tagging because the world does at times appear to function and provide rewards in accordance with chivalric codes.

The confusion of codes and metacognition is especially prominent as Sancho evaluates the enchantment that brings the first volume to a close. Although his apprenticeship has taught him to accept the possibility of magical events, his own senses offer a different perspective, "Señor, para descargo de mi conciencia le quiero decir lo que pasa cerca de su encantamento, y es que aquestos dos que vienen aquí cubiertos los rostros son el cura de nuestro lugar y el barbero" (I.48.573). However, confused source monitoring leads from this valid observation about the physical world to an entirely misguided ToM for the priest and barber; he proposes that the deception has been propagated "de pura envidia que tienen como vuestra merced se les adelanta en hacer famosos hechos" (I.48.573). Of course, the malice he attributes to the two disguised men corresponds to the chivalric world source tag. As

Sancho seeks to understand and navigate a world in which people of elevated social class employ two very different sets of source tags, he devises an ad hoc method for making decisions and using ToM. Rather than seeking to create a formal theory with concrete laws that can be applied universally, he weighs the potential benefits and damages of each new situation and chooses whichever source tag allows him to maximize opportunity and minimize risk.

Early in the second volume, there is a metacognitive scene in which the priest and barber seek to test Don Quixote's return to lucidity. The results are mixed, for he responds to their insulting allegory about the madman with the angry retort,

> Yo, señor barbero, no soy Neptuno, el dios de las aguas, ni procuro que nadie me tenga por discreto no lo siendo; sólo me fatigo por dar a entender al mundo en el error en que está en no renovar en sí el felicísimo tiempo donde campeaba la orden de la andante caballería. (II.1.48)

This speech illustrates the well-known *topos* of the protagonist as "un cuerdo loco"; the representation of both master and squire as paradoxical figures highlights the difficulties in forming an accurate ToM for people or characters who do not conform to psychosocial norms, whose source tagging ability is *sometimes* functional. The early interactions between the half-nude Cardenio and various other characters present a related conundrum; he too, behaves in such an unpredictable manner that establishing a ToM for him is elusive. Don Quixote and Cardenio are of course social outliers, but their quirks provide important insights concerning the variability of human cognitive functioning. As Zunshine notes in her analysis of Richardson's unreliable narrator/character Lovelace, his "metarepresentational ability is selectively compromised and the novel cultivates the scenes that make the reader uncertain" concerning his credibility; I would argue that Cervantes sows similar seeds of reader doubt (98). Thus, I would seek to identify in *Don Quixote* the same complexity that Zunshine posits for *Clarissa* and *Lolita,* whose depictions of ToM

> allo[w] the narrative to engage, train, tease and titillate our metarepresentational ability. Our brain is the focus of the novel's attention, its playground, its raison d'être, its meaning, whereas [the characters] are but the means of delivering this kind of wonderfully rich stimulation to the variety of cognitive adaptations making up our ToM. (*Why* 99)

Zunshine's analysis of Lovelace and of Nabokov's Humbert Humbert focuses on their dual status as both characters with a mind and also unreliable narrators concerning their own and others' ToM. Cervantes, on the other hand, divides these instabilities among a variety of characters and narrators. I believe that both approaches are equally successful in stimulating the kind of readerly engagement that Zunshine reserves for later fictions.

Metacognition plays an important role in the final chapter, both through presence and absence. The chapter begins as the narrator and characters "reweigh" the protagonist and seek to form a new ToM to explain his return to sanity—that is to say, his return to conventional source monitoring. However, as many scholars have noted, the text does not represent the pivotal moment when the knight reverts to his true identity as Alonso Quijano; in cognitive terms, the crucial moment of "reweighing " is absent. As he reclaims the name of Alonso Quijano, the protagonist proclaims,

> —Las misericordias —respondió don Quijote—, sobrina, son las que en este instante ha usado Dios conmigo, a quien, como dije, no las impiden mis pecados. Yo tengo juicio ya libre y claro, sin las sombras caliginosas de la ignorancia que sobre él me pusieron mi amarga y continua leyenda de los detestables libros de las caballerías. (II.74.587)

In a realistic novel that has shunned or demystified all forms of the miraculous for nearly one thousand pages, Alonso's explanation of divine intervention as the source of his reweighing seems no more accurate a source tag than any other he had attributed as Don Quixote. As Alonso overtly rejects the source tagging he had performed previously, his reweighing veers toward the excessive; the stipulation in his will that no man seeking to wed his niece should even know of chivalric tales implies a concern that engaging such fiction is likely to warp *all* readers' s metacognitive ability. In presenting a character whose pivotal act of reweighing is nearly as delusional as his previously warped source tagging, Cervantes anticipates and even exceeds the audacity of contemporary writers who push the envelope concerning such norms by presenting conflicting and ultimately unresolvable metarepresentations.

The profusion of contradictory and self-conscious narrators also contributes to Cervantine metacognition. James Parr, Howard Mancing, and many others have given cogent and exhaustive descriptions of the many different voices and their inconsistencies

(Parr, "On Narration"; Mancing, "Cervantes"). Among the many examples they cite, two moments seem particularly representative of the connection between complex narration and the formation and reweighing of source tags by readers. As the voice that Parr terms the super narrator opens chapter 10, in which the squire convinces his master that a smelly peasant girl is actually an enchanted Dulcinea, we read,

> Llegando el autor desta grande historia a contar lo que en este capítulo cuenta, dice que quisiera pasarle en silencio, temeroso de que no había de ser creído, porque las locuras de don Quijote llegaron aquí al término y raya de las mayores que pueden imaginarse, y aun pasaron dos tiros de ballesta más allá de las mayores. Finalmente, aunque con este miedo y recelo, las escribió de la misma manera que él las hizo. (II.10.103–04)

This passage exemplifies the aesthetic paradigm that Zunshine associates with later writers who provoke frequent modifications of readers' source monitoring; the reader is presented with two different narrative voices even as we are teased concerning what new folly could have so provoked a historian who had already narrated the many follies of the first volume. By the end of the chapter, an additional problem asserts itself, for the adventure is *not* so strange as indicated, and in retrospect the warning appears excessive. In reweighing the Arab historian, are we to decide that he lied, or merely that his sense of discomfort is much greater than our own? Is there a need to modify this narrator's source tag? The Cave of Montesinos chapter repeats and magnifies this extreme metacognition, as the super narrator informs us of comments by the *morisco* translator concerning the notes he had found in the margins of the Arabic manuscript. Not only is the reader presented with three different narrative presences, but also with two contradictory explanations on the part of the protagonist concerning the veracity of his story. The reader's judgment is even more explicitly called upon here, as Cide Hamete refuses to reach a conclusion, "Tú, lector, pues eres prudente, juzga lo que te pareciere" (II.24.223). As this chapter seeks to make abundantly clear, even though the early modern era lacked a neuroscience vocabulary, Cervantes lays bare many aspects of the cognitive activities involved in the reading process; in addition, his innovative narrative techniques caused readers to invent new reading tactics—and to reflect upon them. Zunshine describes and praises the ground-breaking aesthetic of *Lolita*, claiming that, "by tirelessly probing and teasing and stretching our tendency to monitor sources of our representations, Nabokov made the cultivation of mental vertigo in his readers into his trademark as a writer" (118). A more careful and thorough reading reveals the presence of a profusion of metarepresentational tactics in this very first of modern novels. Zunshine's study is aptly entitled *Why We Read Fiction*, for the pleasure to be derived from literary vertigo does indeed help to explain why the Cervantine text is considered a masterpiece and has continued to entice readers for over four centuries.

Reading and the Visual Imagination: Radiant Ignition

Elaine Scarry studies another form of cognitive engagement, the processes by which readers bring to life the words on the printed page. Her particular interest is the types of language that provide readers with concrete and detailed instructions for creating visual images. One of her examples is "radiant ignition," the technique by which words are used to illuminate a scene or a figure part by part, like a spotlight moving across a space or object (80–81). This illuminative practice resembles the medieval blazon and Petrarchan "dismemberment" tactics by which authors provided numerous vivid metaphors to aid readers' creation of a mental image of each of a woman's important physical attributes (Forster 10). As Nancy Vickers has shown, Petrarch's approach to descriptions of the female face and body became the standard in amorous literature of all genres for the following two centuries (95–107). Cervantes utilizes radiant ignition to parody the dismemberment tactic, using both exaggeration and mockery in his depictions of female figures, most of them noteworthy either for supernatural beauty or grotesque ugliness. Many studies have addressed Cervantine representations of female beauty or its opposite; for example, Sherry Velasco and Mary Gossy's studies of masculine women and Arthur Efron's illumination of the shift from idealized beauties in the first volume to more degraded descriptions of the female body in the second. I believe that application of Scarry's concept adds a new dimension to our appreciation of Cervantine parody.

When Don Quixote describes Dulcinea for the benefit of the group heading to Grisóstomo's funeral, his elaboration embodies the ignition or spotlight tactic, moving from one fetishized female feature to another: "sus cabellos son oro, su frente campos elíseos, sus cejas arcos del cielo, sus ojos soles, sus mejillas rosas, sus labios corales, perlas sus dientes, alabastro su cuello, mármol su pecho, marfil sus manos" (I.13.176). However, Cervantes had already undermined this portrayal by his demystificatory preface, "su hermosura, sobrehumana, pues en ella se vienen a hacer verdaderos todos los imposibles y quiméricos atributos de belleza que los poetas dan a sus damas" (I.13.176). Thus, Cervantes signals that the description he is about to provide, which would appear to be a set of instructions to aid the reader or listener in building a mental image, in actuality posits a woman of such perfection that she cannot truly be imagined, cannot possibly exist (Rabin 82). Further, this evocation of a poetic conceit that is already so well known allows the reader to bypass the step-by-step ignition or spotlight tactic and to leap forward to the visualization of the entire cliché ensemble of parts. However, as Vickers has pointed out, and as the Cervantine parody emphasizes, the dismembered description does not allow for the formation of a complete image. Thus, one fatal shortcoming of the blazon description is that it deforms the cognitive act of radiant ignition and fosters instead a highly idiosyncratic and incomplete perspective of women.

Cervantes continues his scrutiny of the blazon in the initial depiction of Dorotea. As Salvador Fajardo has noted, there is a highly "voyeuristic" aspect to the way in which her femininity is gradually revealed (94–95). The radiant ignition model enables us to expand upon Fajardo's observations. In this scene, the verbal spotlight moves across the body of what appears to be a young peasant male, encouraging the formation of a detailed image, one which highlights the differences between the prosaic image to be formed of a male character in distinction with the fanciful blazon paradigm for noble women:

> un mozo vestido como labrador, al cual por tener *inclinado el rostro,* a causa de que se lavaba los pies en el arroyo que por allí corría, no se le pudieron ver por entonces; y ellos llegaron con tanto silencio, que dél no fueron sentidos, ni él estaba a otra cosa atento que a lavarse los pies, que eran tales, que no parecían sino dos pedazos de blanco cristal que entre las otras piedras del arroyo se habían nacido. Suspendióles la blancura y belleza de los pies, pareciéndoles que no estaban hechos a pisar terrones, ni a andar tras el arado y los bueyes, como mostraba el

hábito de su dueño, … el cual traía puesto un capotillo pardo de dos haldas, muy ceñido al cuerpo con una toalla blanca. Traía, ansimesmo, unos calzones y polainas de paño pardo, y en la cabeza una montera parda. Tenía las polainas levantadas hasta la mitad de la pierna, que, sin duda alguna, de blanco alabastro parecía. Acabóse de lavar los hermosos pies, y luego, con un paño de tocar, que sacó debajo de la montera, se los limpió; y al querer quitársele, alzó el rostro, y tuvieron lugar los que mirándole estaban de ver una hermosura incomparable, tal, que Cardenio dijo al cura, con voz baja:

—Ésta, ya que no es Luscinda, no es persona humana, sino divina. El mozo se quitó la montera y, sacudiendo la cabeza a una y a otra parte, se comenzaron a descoger y desparcir unos cabellos, que pudieran los del sol tenerles envidia. Con esto conocieron que el que parecía labrador era mujer … (I.28.345)

The narrator does not begin with a description of the face, in part perhaps because the figure is taken to be masculine and thus subject to a different normative path for radiant ignition to travel—but also for the pragmatic reason that the head is turned away. After three highly prosaic lines that combine descriptions of the figure and his setting, the metaphor of crystal suddenly leaps from the page as the narrator describes "his" improbably beautiful feet. At this point, the reader who is forming a visual image, in conjunction with the priest and barber whose gazes have been moving like the ignition spotlight, begins to sense a discrepancy based on differentiated codes of description and visualization that are guided by class and gender. As the two travelers note, such white and delicate feet do not correspond to the life experiences of a peasant. However, the narrator turns again to ordinary language as the spotlight moves across the various elements of male laborer garb—only to pause once again as alabaster limbs are revealed. In the concluding lines of the description, the spotlight alternates between revealing the garments of a peasant male and exquisite (and thus feminine and aristocratic) body parts. The ignition path that ultimately reveals Dorotea to be a lovely, wealthy young woman is the reverse of the Petrarchan norm, beginning with the feet and moving ever upwards to legs and then head. The final arbiter and determiner of gender identity is her emblematic golden hair; surely the choice of *cabello* over *pelo* and inclusion of the Petrarchan verb *desparcir* is meant to ensure reader awareness of the collision between two imagistic codes.

Such collisions are also emphasized in the descriptions of various unattractive peasant women; the unfortunate Clara Perlerina is a representative example of the parodic effect that ensues when dismembering blazon meets baroque grotesque (Mancing, *Reference* 132). As a humble laborer describes his daughter for the benefit of his new governor, Sancho Panza, each detail passes under the spotlight; in every instance, idealized projection collides with real world deformity:

> ... la doncella es como una perla oriental, y mirada por el lado derecho parece una flor del campo: por el izquierdo no tanto, porque le falta aquel ojo, que se le saltó de viruelas; y aunque los hoyos del rostro son muchos y grandes, dicen los que la quieren bien que aquellos no son hoyos, sino sepulturas donde se sepultan las almas de sus amantes. Es tan limpia, que por no ensuciar la cara trae las narices, como dicen, arremangadas, que no parece sino que van huyendo de la boca; y, con todo esto, parece bien por estremo, porque tiene la boca grande, y, a no faltarle diez o doce dientes y muelas, pudiera pasar y echar raya entre las más bien formadas. De los labios no tengo que decir, porque son tan sutiles y delicados, que, si se usaran aspar labios, pudieran hacer dellos una madeja; pero como tienen diferente color de la que en los labios se usa comúnmente, parecen milagrosos, porque son jaspeados de azul y verde y aberenjenado. (II.47.393)

Eyes, skin, teeth, lips—each fetishized feature in turn is evoked, imagined, and then deconstructed as absent or imperfect, with metaphors mixed to hideous effect. Such lingering over negative details is more typical of moralistic literature in which character flaws are said to be revealed by one's outer façade—or in later eras, of Gothic and horror fiction. The purpose for the spotlighting of unattractive details is both parodic and ideological; just as no aristocratic woman could be as beautiful as Dulcinea and her poetic compatriots, neither is it plausible that the plethora of peasant women across the two volumes could all be so utterly lacking in beauty. Through the repeated use of radiant ignition to lambaste cultural preoccupation with the blazon from a variety of angles, Cervantes encourages readers to be aware of and wary of the ways in which literary description affirms social inequity even as it stimulates the visual imagination.

Clara's father further lays bare the spotlight tactic as he comments upon his own description: "Y perdóneme el señor gobernador si por tan menudo voy pintando las partes de la que al fin al fin ha de ser mi hija, que la quiero bien y no me parece mal" (II.47.393). At all levels of society, women serve as exchange commodities in one way or another, and the quality of their teeth is as relevant as those of a horse to be traded. If a woman cannot elicit love for her beauty and a propitious marriage, then perhaps a recitation of her defects can move Sancho to pity, and more important, to provide governmental charity. Although there is no such final vindication, nonetheless Sancho does express appreciation for this novel form of entertainment: "—Pintad lo que quisiéredes —dijo Sancho—, que yo me voy recreando en la pintura, y, si hubiera comido, no hubiera mejor postre para mí que vuestro retrato" (II.47.393). Sancho reveals that for readers and listeners alike, the mental activity associated with radiant ignition, which consists of the gradual formation of a mental portrait based on verbal imagery, is a pleasurable activity. His own metaphoric comparison of visual imagining and eating a sweet is particularly significant at this moment when the Duke's servants have been starving him.

Cervantes's very first verbal portrait had provided an initial indication that the text would not follow descriptive norms. After dedicating several lines to the culinary habits of his protagonist, his depiction of the protagonist is brief and even terse, "era de complexión recia, seco de carnes, enjuto de rostro" (I.1.71). The process of radiant ignition is given no spark but is instead doused; the reader's construction of Don Quixote will depend far more upon events than adjectives; for example, we learn that he had had a full set of teeth only at the point when he loses several molars, "en toda mi vida me han sacado diente ni muela de la boca, no se me ha caído ni comido de neguijón ni de reuma alguna" (I.18.227). And even when Sancho informs his master and the reader that his master's appearance has taken a decided turn for the worse, details are still scant, "verdaderamente tiene vuestra merced la más mala figura, de poco acá, que jamás he visto; y débelo de haber causado, o ya el cansancio deste combate, o ya la falta de las muelas y dientes" (I.19.234). Sancho later adds that malnutrition has also taken its toll (I.19.235). Cervantes deconstructs the radiant ignition process by scattering specific details concerning his protagonist across many hundreds of pages; as the book progresses, the gradual addition of facts serves mainly to alert the reader to this departure from descriptive norms, rather than to facilitate radiant ignition. There are many other examples of Cervantine innovations concerning the spotlight technique: for female characters of all ages and social states, in the initial encounters with Cardenio and the Duchess, and in the descriptions of Vicente de la Rosa's wardrobe, to name just a few.

As this and previous chapters have demonstrated, the many subfields of cognitive theory offer a rich new array of paradigms that enable scholars to shed new light on the tactics through which early modern Spain circulated class and gender norms. The language of cognitive theory also allows for a fuller exploration of the imaginative and constructive aspects of reading as performed by readers within and of this text. It also increases awareness of the particular formal elements that stimulate various types of response, from emotional identification to radiant ignition to gap-filling activities that readers employ where writers provide insufficient detail (see also *Cognitive Cervantes,* a special issue that appeared as this book was going to press). Cognitive study provides important new theories and data that allow scholars to reconceptualize the intensive mental and emotional energy that readers invest in order to bring settings and characters to life; because Don Quixote is above all else a reader, this new area of research cannot help but illuminate the character and the text.

Conclusion

The Practice of Cognitive Cultural Studies

In a recent study entitled *Macachiavellian Intelligence: How Rhesus Macaques and Humans Have Conquered the World*, Dario Maestripieri delineates the ways in which the ability to wield the cognitive tools (or arms) known as Machiavellian Intelligence have enabled rhesus macaques and humans to emerge as two of the most successful primate groups on planet Earth. Within both species, "as groups became larger and more opportunities for complex patterns of cooperation and competition both within and between groups arose, pressures mounted for an increase in Machiavellian intelligence" (171). Some of the most important survival characteristics, including the capacity for deception and reactions of curiosity rather than fear in the face of unfamiliar stimuli or beings, are connected to our social intelligence capacity. Maestripieri readily concedes that this cognitive system has led to "highly despotic and nepotistic social organization" and describes Machiavellian brains as "effective war machines" (171). All of these negative aspects of social intelligence are on display within the texts analyzed in the preceding seven chapters, especially in the sections that address representations of courtship, honor, and class mobility. However, we have also seen that characters and authors can use social intelligence to assess or even thwart hierarchies: paternalism, patriarchy, and elitism alike are laid bare to a critical gaze. This study has shown that the paradigm of Theory of Mind and its subdomain of Machiavellian cognitive activity offer a multivalent, flexible, and ultimately productive approach to exploring the ideologies and aesthetics of early modern Spain's literary corpus.

In recent years, the cognitive activities associated with Theory of Mind have been studied in a neurological context, using fMRI scanning (a functional MRI, which provides more detailed information on brain activity than older tests) in order to identify the biological mechanisms involved in mentalist activity. Rebecca Saxe and Simon Baron-Cohen conclude that ToM involves a highly complex interaction among domain-specific and domain-general regions of the brain, with cognitive and empathic activity in different loci (vi). They also emphasize the significant supporting roles played by genetics, the psychology of language development, and variances in the subjects' early environment (vi–viii). They conclude that future studies of ToM must be pursued from an "integrated" perspective of "social neuroscien[ce]" (viii). This diffuse and complex perspective of interdisciplinary study is consistent with the "contextualist" model of cognitive activity that I propose.

Concerns about the validity of cognitive approaches to literature may still arise for literary scholars who associate neuroscience with deterministic models of human behavior, which can be used in particularly deleterious discourses against persons occupying marginalized gender and class positions. The contextualist paradigm of interactive cognition and the newly emerging discipline of Social Neuroscience (a journal by that name was launched in 2006) are two important indicators that facile determinism is on the wane. Both of these approaches are consistent with "ecological" cognitivism. As John Sanders explains,

> The "ecological approach" to this-and-that follows a pattern that was probably first recommended for evolutionary biology. It encourages attempts to understand particular areas of interest through emphasis of the importance of large(r) interacting systems. Thus to fully understand a biological organism, one must (at least) understand that organism as a member of a species which is itself the product of a long process of natural selection within a changing environment ... And the "organism" is understood as, in an important sense, both shaped by and shaper of this environment. It is this system orientation, with its emphasis upon symbiotic relations among elements within the system, that is to be emphasized in any "ecological" approach. (5)

The ecological model proposes an interactive model of brain, individual psyche, and environment. This approach is embodied but resolutely anti-deterministic, "There can be no doubt about the absolutely vital role played by the brain as we go about learning, searching, and acting. But the unit of analysis should be the organism, not the brain" (Sanders 10). Sanders views this model as compatible with Marxist -based sociocultural analysis, although not with the strict formulations of economic determinism. He explains,

> the opposition of the ecological approach to "materialism" in the narrower sense is not opposition come-what-may, in all contexts of inquiry; rather, again, the claim of the ecological approach is only that, at the present time, under the circumstances of the problem situations that dominate cognitive science, it is relatively more important to try to understand cognition in terms of its role in its broader environment than it is to try to further understand its internal construction and its basis in matter-energy. (20)

As we can see, the most recent developments in ecological approaches to the cognitive sciences bear little resemblance to the deterministic positions that Artificial Intelligence and Behaviorist models proposed half a century ago.

Ecological cognition grows out of revised studies of visual perception, which propose *active* perceivers who interact with stimuli as opposed to the previous theory of a passive perceiver, "a motionless creature haplessly bombarded by stimuli" (Gibson and Pick 15). Ecological cognition applies this model of mutuality to all forms of perception, and asserts that cognitive activity arises out of the interaction between subjects' perceptions and actions and the "affordances" of the material world. Affordances is the term used to describe the material world in a non-deterministic fashion: as the "properties of the environment as they are related to [sentient beings'] capabilities for using them" (Gibson and Pick 16). A very basic example is Goldilocks in her encounters with the differing affordances of the three bowls of porridge, three chairs, three beds in the bears' domicile (Gibson and Pick 16). This ecological model goes beyond both the Cartesian model of the brain as the dominant cognitive force, and simple models of environmental determinism as the determining factor. Although no author that I consulted specifically addresses this issue, the readings I offer of the social functions of Theory of Mind, contextualism, and skepticism in early modern texts posit interactive forms of cognitive theory that are in alignment with the ecological model. The cognitive models for reading are also compatible.

This study demonstrates that ToM and MI almost never entail a unidimensional process in which one active and dominant subject uses cognitive skills to comprehend and impact another. Rather, the texts under consideration offer new perspectives on social identity that derive from delineating complex cognitive interactions between minds of marginalized and dominant social groups. These subjects may not always succeed in using cognitive skills to achieve more stable or influential positions in their social hierarchy, but nonetheless most of the authors (with the exceptions of Agustín Moreto and Quevedo) depict female or low-born characters that demonstrate cognitive potential and growth in ways that contest orthodox views of intellectual potential.

Contextualist cognitive models depict the brain as a complex and highly interactive system. In moving beyond linear and modular models of circuitry, contextualism views the brain itself as an ecological system. Spolsky's "satisfying skepticism" features characters who actively examine competing information streams that derive from embodied, sensorial, and abstract knowledges. The cognitively competent heroes—and heroines—of "tragicomic" honor texts are precisely those figures who move beyond stimuli bombardment to evaluate and interact in ways that lead to cognitive enlightenment. Tragic figures are those who fail to employ the full potential of the cognitive ecology.

The ecological approach to cognitive cultural studies is a deliberate rejection of Foucauldian and New Historicist models of cultural study that posit humans as powerless or hapless in the face of structures of domination. I envision cognitive cultural studies as a continuation and development of British cultural and feminist materialism, offering explorations of cognition as an additional factor to consider in exploring literary representations of social resistance and individual agency (Zunshine, *Cognitive* 5–8). I have used this ecological model of interactivity as one of the bases for analysis of the ideological dimensions of early modern literature. Each chapter delineates the ways in which authors support or challenge early modern Spain's normative projections concerning the cognitive functions of humans who are born into specific subject positions related to class, gender, or religious affiliation. Each chapter demonstrates that the cognitive cultural studies model provides scholars with new tools to analyze early modern

Spanish society. In particular, this approach allows us to offer new insights concerning the role that representations of cognition played in challenging the status quo. Through their depictions of a continuum of honesty and deception, truth-seeking and specious rationalizations, early modern Spanish texts scrutinize, critique, and even condemn the validity of hierarchical models of subjectivity and cognitive function.

Works Cited

Abel, Lionel. *Metatheatre: A New View of Dramatic Form.* New York: Hill & Wang, 1963. Print.

Alcalá Galán, Mercedes. *Escritura desatada: poéticas de la representación en Cervantes.* Alcalá de Henares: Centro de estudios cervantinos, 2009. Print.

Alemán, Mateo. *Guzmán de Alfarache. Libros de arena* (ibl). Web. 16 Jan. 2013. <http://www.librosdearena.es/Biblioteca_pdf/GuzmandeAlfarache. pdf>.

Alter, Robert. *Partial Magic: The Novel as a Self-Conscious Genre.* Berkeley: California UP, 1975. Print.

———. *Rogue's Progress: Studies in the Picaresque Novel.* Cambridge, MA: Harvard UP, 1964. Print.

Arbesú Fernández, David. "Auctoritas y experiencia en 'El curioso impertinente.'" *Cervantes* 25.1 (Spring 2005): 23–43. Print.

Armon, Shifra. *Picking Wedlock: Women and the Courtship Novel in Spain.* Lanham, MD: Rowman and Littlefield, 2002. Print.

Astington, Janet. "What Is *Theoretical* about the Child's Theory of Mind? A Vygotskian View of Its Development." Carruthers and Smith 184–99. Print.

Avalle-Arce, Juan B. *Nuevos deslindes cervantinos.* Barcelona: Ariel, 1975. Print.

Ayala, Francisco. "Los dos amigos." *Revista de Occidente* 111 (1965): 287–305. Print.

Azevedo, Angela de. *La margarita del Tajo que dio nombre a Santarén.* Soufas, *Women's Acts* 45–90. Print.

———. *El muerto disimulado.* Soufas, *Women's Acts* 91–132. Print.

Bailey, Frederick G. *The Prevalence of Deceit.* Ithaca: Cornell UP, 1991. Print.

Bakhtin, Mikhail M. *The Dialogic Imagination: Four Essays.* Ed. Michael Holquist. Austin, TX: U of Texas P, 1982. Print.

Bayliss, Robert. "Feminism and María de Zayas's Exemplary Comedy, *La traición en la amistad.*" *Hispanic Review* 76.1 (2008): 1–17. Print.

Benabu, Isaac. "Who Is the Protagonist? Gutierre on the Stand." *Indiana Journal of Hispanic Literatures* 2.2 (1994): 13–25. Print.

Berceo, Gonzalo de. *Milagros de Nuestra Señora. Cervantes Virtual.* Web. 1 July 2011. <http://www.cervantesvirtual.com/obra/milagros-de-nuestra-senora--0/>

Berger, Harry, Jr. *The Absence of Grace: Sprezzatura and Suspicion in Two Renaissance Courtesy Books.* Palo Alto, CA: Stanford UP, 2000. Print.

Blackburn, Alexander. *The Myth of the Pícaro: Continuity and Transformation of the Picaresque Novel, 1554–1954.* Chapel Hill: U of North Carolina P, 1979. Print.

Blue, William R. "Echoing Desire, Mirroring Disdain: Moreto's *El desdén con el desdén.*" *Bulletin of the Comediantes* 38 (1986): 137–46. Print.

———. "*El médico de su honra* and the Politics of Reading." *Hispania* 82.3 (Sept. 1999): 408–16. Print.

———. *Spanish Comedy and Historical Contexts in the 1620s.* University Park: Pennsylvania State UP, 1996. Print.

Boehm, Christopher. "Egalitarian Behavior and the Evolution of Political Intelligence." Byrne and Whiten 1988, 341–64. Print.

Boyer, H. Patsy, trans. *The Disenchantments of Love: A Translation of the Desengaños Amorosos.* By María de Zayas y Sotomayor. Albany: SUNY P, 1997. Print.

Braudel, Fernand. *The Mediterranean and the Mediterranean World in the Age of Philip II.* Vol. 1. Berkeley: U of California P, 1995. Print.

Brown, Jonathan, and John H. Elliott. *A Palace for a King: The Buen Retiro and the Court of Phillip IV.* New Haven, CT: Yale UP, 2004. Print.

Brownlee, Marina S. *The Cultural Labyrinth of María de Zayas.* Philadelphia: U of Pennsylvania P, 2000. Print.

Bruner, Jerome. *Actual Minds, Possible Worlds.* Cambridge, MA: Harvard UP, 1986. Print.

———. "The Narrative Construction of Reality." *Critical Inquiry* 18 (1991): 1–21. Print.

Burke, Peter. *The Fortunes of the Courtier: The European Reception of Castiglione's Cortegiano.* University Park: Pennsylvania State UP, 1996. Print.

Burningham, Bruce R. *Radical Theatricality: Jongleuresque Performance on the Early Spanish Stage.* Purdue Studies in Romance Literatures 39. West Lafayette, IN: Purdue UP, 2007. Print.

———. *Tilting Cervantes: Baroque Reflections on Postmodern Culture.* Nashville, TN: Vanderbilt UP, 2008. Print.

Butte, George. *I Know That You Know That I Know: Narrating Subjects from Moll Flanders to Marnie.* Columbus: Ohio State UP, 2004. Print.

Byrne, Richard W. "The Technical Intelligence Hypothesis: An Additional Evolutionary Stimulus to Intelligence?" Byrne and Whiten 1997, 289–311. Print.

Byrne, Richard W., and Andrew Whiten, eds. and preface. *Machiavellian Intelligence: Social Expertise and the Evolution of Intellect in Monkeys, Apes, and Humans.* Oxford: Oxford UP, 1988. Print.

————, eds. and preface. *Machiavellian Intelligence II: Extensions and Evaluations.* Cambridge: Cambridge UP, 1997. Print.

————. "Machiavellian Intelligence." Byrne and Whiten 1997, 1–23. Print.

————. "The Manipulation of Attention in Primate Tactical Deception." Byrne and Whiten 1988, 211–33. Print.

————. "Tactical Deception of Familiar Individuals in Baboons." Byrne and Whiten 1988, 205–10. Print.

Calderón de la Barca, Pedro. *El médico de su honra. Association for Hispanic Classic Theater.* Web. 1 July 2011. <http://www.comedias.org/textlist.html#Calderón>.

Campbell, Gwyn E. "(En)Gendering Fenisa in María de Zayas's *La traición en la amistad." Romance Languages Annual* 1998. Vol. 10 (1999): 482–87. Print.

Caro Mallén de Soto, Ana. *El conde Partinuplés.* Soufas, *Women's Acts* 137–62. Print.

————. *Valor, agravio y mujer.* Soufas, *Women's Acts* 163–94. Print.

Carrión, María Mercedes. "The Burden of Evidence: Performances of Marriage, Violence, and the Law in *El médico de su honra."Revista Canadiense de Estudios Hispánicos* 27.3 (2003 Spring): 447–68. Print.

————. "Portrait of a Lady: Marriage, Postponement, and Representation in Ana Caro's *El conde Partinuplés."* Hispanic Issue. *MLN* 114.2 (Mar. 1999): 241–68. Print.

Carruthers, Peter. "Simulation and Self Knowledge." Carruthers and Smith 22–38. Print.

Carruthers, Peter, and Peter K. Smith, eds. and introd. *Theories of Theories of Mind.* Cambridge: Cambridge UP, 1996. Print.

Casa, Frank P. "Some Remarks on Professor O'Connor's Article 'Is the Spanish *Comedia* a Metatheater?'" *Bulletin of the Comediantes* 28 (1976): 27–31. Print.

Cascardi, Anthony J. *The Bounds of Reason: Cervantes, Dostoevsky, Flaubert.* New York: Columbia UP, 1986. Print.

————. *The Limits of Illusion: A Critical Study of Calderón.* Cambridge: Cambridge UP, 1984. Print.

Case, Thomas E. "Metatheater and World View in Lope's *El divino africano." Bulletin of the Comediantes* 42.1 (Summer 1990): 129–42. Print.

Castiglione, Baldassarre. *The Book of the Courtier.* New York: AMS P, 1967. Print.

Castillo, David. *(A)wry Views: Anamorphosis, Cervantes, and the Early Picaresque.* Purdue Studies in Romance Literatures 23. West Lafayette, IN: Purdue UP, 2001. Print.

Cavillac, Michel. *Pícaros y mercaderes en el Guzmán de Alfarache: reformismo burgués y mentalidad aristocrática en la España del Siglo de Oro.* Granada: Universidad de Granada, 1994. Print.

Cervantes y Saavedra, Miguel de. *Don Quixote. Cervantes Virtual.* Web. 1 July 2011. <http://www.cervantesvirtual.com/servlet/Sirve Obras/24650507767132507754491/index.htm>.

Chaudhuri, Sukanta. *Infirm Glory: Shakespeare and the Renaissance Image of Man.* Oxford: Oxford UP, 1981. Print.

Churchland, Patricia. *Neurophilosophy: Toward a Unified Science of the Mind-Brain.* Cambridge, MA: MIT P, 1986. Print.

Cognitive Cervantes. Ed. Julien Simon, Howard Mancing, Barbara Simerka, and Bruce Burningham. Spec. issue of *Cervantes* 31.2 (Spring 2012). Print.

Concha, Jaime. "El tema del segundón en *La verdad sospechosa." Texto y sociedad: problemas de historia literaria.* Ed. Bridget Aldaraca, Edward Baker, and John Beverley. Atlanta: Rodopi, 1990. 253–79. Print.

Connor, Catherine. "Why We Don't Get No Respect and What We Are Doing about It, or The Rapprochement of Body and Mind and the Return of *Comedia* Studies." *Bulletin of the Comediantes* 56.1 (2004): 153–62. Print.

Crane, Mary Thomas. "Analogy, Metaphor and the New Science: Cognitive Science and Early Modern Epistemology." Zunshine, *Cognitive* 103–14. Print.

———. *Shakespeare's Brain: Reading with Cognitive Theory.* Princeton, NJ: Princeton UP, 2001. Print.

Cruz, Anne J. *Discourses of Poverty: Social Reform and the Picaresque Novel in Early Modern Spain.* Toronto and Buffalo: U of Toronto P, 1999. Print.

Damasio, Antonio. *The Feeling of What Happens: Body and Emotion in the Making of Consciousness.* New York: Houghton Mifflin Harcourt, 1999. Print.

Darbord, Michel. "Cervantes et le théâtre." *Vérité et illusion dans le théâtre au temps de la Renaissance.* Ed. Marie-Thérèse Jones-Davies. Paris: Touzot, 1983. 21–25. Print.

Davies, M., and T. Stone, eds. and introd. *Folk Psychology: The Theory of Mind Debate.* 1st ed. Oxford: Blackwell, 1995. Print.

Davis, Nina Cox. *Autobiography as Burla in the Guzmán de Alfarache.* Cranbury, NJ: Associated U Presses, 1991. Print.

De Armas, Frederick A. "The Burning at Ephesus: Cervantes and Alarcón's *La verdad sospechos*a." *Studies in Honor of Gilberto Paolini.* Ed. and introd. Mercedes Vidal Tibbitts. Newark, DE: Juan de la Cuesta, 1996. 41–56. Print.

—. *The Invisible Mistress: Aspects of Feminism and Fantasy in the Golden Age.* Charlottesville, VA: Biblioteca Siglo de Oro, 1976. Print.

—. "Lope de Vega's *La quinta de Florencia*: An Example of Iconic Role-Playing." *Hispanófila* 28.3 (May 1985): 31–42. Print.

Dennett, Daniel. *The Intentional Stance.* Cambridge, MA: MIT P, 1987. Print.

Deyermond, Alan D. *Lazarillo de Tormes: A Critical Guide.* London: Tamesis, 1975. Print.

DiLillo, Leonard M. "Moral Purpose in Ruíz de Alarcón's 'La Verdad Sospechosa.'" *Hispania* 56 (Apr. 1973): 254–59. Print.

DiPuccio, Denise M. "Saints Meet Sinners: The Hagiographic and Mythological Traditions in the *Comedia.*" *Hispanic Journal* 22.2 (Fall 2001): 383–400. Print.

Doležel, Lubomír. *Heterocosmica: Fiction and Possible Worlds.* Baltimore: Johns Hopkins UP, 1997. Print.

Dopico Black, Georgina. *Perfect Wives, Other Women: Adultery and Inquisition in Early Modern Spain.* Durham, NC: Duke UP, 2001. Print.

Dunn, Peter. *Spanish Picaresque Fiction: A New Literary History.* Ithaca: Cornell UP, 1993. Print.

Edelman, Gerald. *Neural Darwinism: The Theory of Neuronal Group Selection.* New York: Basic Books, 1987. Print.

Efron, Arthur. "Bearded Waiting Women, Lovely Lethal Female Piratemen: Sexual Boundary Shifts in Don Quixote, Part II." *Cervantes* 2.2 (1982): 155–64. Print.

—. "On Some Central Issues in Quixote Criticism: Society and the Sexual Body." *Cervantes* 2.2 (1982): 171–80. Print.

Egginton, William. "Gracián and the Emergence of the Modern Subject." Spadaccini and Talens 151–69. Print.

—. *How the World Became a Stage: Presence, Theatricality, and the Question of Modernity.* Albany: SUNY P, 2003. Print.

Ekstein, Nina C. "The Conversion of *Polyeucte's* Félix: The Problem of Religion and Theater." *French Forum* 34.1 (Winter 2009):1–17. Print.

Elliott, John H. *Imperial Spain: 1469–1716.* 2nd ed. New York: Penguin, 2002. Print.

El Saffar, Ruth. "Ana/Lysis/Zayas: Reflections on Courtship and Literary Women in the *Novelas ejemplares y amorosas.*" Williamsen and Whitenack 192–218. Print.

—. "Anxiety of Identity: Gutierre's Case in *El médico de su honra.*" *Studies in Honor of Bruce W. Wardropper.* Ed . Dian Fox, Harry Sieber, and Robert ter Horst. Newark, DE: Juan de la Cuesta, 1989. 105–24. Print.

Esrock, Ellen J. *The Reader's Eye: Visual Imaging as Reader Response*. Baltimore: Johns Hopkins UP, 1994. Print.

Fajardo, Salvador J. "Unveiling Dorotea or the Reader as Voyeur." *Cervantes* 4.2 (1984): 89–108. Print.

Fischer, Susan L. "Art-Within-Art: The Significance of the Hercules Painting in *El pintor de su deshonra*." *Critical Perspectives on Calderón de la Barca*. Ed. Frederick de Armas, David M. Gitlitz, and José A. Madrigal. Lincoln, NE: Society of Spanish and Spanish-American Studies, U of Nebraska, 1981. 69–79. Print.

———. "Calderón's *Los caballos de Absalón*: A Metatheater of Unbridled Passion." *Bulletin of the Comediantes* 28 (1976): 73–79. Print.

———. "Lope's *Lo fingido verdadero* and the Dramatization of the Theatrical Experience." *Revista Hispánica Moderna* 39 (1976–77): 156–66. Print.

Fiore, Robert L. "The Interaction of Motives and Mores in *La verdad sospechosa*." *Hispanófila* 61 (1977): 11–21. Print.

Fly, Richard. "The Evolution of Shakespearean Metadrama: Abel, Burckhardt, and Calderwood." *Comparative Drama* 20.2 (Summer 1986): 124–39. Print.

Foa, Sandra M. *Feminismo y forma narrativa: estudio del tema y las técnicas de María de Zayas y Sotomayor*. Valencia: Albatros Hispanófila, 1979. Print.

Fodor, Jerry. *The Modularity of Mind*. Cambridge, MA: MIT P, 1983. Print.

Forster, Leonard. *The Icy Fire: Five Studies in European Petrarchism*. Cambridge: Cambridge UP, 1969. Print.

Fothergill-Payne, Louise. "La justicia poética de *La verdad sospechos*a." *Romanische Forshungen* 83 (1971): 588–95. Print.

Foucault, Michel. *The History of Sexuality: An Introduction*. New York: Vintage, 1990. Print.

Fox, Dian. *Kings in Calderón: A Study in Characterization and Political Theory*. London: Tamesis, 1986. Print.

Friedman, Edward H. *The Antiheroine's Voice: Narrative Discourse and Transformations of the Picaresque*. Columbia: U of Missouri P, 1987. Print.

———. "*Executing the Will*: The End of the Road in Don Quixote." *Indiana Journal of Hispanic Literature* 5 (Fall 1994): 105–25. Print.

Fuchs, Barbara. *Passing for Spain: Cervantes and the Fictions of Identity*. Urbana: Illinois UP, 2003. Print.

Fuster, Joaquín. *Cortex and Mind: Unifying Cognition*. Oxford: Oxford UP, 2005. Print.

Gabriele, John P. "Engendering Narrative Equality in Angela de Azevedo's *El muerto disimulado.*" *Bulletin of the Comediantes* 60.1 (2008): 127–38. Print.

Gallese, Vittorio, and Alvin Goldman. "Mirror Neurons and the Simulation Theory of Mind-Reading." *Trends in Cognitive Sciences* 2 (1998): 493–501. Print.

Gamboa Tusquets, Yolanda. *Cartografía social en la narrativa de María de Zayas.* Madrid: Biblioteca Nueva, 2009. Print.

García Gómez, Ángel M. "*El médico de su honra*: perfil y función de Coquín." *Calderón: actas del congreso internacional sobre Calderón y el teatro español del siglo de oro.* Ed. Luciano García Lorenzo. Madrid: Consejo Superior de Investigaciones Científicas, 1983. 1025–37. Print.

Gascón, Christopher D. "Female and Male Mediation in the Plays of Angela de Azevedo." *Bulletin of the Comediantes* 57.1 (2005): 125–45. Print.

Gaylord, Mary Malcolm. "The Telling Lies of *La verdad sospechosa.*" *MLN* 103.2 (Mar. 1988): 223–38. *JSTOR.* Web. 1 July 2011. <http://www.jstor.org/stable/2905340>.

Gerli, E. Michael. "Truth, Lies, and Representation: The Crux of 'El curioso impertinente.'" *Cervantes for the 21st Century / Cervantes para el siglo XXI: Studies in Honor of Edward Dudley.* Ed. Francisco La Rubia Prado. Newark, DE: Juan de la Cuesta, 2000. 107–22. Print.

Gerrig, Richard J. *Experiencing Narrative Worlds: On the Psychological Activities of Reading.* New Haven, CT: Yale UP, 1993. Print.

Gibson, Eleanor J., and Anne D. Pick. *An Ecological Approach to Perceptual Learning and Development.* 1st ed. New York: Oxford UP USA, 2003. Print.

Gigerenzer, Gerd. "The Modularity of Social Intelligence." Byrne and Whiten 1997, 264–88. Print.

Gilbert-Santamaría, Donald. *Writers on the Market: Consuming Literature in Early Seventeenth-Century Spain.* Lewisburg, PA: Bucknell UP, 2005. Print.

Gillespie, Diane. *The Mind's We: Contextualism in Cognitive Psychology.* Carbondale: Southern Illinois UP, 1992. Print.

Gilligan, Carol. *In a Different Voice: Psychological Theory and Women's Development.* Cambridge, MA: Harvard UP, 1982. Print.

Gil-Oslé, Juan Pablo. "El examen de maridos en *El conde Partinuplés* de Ana Caro: la agencia femenina en el Juicio de Paris." *Bulletin of the Comediantes* 61.2 (2009): 103–19. Print.

Girard, René. *Deceit, Desire, and the Novel: Self and Other in Literary Structure*. Baltimore: Johns Hopkins UP, 1976. Print.

Goffman, Erving. *The Presentation of Self in Everyday Life*. New York: Anchor–Doubleday, 1959. Print.

Goldman, Alvin. "Interpretation Psychologized." Davies and Stone 74–99. Print.

Gómez, Jesús. "Alusiones metateatrales en las comedias de Lope de Vega." *Boletín de la Real Academia Española* 79.277 (May–Aug. 1999): 221–47. Print.

Gopnik, Alison. "The Theory Theory as an Alternative to the Innateness Hypothesis." *Chomsky and His Critics*. Ed. Louise Antony and Norbert Hornstein. New York: Blackwell, 2003. 238–54. Print.

Gordon, Robert M. "The Simulation Theory: Objections and Misconceptions." *Mind and Language* 7.1–2 (1992): 11–34. Print.

Gorfkle, Laura. "Female Communities, Female Friendships and Social Control in María de Zayas's *La traición en la amistad*: A Historical Perspective." *Romance Languages Annual* 1998. Vol. 10 (1999): 615–20. *RLA Archive*. Web. 1 July 2011. <http://tell.fll.purdue.edu/RLA-Archive/1998/spanish-html/Gorfkle,%20Laura.htm>.

Gossy, Mary S. "Aldonza as Butch: Narrative and the Play of Gender in *Don Quijote*." *¿Entiendes? Queer Readings, Hispanic Writings*. Ed. Emilie L. Bergmann and Paul Julian Smith. Durham: Duke UP, 1995. 17–28. Print.

Gracián, Baltasar. *Oráculo manual y arte de prudencia. Cervantes Virtual*. Web. 1 July 2011. <http://www.cervantesvirtual.com/servlet/SirveObras/02493842322571839644424/p0000001.htm>.

Gracián Dantisco, Lucas. *Galateo español*. Madrid: Consejo Superior de Investigaciones Científicas, 1968. Print.

Green, Otis. *Spain and the Western Tradition*. 4 vols. Madison: U of Wisconsin P, 1964. Print.

Greenblatt, Stephen. *Renaissance Self-Fashioning: From More to Shakespeare*. Chicago: U of Chicago P, 1980. Print.

Greer, Margaret Rich. *María de Zayas Tells Baroque Tales of Love and the Cruelty of Men*. University Park: Pennsylvania State UP, 2000. Print.

———. "The M(Other) Plot: Houses of God, Man and Mother in María de Zayas." Williamsen and Whitenack 90–116. Print.

Grieve, Patricia E. "Embroidering with Saintly Threads: María de Zayas Challenges Cervantes and the Church." *Renaissance Quarterly* 44 (Spring 1991): 86–106. Print.

Guevara, Antonio de. *Menospecio de corte y alabanza de aldea*. Madrid: Espasa-Calpe, 1952.

Hafter, Monroe Z. *Gracián and Perfection: Spanish Moralists of the Seventeenth Century*. Cambridge, MA: Harvard UP, 1966. Print.

Hall, H. Gaston. "Illusion et vérité dans deux pièces de Lope de Vega: *La Fiction vraie* et *Le Chien du jardinier*." *Vérité et illusion dans le théâtre au temps de la Renaissance*. Ed. Marie-Thérèse Jones-Davies. Paris: Touzot, 1983. 41–54. Print.

Harris, Paul. "From Simulation to Folk Psychology: The Case for Development." Davies and Stone 207–31. Print.

Heal, Jane. "*Simulation, Theory, and Content*." Carruthers and Smith 75–89. Print.

Hegstrom Oakey, Valerie. "The Fallacy of False Dichotomy in María de Zayas's *La traición en la amistad*." *Bulletin of the Comediantes* 46.1 (Summer 1994): 59–70. Print.

Herman, David, ed. *Narrative Theory and the Cognitive Sciences*. Chicago: U of Chicago P, 2003. Print.

———. *Narratologies: New Perspectives on Narrative Analysis*. Columbus: Ohio State UP, 1999. Print.

Hjort, Mette, and Sue Laver, eds. *Emotion and the Arts*. New York: Oxford UP, 1997. Print.

Hogan, Patrick Colm. *The Mind and Its Stories: Narrative Universals and Human Emotion*. Cambridge: Cambridge UP, 2003. Print.

Holland, Norman N. *The Brain of Robert Frost: A Cognitive Approach to Literature*. New York: Routledge, 1988. Print.

Honig, Edwin. *Calderón and the Seizures of Honor*. Cambridge, MA: Harvard UP, 1972. Print.

Hornby, Richard. *Drama, Metadrama, and Perception*. Cranbury, NJ: Associated U Presses, 1986. Print.

Howe, Elizabeth Teresa. *Education and Women in the Early Modern Hispanic World*. Aldershot, UK: Ashgate, 2008. Print.

Ife, Barry W. *Reading and Fiction in Golden-Age Spain: A Platonist Critique and Some Picaresque Replies*. Cambridge: Cambridge UP, 1985. Print.

Ihrie, Maureen. *Skepticism in Cervantes*. London: Tamesis, 1982. Print.

Ínsula: Revista de Letras y Ciencias Humanas. Spec. issue: *Levante sus primores la agudeza: Baltasar Gracián (1601–2001)*. No. 655–56 (July–Aug. 2001). Print.

Jackendoff, Ray. *Consciousness and the Computational Mind.* Cambridge, MA: MIT P, 1987. Print.

Jaggar, Alison Mary. "Love and Knowledge: Emotion in Feminist Epistemology." *Gender/Body/Knowledge: Feminist Reconstructions of Being and Knowing.* Ed. Alison M. Jaggar and Susan Bordo. New Brunswick, NJ: Rutgers UP, 1992. 149–63. Print.

Jehenson, Yvonne. "Masochisma versus Machismo or: Camila's Re-writing of Gender Assignations in Cervantes's Tale of Foolish Curiosity." *Cervantes* 18.2 (1998): 26–52. Print.

Johnson, Carroll. "Defining the Picaresque: Authority and the Subject in *Guzmán de Alfarache.*" *The Picaresque: Tradition and Displacement.* Ed. Giancarlo Maiorino. Minneapolis: U of Minnesota P, 1996. 159–82. Print.

———. *Inside Guzmán de Alfarache.* Berkeley: U of California P, 1978. Print.

Johnston, Robert M. "The Spectator's Mirror: Mencía of Calderón's *El médico de su honra.*" *Indiana Journal of Hispanic Literatures* 2.2 (Spring 1994): 39–48. Print.

Jones, Michael. "Five Liars: French, English and Italian Imitations of *La verdad sospechosa.*" *AUMLA: Journal of the Australasian Universities Language and Literature Association* 62 (1984): 192–207. Print.

Jütte, Robert. *Poverty and Deviance in Early Modern Europe.* Cambridge: Cambridge UP, 1994. Print.

Kamen, Henry. *Early Modern European Society.* London: Routledge, 2000. Print.

———. *Spain 1469–1714: A Society of Conflict.* London and New York: Longman, 2005. Print.

Kaplan, David. "The Lover's Test Theme in Cervantes and Madame de Lafayette." *French Review* 26.4 (1953): 285–90. Print.

Karmiloff-Smith, Annette. *Beyond Modularity: A Developmental Perspective on Cognitive Science.* Cambridge, MA: MIT P, 1986. Print.

Kirby, Carol Bingham. "Theater and the Quest for Anointment in *El rey don Pedro en Madrid.*" *Bulletin of the Comediantes* 33.2 (Fall 1981): 149–59. Print.

Kors, Alan Charles. *Atheism in France, 1650–1729.* Vol. 1. Princeton, NJ: Princeton UP, 1990. Print.

Krueger, Alison E. "Cervantes's Laboratory: The Thought Experiment of 'El curioso impertinente.'" *Cervantes* 29.1 (Spring 2009): 117–65. Print.

LaFrenière, Peter. "The Ontogeny of Tactical Deception in Humans." Byrne and Whiten 1988, 238–55.

Larson, Catherine. "Gender, Reading, and Intertextuality: Don Juan's Legacy in María de Zayas's *La traición en la amistad*." *Inti: Revista de Literatura Hispánica* 40–41 (1994–95): 129–38. Print.

———. "Metatheater and the *Comedia*: Past, Present, and Future." *The Golden Age Comedia: Text, Theory, and Performance*. Ed. and introd. Charles Ganelin and Howard Mancing. West Lafayette, IN: Purdue UP, 1994. 204–21. Print.

László, János. *Cognition and Representation in Literature: The Psychology of Literary Narratives*. Budapest: Akadémiai Kiadó, 1999. Print.

Lazarillo de Tormes. (Anonymous). Interp. ed. Alcalá. Burgos, 1554. *Project Gutenberg*. Web. 1 July 2011. <http://www.gutenberg.org/files/320/>.

Leoni, Mónica. "María de Zayas and *La traición en la amistad*: The Convenient Demonization of Fenisa." *Bulletin of the Comediantes* 59.1 (2007): 149–66. Print.

———. "María de Zayas's *La traición en la amistad*: Female Friendship Politicized?" *South Atlantic Review* 68.4 (Fall 2003): 62–84. Print.

Leverage, Paula, Howard Mancing, Richard Schweickert, and Jennifer Marston William, eds. *Theory of Mind and Literature*. West Lafayette, IN: Purdue UP, 2010. Print.

Levinson, Jerrold. "Emotion in Response to Art: A Survey of the Terrain." Hjort and Laver 20–35. Print.

López-Peláez Casellas, Jesús. "Woman as Text in *Othello* and in Calderón's *Dramas de Honor*." *SEDERI* 6 (2006): 93–98. Web. 1 July 2011. <http://sederi.org/docs/yearbooks/06/6_10_lopez-pelaez.pdf>.

Lo Ré, Anthony G. "The Three Deaths of Don Quixote: Comments in Favor of the Romantic Critical Approach." *Cervantes* 9.2 (1989): 21–41. Print.

Lynch, John. *The Hispanic World in Crisis and Change, 1598–1700*. Oxford: Oxford UP, 1992. Print.

Maestripieri, Dario. *Macachiavellian Intelligence: How Rhesus Macaques and Humans Have Conquered the World*. Chicago: U of Chicago P, 2007. Print.

Maia Neto, José Raimundo. *Machado de Assis, The Brazilian Pyrrhonian*. Purdue Studies in Romance Literatures 5. West Lafayette, IN: Purdue UP, 1994. Print.

Maiorino, Giancarlo. *At the Margins of the Renaissance: Lazarillo de Tormes and the Picaresque Art of Survival*. University Park: Pennsylvania State UP, 2003. Print.

Mancing, Howard. "Camila's Story." *Cervantes* 25.1 (2005 [2006]): 9–22. Print.

Mancing, Howard. "Cervantes as Narrator of *Don Quijote*." *Cervantes* 23.1 (2003): 117–40. Print.

———. *Cervantes' Don Quixote: A Reference Guide*. Westport, CT: Greenwood, 2006. Print.

———. "Embodied Cognitive Science and the Study of Literature." *Cervantes* 31.2 (Spring 2012): 25–69. Print.

———. "James Parr's Theory of Mind." *Critical Reflections: Essays on Golden Age Spanish Literature (In Honor of James A. Parr.)*. Ed. Barbara Simerka and Amy Williamsen. Lewisburg, PA: Bucknell UP, 2006. 125–43. Print.

———. "Sancho Panza's Theory of Mind." *Theory of Mind and Literature*. Ed. Paula Leverage et al. West Lafayette IN: Purdue UP, 2010. 123–32. Print.

———. "Voices in Everything: Restoring the Human Context to Literary Theory." Unpublished manuscript. Print.

Mariscal, George. *Contradictory Subjects: Quevedo, Cervantes, and Seventeenth Century Spanish Culture*. Ithaca: Cornell UP, 1991. Print.

Maroto Camino, Mercedes. "Negotiating Woman: Ana Caro's *El conde Partinuplés* and Pedro Calderón de la Barca's *La vida es sueño*." *Tulsa Studies in Women's Literature* 26.2 (2007): 199–216. Print.

———. "Spindles for Swords: The Re/Dis-Covery of María de Zayas' Presence." *Hispanic Review* 62.4 (Autumn 1994): 519–36. *JSTOR*. Web. 1 July 2010. <http://www.jstor.org/stable/475007>.

———. "Transvestism, Translation and Transgression: Angela de Azevedo's *El muerto disimulado*." *Forum for Modern Language Studies* 37.3 (2001): 314–25. Print.

Martin, Randall A. "Metatheater, Gender, and Subjectivity in *Richard II* and *Henry IV*, Part I." *Comparative Drama* 23.3 (1989): 255–64. Print.

Matos-Nin, Ingrid. *The Novels of Maria de Zayas (1590–1650): The Supernatural and the Occult in Spanish Women's Literature of the Seventeenth Century*. New York: Mellen, 2010. Print.

May, Julian. *Jack the Bodiless* (The Galactic Milieu Trilogy I). New York: Del Rey–Ballantine, 1993. Print.

McConachie, Bruce, and F. Elizabeth Hart, eds. and introd. *Performance and Cognition: Theatre Studies and the Cognitive Turn*. New York: Routledge, 2010. Print.

McGaha, Michael, trans. *Lo fingido verdadero: Acting Is Believing*. San Antonio, TX: Trinity UP, 1986. Print.

McKendrick, Melveena. "Anticipating Brecht: Alienation and Agency in Calderón's Wife-Murder Plays." *Bulletin of Hispanic Studies* 77 (2000): 217–36. Print.

Miall, David S. *Literary Reading: Empirical and Theoretical Studies*. New York: Peter Lang, 2006. Print.

Miller, Geoffrey. "Protean Primates: The Evolution of Adaptive Unpredictability in Competition and Courtship." Byrne and Whiten 1997, 312–40. Print.

Milton, Katharine. "Foraging Behaviour and the Evolution of Primate Cognition." Byrne and Whiten 1988, 285–308. Print.

Mitchell, Jason P. "The False Dichotomy between Simulation and Theory-Theory: The Argument's Error." *Trends in Cognitive Sciences* 9.8 (2005): 363–64. Print.

Moore, Roger. "Metatheater and Magic in *El mágico prodigioso*." *Bulletin of the Comediantes* 33.2 (Fall 1981): 129–37. Print.

Moreto, Agustín. *El desdén con el desdén*. *Association for Hispanic Classic Theater*. Web. 1 July 2011. <http://www.comedias.org/textlist.html#Moreto>.

Morton, John G. "Alarcon's *La verdad sospechosa*: Meaning and Didacticism." *Bulletin of the Comediantes* 26 (1974): 51–57. Print.

Mujica, Barbara. "Cervantes' Use of Skepticism in *El retablo de las maravillas*." *Looking at the Comedia in the Year of the Quincentennial*. Ed. Barbara Mujica, Sharon Voros, and Matthew D. Stroud. Lanham, MD: UP of America, 1992. 149–58. Print.

———. *Women Writers of Early Modern Spain: Sophia's Daughters*. New Haven, CT: Yale UP, 2004. Print.

Mulryne, J. Ronnie. "'What is truth' said joking Pilate? The Truth of Illusion in Shakespeare and Webster." *Vérité et illusion dans le théâtre au temps de la Renaissance*. Ed. Marie-Thérèse Jones-Davies. Paris: Touzot, 1983. 57–73. Print.

Murray, Janet. *Hamlet on the Holodeck: The Future of Narrative in Cyberspace*. Cambridge, MA: MIT P, 1998. Print.

Múzquiz-Guerreiro, Darlene. "Symbolic Inversions in Angela de Azevedo's *El muerto disimulado*." *Bulletin of the Comediantes* 57.1 (2005): 147–63. Print.

Neisser, Ulric. *Cognition and Reality: Principles and Implications of Cognitive Psychology*. Cranbury, NJ: Freeman, 1996. Print.

Nell, Victor. *Lost in a Book: The Psychology of Reading for Pleasure*. New Haven, CT: Yale UP, 1988. Print.

Nelson, Robert. *Play within a Play: The Dramatist's Conception of His Art: Shakespeare to Anouilh*. New Haven, CT: Yale UP, 1958. Print.

Nichols, Shaun, and Stephen Stich. *Mindreading: An Integrated Account of Pretence, Self-Awareness, and Understanding of Other Minds*. Oxford: Oxford UP, 2003. Print.

Oatley, Keith, and Mitra Gholomain. "Emotions and Identification: Connections between Readers and Fiction." Hjort and Laver 263–72. Print.

O'Brien, Eavan. *Women in the Prose of María de Zayas.* Woodbridge, UK: Tamesis, 2010. Print.

O'Connell, Sanjida. *Mindreading: An Investigation into How We Learn to Love and Lie.* New York: Doubleday, 1998. Print.

O'Connor, Thomas. "The Interplay of Prudence and Imprudence in *El médico de su honra.*" *Romanistisches Jahrbuch* (1973): 303–22. Print.

———. "Is the Spanish *Comedia* a Metatheater?" *Hispanic Review* 43 (1975): 275–89. Print.

———. "Metatheater and the *Comedia*: A Further Comment." *MLN* 92 (1977): 336–38. Print.

———. "*La vida es sueño*: A View from Metatheater." *Kentucky Romance Quarterly* 25 (1979): 13–26. Print.

Ong, Walter. *Orality and Literacy: The Technologizing of the Word.* New York: Routledge, 1982. Print.

Ordoñez, Elizabeth J. "Woman and Her Text in the Works of María de Zayas and Ana Caro." *Revista de Estudios Hispánicos* 19.1 (1985): 3–15. Print.

Orgel, Stephen. *The Illusion of Power.* Berkeley: U California P, 1975. Print.

Palmer, Alan. *Fictional Minds.* Lincoln: U of Nebraska P, 2004. Print.

———. *Social Minds in the Novel.* Columbus: Ohio State UP, 2010. Print.

Paredes, Alejandro. "Nuevamente la cuestión del metateatro: *La cisma de Inglaterra.*" *Calderón: actas del congreso internacional sobre Calderón y el teatro español del siglo de oro.* Ed. Luciano García Lorenzo. Vol. 1. Madrid: Consejo Superior de Investigaciones Científicas, 1983. 541–48. Print.

Parker, Alexander A. *Literature and the Delinquent: The Picaresque Novel in Spain and Europe 1599–1753.* Edinburgh: Edinburgh UP, 1967. Print.

Parr, James A. *After Its Kind: Approaches to the Comedia.* Kassel: Reichenberger, 1991.

———. "On Narration and Theory." *Cervantes* 24.2 (Fall 2004): 119–35. Print.

Pasto, David J. "The Independent Heroines in Ruíz de Alarcón's Major Comedias." *Bulletin of the Comediantes* 40.2 (1988): 227–35. Print.

Paterson, Alan K. G. "Reversal and Multiple Role Playing in Alarcón's *La verdad sospechosa.*" *Bulletin of Hispanic Studies* 61 (1984): 361–68. Print.

Pavel, Thomas. *Fictional Worlds*. Cambridge, MA: Harvard UP, 1986. Print.

Perry, Mary Elizabeth. *The Handless Maiden: Moriscos and the Politics of Religion in Early Modern Spain*. Princeton, NJ: Princeton, NJ UP, 2005. Print.

———. *Gender and Disorder in Early Modern Seville*. Princeton, NJ: Princeton UP, 1990. Print.

Piaget, Jean. *The Language and Thought of the Child*. New York: Routledge, 2002. Print.

Ponce, Joaquín. *Metateatro: su aplicación a tres dramas de honor de Calderón*. Diss. U of Georgia, 1984. *DIA* (45:46 [1772]). Microfiche.

Popkin, Richard. *The History of Skepticism from Erasmus to Spinoza*. Berkeley: U of California P, 1979. Print.

Quevedo, Francisco de. *Historia de la vida del Buscón*. *Cervantes Virtual*. Web. 1 July 2011. <http://www.cervantesvirtual.com/servlet/Sirve Obras/02426175211793617422202/ index.htm>.

Rabin, Lisa. "The Reluctant Companion of Empire: Petrarch and Dulcinea in *Don Quijote de la Mancha*." *Cervantes* 14.2 (1994): 81–91. Print.

Radway, Janice A. *Reading the Romance: Women, Patriarchy, and Popular Literature*. Chapel Hill: U of North Carolina P, 1984. Print.

Reed, Cory. "'No está olvidada la ciencia': Science, Chaos Theory, and Tragedy in *El médico de su honra*." *South Central Review* 13.1 (1996): 26–39. Print.

Reed, Helen H. *The Reader in the Picaresque Novel*. London: Tamesis, 1984. Print.

Reichenberger, Arnold G. "A Postscript to Professor Thomas Austin O'Connor's Article on the *Comedia*." *Hispanic Review* 43 (1975): 289–91. Print.

Reiss, Timothy J. *Toward Dramatic Illusion: Theatrical Technique and Meaning from Hardy to Horace*. New Haven, CT: Yale UP, 1971. Print.

Ribbans, Geoffrey. "'La Verdad Sospechosa': Lying and Dramatic Structure Once More." *RILCE: Revista de Filología Hispánica* 26.1 (2010): 139–56. Print.

Richardson, Alan. *The Neural Sublime: Cognitive Theories and Romantic Texts*. Baltimore: Johns Hopkins UP, 2010.

Richardson, Alan, and Ellen Spolsky. *The Work of Fiction: Cognition, Culture, and Complexity*. Aldershot, UK: Ashgate, 2004. Print.

Rico, Francisco. *La novela picaresca y el punto de vista*. 2nd ed. corr. and augm. Barcelona: Seix Barral, 1973. Print.

Rico-Ferrer, José Antonio. "In Earnest and in Jest: Disciplining Masculinity through Narration and Humor in *The Spanish Galateo*." *The Poetics of Masculinity in Early Modern Italy and Spain*. Ed. Gerry Milligan, Jane Tylus, and Josiah Blackmore. Toronto: Centre for Reformation and Renaissance Studies, 2010. 267–91. Print.

———. *Re-Readings of the Figure of the Courtier: Subjectivity and Ambivalence in Boscán, Vives, Quevedo y Gracián*. Diss. Emory U, 2001. *DIA*, Section A: The Humanities and Social Sciences 62.11 (May 2002): p3807. Microfiche.

———. *Los tratadistas ibéricos de conducta áulica: representación, masculinidad y colaboración auriseculares*. Vigo: Editorial Academia del Hispanismo, 2011. Print.

Riley, Edward C. "Alarcón's *mentiroso* in the Light of Contemporary Theory of Character." *Hispanic Studies in Honour of I. González Llubera*. Ed. F. Pierce. Oxford: Dolphin, 1959. 287–97.

Rissel, Hilda. "Agustín Moreto y Cabaña: A Transitional Playwright and His Heroines." *Bulletin of the Comediantes* 46.2 (Winter 1994): 219–28. Print.

Rokotnitz, Naomi. "'It Is Required You Do Awake Your Faith': Learning to Trust the Body through Performing *The Winter's Tale*." McConachie and Hart 122–46. Print.

Romano, James Vincent. *Baltasar Gracián and the Fabrication of Subjects: The "Oráculo Manual" as "Self-Help" Writing*. Diss. U of Minnesota, 1997. *DIA*. Section A: The Humanities and Social Sciences 58.11 (May 1998): p4293. Microfiche.

Romero-Díaz, Nieves. "En los límites de la representación: la traición de María de Zayas." *Revista Canadiense de Estudios Hispánicos* 26.3 (2002): 475–92. Print.

———. "Revisiting the Culture of the Baroque: Nobility, City, and Post-Cervantine Novella." *Hispanic Baroques: Reading Cultures in Context*. Ed. Nicholas Spadaccini and Luis Martín-Estudillo. Hispanic Issues 31. Nashville,TN: Vanderbilt UP, 2005. 162–205. Print.

Ruan, Felipe. *Pícaro and Cortesano: Identity and the Forms of Capital in Early Modern Spanish Picaresque Narrative and Courtesy Literature*. Lewisburg, PA: Bucknell UP, 2011. Print.

———. "A Taste for Symbolic Wealth: Gusto and Cultural Capital in Baltasar Gracián." *Revista Canadiense de Estudios Hispánicos* 32.2 (2008): 315–31. Print.

Ruíz de Alarcón, Juan. *La verdad sospechosa*. *Association for Hispanic Classic Theater*. Web. 1 July 2011. <http://www.comedias.org/textlist.html#Alarcón>.

Ruíz Ramón, Francisco. *Calderón y la tragedia*. Madrid: Alhambra, 1984. Print.

Russon, Anne. "Exploiting the Expertise of Others." Byrne and Whiten 1997, 174–206. Print.

Ryan, Marie-Laure. *Possible Worlds, Artificial Intelligence, and Narrative Theory*. Bloomington: Indiana UP, 1991. Print.

Sacks, Oliver. *The Mind's Eye*. New York: Knopf, 2010. Print.

Sánchez, Elizabeth. "From World to Word: Realism and Reflexivity in *Don Quijote* and *La Regenta*." *Hispanic Review* 55.1 (Winter 1987): 27–39. Print.

Sánchez, Francisco J. *An Early Bourgeois Literature in Golden Age Spain. Lazarillo de Tormes, Guzmán de Alfarache and Baltasar Gracián*. Studies in the Romance Languages and Literatures. Chapel Hill: U of North Carolina P, 2003. Print.

———. "Symbolic Wealth and Theatricality in Gracián." Spadaccini and Talens 209–29. Print.

Sanders, John T. "An Ecological Approach to Cognitive Science." *The Electronic Journal of Analytic Philosophy* 4 (Spring 1996): n.pag. Web. 1 July 2011. <http://ejap.louisiana.edu/EJAP/1996.spring/sanders.1996.spring.html>.

Sanderson, Richard K. "Suicide as Message and Metadrama in English Renaissance Tragedy." *Comparative Drama* 26.3 (Fall 1992): 199–217. Print.

Saxe, Rebecca, and Simon Baron-Cohen, eds. and introd. *Theory of Mind. A Special Issue of Social Neuroscience*. New York: Routledge, 2007. Print.

Scarry, Elaine. *Dreaming by the Book*. New York: Farrar, Strauss, and Giroux, 1999. Print.

Schank, Roger. *Tell Me a Story: Narrative and Intelligence*. Chicago: Northwestern UP, 1995. Print.

Schmitt, Alain, and Karl Grammer. "Social Intelligence and Success: Don't Be Too Clever in Order to Be Smart." Byrne and Whiten 1997, 86–111. Print.

Sedgwick, Eve Kosofsky. *Between Men: English Literature and Male Homosocial Desire*. New York: Columbia UP, 1985. Print.

Sieber, Harry. *The Picaresque*. New York: Harper & Row, 1977. Print.

Simerka, Barbara. "Dramatic and Discursive Genres: *La verdad sospechosa* as Problem Comedy and Marriage Treatise." *El arte nuevo de estudiar comedias*. Ed. Simerka. Lewisburg, PA: Bucknell UP, 1996. 187–205. Print.

249

Simerka, Barbara. "Early Modern Literature and Contemporary Feminist Philosophy: Alison Jaggar, Carol Gilligan, and Ana Caro's *El conde Partinuplés*." *Revista de Estudios Hispánicos* 33.3 (Oct. 1999): 495–512. Print.

———. "Early Modern Skepticism and Unbelief and the Demystification of Providential Ideology in *El burlador de Sevilla*." *Gestos* 23 (Apr.1997): 39–66. Print.

———. "Homosociality and Dramatic Conflict: A Reconsideration of Early Modern Spanish Comedy." *Hispanic Review* 70.4 (Fall 2002): 521–33. Print.

Sito Alba, Manuel. "Metateatro en Calderón: *El gran teatro del mundo*." *Calderón: actas del congreso internacional sobre Calderón y el teatro español del siglo de oro.* Ed. Luciano García Lorenzo. Vol. 2. Madrid: Consejo Superior de Investigaciones Científicas, 1983. 789–802. Print.

Smith, Dawn L. "Cervantes and His Audience: Aspects of Reception Theory in *El retablo de las maravillas*." *The Golden Age Comedia: Text, Theory, and Performance.* Ed. and introd. Charles Ganelin and Howard Mancing. West Lafayette, IN: Purdue UP, 1994. 249–61. Print.

Soufas, Teresa Scott. "Calderón's Melancholy Wife-Murderers." *Hispanic Review* 52.2 (Spring 1984): 181–203. Print.

———. *Dramas of Distinction: A Study of Plays by Golden Age Women.* Lexington: UP of Kentucky, 1997. Print.

———. "A Feminist Approach to a Golden Age Dramaturga's Play." *El arte nuevo de estudiar comedias: Literary Theory and Spanish Golden Age Drama.* Ed. Barbara Simerka. Lewisburg, PA: Bucknell UP, 1996. 127–42. Print.

———. *Melancholy and the Secular Mind in Spanish Golden Age Literature.* Columbia: U of Missouri P, 1990.

———, ed. *Women's Acts: Plays by Women Dramatists of Spain's Golden Age.* Lexington: UP of Kentucky, 1997. Print.

Spadaccini, Nicholas, and Jenaro Talens, eds. *Rhetoric and Politics: Baltasar Gracián and the New World Order.* Minneapolis: U of Minnesota P, 1997. Print.

Spolsky, Ellen. *Gaps in Nature: Literary Interpretation and the Modular Mind.* Albany: SUNY P, 1993. Print.

———. "Making 'Quite Anew': Brain Modularity and Creativity." Zunshine, *Cognitive* 84–102. Print.

———. *Satisfying Skepticism: Embodied Knowledge in the Early Modern World.* Aldershot, UK: Ashgate, 2001. Print

———. "Women's Work Is Chastity: Lucretia, Cymbeline, and Cognitive Impenetrability." Richardson and Spolsky 51–84. Print.

Stich, Stephen, and Shaun Nichols. "Folk Psychology: Simulation or Tacit Theory?" Davies and Stone 123–58. Print.

———. *Mind Reading: An Integrated Account of Pretense, Self-Awareness and Understanding Other Minds.* Oxford: Oxford UP, 2003. Print.

Stockwell, Peter. *Cognitive Poetics: An Introduction.* London: Routledge, 2002. Print.

Stoll, Anita K. "Staging, Metadrama, and Religion in Lope's *Los locos por el cielo.*" *Neophilologus* 78.2 (Apr. 1994): 233–41. Print.

Stroud, Matthew D. *Fatal Union: A Pluralistic Approach to the Spanish Wife-Murder Comedias.* Lewisburg, PA: Bucknell UP, 1990. Print.

———. "Love, Friendship, and Deceit in *La traición en la amistad,* by María de Zayas." *Neophilologus* 69 (1985): 539–47. Print.

Strum, Shirley C., Deborah Forster, and Edwin Hutchins. "Why Machiavellian Intelligence May Not Be Machiavellian." Byrne and Whiten 1997, 50–85. Print.

Sugiera, Malgorzata. "Theatricality and Cognitive Science: The Audience's Perception and Reception." *SubStance* 31.2–3 (2002): 225–35. Print.

Sullivan, Henry. *Tirso de Molina and the Drama of the Counter Reformation.* Amsterdam: Rodopi, 1976. Print.

Teresa de Ávila. *Las moradas / Libro de su vida.* Mexico City: Porrúa, 1998. Print.

Thacker, Jonathan. *Role-Play and the World as Stage in the Comedia.* Liverpool: Liverpool UP, 2002. Print.

Thelen, Esther, and Linda B. Smith. *A Dynamic Systems Approach to the Development of Cognition and Action.* Cambridge, MA: MIT P, 1996. Print.

Thompson, Clive. "What Is I.B.M.'s Watson?" *New York Times Magazine. New York Times.* 1 July 2010. Web. 1 July 2011. <http://www.nytimes.com/2010/06/20/magazine/ 20Computer-t.html>.

Thompson, Douglas F. S., ed. and introd. *That Nothing Is Known: Francisco Sánchez.* Cambridge: Cambridge UP, 1989. Print.

Tierno Galván, Enrique. *Sobre la novela picaresca y otros escritos.* Madrid: Tecnos, 1974. Print.

Trueblood, Alan S. "Role-Playing and the Sense of Illusion in Lope de Vega." *Hispanic Review* 32 (1964): 305–18. Print.

Tsur, Reuven. *Poetic Rhythm: Structure and Performance: An Empirical Study in Cognitive Poetics.* Berne: Peter Lang, 1998. Print.

———. *Toward a Theory of Cognitive Poetics.* Amsterdam: North-Holland, 1992. Print.

Turner, Mark. *Reading Minds: The Study of English in the Age of Cognitive Science.* Princeton, NJ: Princeton UP, 1991. Print.

Urbina, Eduardo. "'La razón de más fuerça': triple juego en *La verdad sospechosa.*" *Hispania* 70.4 (Dec. 1987): 724–30. *JSTOR.* Web. 1 July 2011 <http://www.jstor.org/stable/342514>.

Varela, Francisco J., Evan Thompson, and Eleanor Rosch. *The Embodied Mind: Cognitive Science and Human Experience.* Cambridge, MA: MIT P, 1991. Print.

Vega y Carpio, Lope de. *El animal de Hungría.* Charleston, SC: BiblioBazaar, 2007. Print.

———. *Lo fingido verdadero. SCRIBD.* Web. 17 Sept 2012. <http://www. scribd.com/doc/70894270/Lo-Fingido-Verdadero-PDF>.

———. *Lo fingido verdadero / Acting Is Believing: A Tragicomedy in Three Acts.* Trans. Michael McGaha. San Antonio, TX: Trinity UP, 1986. Print.

Velasco, Sherry. "Marimachos, hombrunas, barbudas: The Masculine Woman in Cervantes." *Cervantes* 20.1 (2000): 69–78. Print.

Vermeule, Blakey. *Why Do We Care about Literary Characters?* Baltimore: Johns Hopkins UP, 2009. Print.

Vickers, Nancy. "Diana Described: Scattered Woman and Scattered Rhyme." *Writing and Sexual Difference.* Ed. Elizabeth Abel. Chicago: U of Chicago P, 1982. 95–109. Print.

Vollendorf, Lisa. "The Future of Early Modern Women's Studies: The Case of Same-Sex Friendship and Desire in Zayas and Carvajal." *Arizona Journal of Hispanic Cultural Studies* 4 (2000): 265–84. *JSTOR.* Web. 1 July 2011. <http://www.jstor.org/pss/20641508>.

———. *The Lives of Women: A New History of Inquisitional Spain.* Nashville, TN: Vanderbilt UP, 2005. Print.

———. *Reclaiming the Body: María de Zayas's Early Modern Feminism.* Chapel Hill: U of North Carolina P, 2001. Print.

———, ed. and introd. *Recovering Spain's Feminist Tradition.* New York: MLA, 2001. Print.

Vuillemin, Jean-Claude. "Illusions comiques et dramaturgie baroque: Corneille, Rotrou et quelques autres." *Papers on French Seventeeth-Century Literature* 28.55 (2001): 307– 25. Print.

Wagschal, Steven. *The Literature of Jealousy in the Age of Cervantes.* Columbia: U of Missouri P, 2006. Print.

Walton, Kendall. "Spelunking, Simulation, and Slime." Hjort and Laver 37–49. Print.

Wardropper, Bruce. "Poesía y drama en *El médico de su honra.*" *Calderón y la crítica: historia y antología,* II. Ed. Manuel Durán and Roberto González Echevarría. Madrid: Gredos, 1976. 582–97. Print.

Warnke, Frank. *Versions of Baroque: European Literature in the Seventeenth Century.* New Haven, CT: Yale UP, 1972. Print.

Weimer, Christopher B. "Ana Caro's *El conde Partinuplés* and Calderón's *La vida es sueño*: Protofeminism and Heuristic Imitation." *Bulletin of the Comediantes* 52.1 (2000): 123–46. Print.

Whicker, Jules. *The Plays of Juan Ruiz de Alarcón.* Woodbridge, UK: Tamesis, 2003. Print.

Whiten, Andrew. "The Machiavellian Mindreader." Byrne and Whiten 1997, 144–73. Print.

Whitenack, Judith A. "'Lo que ha menester': Erotic Enchantment in 'La inocencia castigada.'" Williamsen and Whitenack 170–91. Print.

Wicks, Ulrich. *Picaresque Narrative, Picaresque Fictions: A Theory and Research Guide.* New York: Greenwood, 1989. Print.

Wilkins, Constance. "Subversion through Comedy? Two Plays by Sor Juana Inés de la Cruz and María de Zayas." *The Perception of Women in Spanish Theater of the Golden Age.* Ed. Anita K. Stoll and Dawn L. Smith. Lewisburg, PA: Bucknell UP, 1991. 107–20. Print.

Williams, Raymond. *The Country and the City.* Oxford: Oxford UP, 1973. Print.

———. *Marxism and Literature.* Oxford: Oxford UP, 1977. Print.

Williamsen, Amy R. "Challenging the Code: Honor in Maria de Zayas." Williams and Whitenack 133–54. Print.

———. "Fatal Formulas: Mencía, Men, and Verbal Manipulation." *Indiana Journal of Hispanic Literatures* 2.2 (Spring 1994): 27–37. Print.

Williamsen, Amy R., and Judith A. Whitenack. *María de Zayas: The Dynamics of Discourse.* Madison, NJ: Fairleigh Dickinson UP, 1995. Print.

Wilson, R. Rawdon. "Narrative Reflexivity in Shakespeare." *Poetics Today* 10.4 (Winter 1989): 771–91. Print.

Wimmer, H., and J. Perner. "Beliefs about Beliefs: Representation and Constraining Function of Wrong Beliefs in Young Children's Understanding of Deception." *Cognition* 13 (1983): 103–28. Print.

Witt, Mary Ann Frese. "From Saint Genesius to Kean: Actors, Martyrs, and Metatheater." *Comparative Drama* 43.1 (May 2009): 19–44. Print.

Wooton, David. "New Histories of Atheism." *Atheism from the Renaissance to the Enlightenment*. Ed. Michael Hunter and David Wooton. New York: Oxford UP, 1992. 13–53. Print.

Yarbro-Bejarano, Yvonne. *Feminism and the Honor Plays of Lope de Vega*. Purdue Studies in Romance Literatures 4. West Lafayette, IN: Purdue UP, 1994. Print.

Yllera, Alicia, ed. and introd. *Desengaños amorosos: parte segunda del sarao y entretenimiento honesto*. By María de Zayas y Sotomayor. 2nd ed. Madrid: Cátedra, 1983. Print.

Zayas y Sotomayor, María de. *Desengaños amoroso: parte segunda del sarao y entretenimiento honesto*. 2nd ed. Madrid: Cátedra, 1983. Print.

———. *La traición en la amistad*. Soufas, *Women's Acts* 277–308. Print.

Zunshine, Lisa. "Essentialism and Comedy: A Cognitive Reading of the Motif of Mislaid Identity in Dryden's *Amphitryon* (1690)." McConachie and Hart 97–121. Print.

———, ed. *Introduction to Cognitive Cultural Studies*. Baltimore: Johns Hopkins UP, 2010. Print.

———. "Richardson's *Clarissa* and a Theory of Mind." Richardson and Spolsky 127–43. Print.

———. *Why We Read Fiction: Theory of Mind and the Novel*. Columbus: Ohio State UP, 2006. Print.

Index

About the Author

Barbara Simerka, Queens College/CUNY, is the author of *Discourses of Empire*. She is editor or co-editor of three volumes of critical essays and of a special issue of *Cervantes*. She has published over twenty essays, with emphasis on interdisciplinary and feminist approaches. With Christopher Weimer, she co-authored several articles on Don Quixote and postmodern film and founded the electronic journal *Laberinto*. Her most recent works employ cognitive theories to study tragic drama and genre theory, political drama (*privanza*), and contemporary feminist science fiction.